**Essay Index**

# HERALDS OF AMERICAN
# LITERATURE

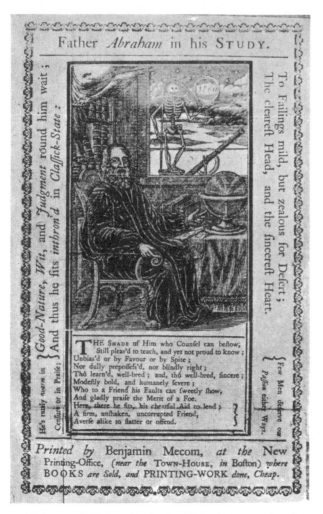

Title-page of *Father Abraham's Advice*, Boston, 1760; from copy in Boston Public Library.

# Heralds of American Literature

A GROUP OF PATRIOT WRITERS OF THE
REVOLUTIONARY AND NATIONAL PERIODS

*By*
ANNIE RUSSELL MARBLE, M.A.

*Essay Index Reprint Series*

## Essay Index

BOOKS FOR LIBRARIES PRESS
FREEPORT, NEW YORK

First Published 1907
Reprinted 1967

INTERNATIONAL STANDARD BOOK NUMBER
0-8369-0675-6


LIBRARY OF CONGRESS CATALOG CARD NUMBER:
67-26761


PRINTED IN THE UNITED STATES OF AMERICA

# PREFACE

Each decade calls forth a more detailed study of the beginnings of American history. The lives of our pioneer soldiers and statesmen have been narrated in many volumes. On the other hand, the writers who prophesied, and sought to promote, a national literature during the early days of American independence have not been so generally studied, except in groups. Moses Coit Tyler individualized scores of Colonial and Revolutionary versifiers and satirists, but the self-imposed limits of his theme prevented him from completing the later services of some of these writers, after the Revolution. He did not live to accomplish a similar work in biography for the patriot-writers of the National period in which American government, industry, and education were slowly established. The aim of this book is to recount, in detailed study and largely from original sources, the lives and services of a group of typical writers during the pioneer days of national growth, who revealed the standards and aspirations of their time and who announced the dawn of a national literature, although their own products were often immature and crude.

In my researches, which have extended over many years, I have had valuable assistance from librarians at Harvard, Yale, Brown, and Princeton Universities, the Library of Congress, the Lenox Library of New York, the Athenaeum and Public Library of Boston, the American Antiquarian Society and Public Library at Worcester, and Pequot Library at Southport, Connecticut. I would also acknowledge indebtedness to the Historical Societies of New York, New Jersey, Pennsylvania, Connecticut, and Massachusetts. For editorial suggestions I am grateful to members of the faculty of the University of Chicago. Descendants of some of these early writers, and many individuals, have given me generous interest and co-operation. Four of the chapters, in abbreviated form, have been printed in the *New England Magazine,* and one in the *Critic.* Thanks are due the editors of these journals for permission to reprint.

A. R. M.

# LIST OF ILLUSTRATIONS

# CONTENTS

INTRODUCTORY: SIGNS OF THE DAWN
—THE IMPULSE OF FRANKLIN

# I

## INTRODUCTORY: SIGNS OF THE DAWN
## —THE IMPULSE OF FRANKLIN

The strong impulses of every epoch in a nation's life are impressed upon the pages of contemporary literature. The awakening, on the part of the American colonists, of a spirit of remonstrance against English misrule, the drift of sentiment toward independence, and the slow, toilsome victory in war and establishment of a republic, were expressions of a vital period in the world's history. The motives behind the events were prophesied and narrated by the writers of this age of transition, who lived amid its scenes. In literary style their work does not rank high; but their services to America, in her political agitations and her initial progress in arts and education, deserve some attention beyond the usual "honorable mention."

Research among the unfamiliar writings by American patriots of the past has compensation for much which baffles and disappoints. Within their lives were heroic deeds and blighting failures, and the varied incidents form an interesting record. They portrayed the customs and standards of their own time, in industry, society, and morals, with a realism and faithfulness which cannot be fully reproduced. The bulk of what is called American literature, from 1765 to 1815, was immature and crude, according to the rules of criticism, but within it are suggestions of nature-study, poetry, and romance, against a background of native scenery. Later authors wove these elements into effective fabrics.

For many years the question has been discussed: Has America a literature of her own; and, if so, when did it begin? Only within recent times would one venture to affirm the independent existence of such a literature. The specious argument, that everything written in the English language belongs to English literature exclusively, has been nullified. We identify patriots today by the spirit, not by the letter, of their writings.

American nationality was evolved and established between 1765 and 1815. The inherent aims of the new nation were gradually dissociated from those of England, and the divorce was recognized for many decades. During the latter part of the nineteenth century the true racial bonds have again been openly emphasized. Why should the writings of this formative era of American federation, the direct impressions and records of the dawning national spirit, be still discounted as American literature? The themes of these early writers were localized, and their vision was often distorted; yet a unity of purpose distinguished their prose and crude verse from the products of the British colonists in America prior to 1765. The dominant quality of the later writings was that rugged sincerity which is "the essence of originality," as Carlyle has declared.

Colonial verse showed a marked advance from the mawkish couplets of Wigglesworth and grotesque musings of Mistress Anne Bradstreet, to the ballads and lyrics of Dr. Benjamin Prime and William Livingstone, which were popular during the last half of the eighteenth century. In prose also there was progress in literary form, which is seen by comparing the labored pages of the early annalists and preachers with the compulsive logic of Jonathan Edwards, the *Journal* of John Woolman, and the varied writings of Benjamin Franklin.

As statesman, as ingenious scientist, and as writer of pure, strong English, Franklin has gained a world-wide recognition for which it is not necessary to argue. He was a representative of the highest Colonial development along industrial and educational paths. His style was confessedly modeled after that of the best English essayists, and it was disturbed by no uncouth efforts to seem "American." At the same time, perhaps unconsciously, Franklin introduced notes

of democracy and Americanism into his epigrams
and treatises, long before the ideas or the words
had come into vogue, and while the colonists in
America were loyal and contented subjects of
Great Britain.

One of the people by birth and hard-won success, Franklin wrote for the common people, not
for the aristocracy or the lettered.  His *Alma-
nacks*, and his counsels by Father Abraham and
Poor Richard appealed to the mind and ambition
of the populace.  In his later life, famous as
scientist, diplomat, and wit, he was in favor with
the élite of Europe; but in his early manhood,
and in most of his writings, he was democratic
in thought and associations.  He familiarized the
common people with the wit and wisdom of the
English essayists whom he admired.  He believed
that he could increase the thrift and industry of
the masses, even as he could lighten their drudgery, by pungent sentences which would be easily
acquired and quoted.  His activities and his writings were utilitarian in aim.  He advised the individual to increase his material resources, but also
to broaden and sweeten his mind by contact with
good literature of practical value.[1]  His pages

[1] Of the 748 titles and editions enumerated by Paul
Leicester Ford in his *Bibliography of Franklin* (Brooklyn,
1889), nearly all indicate the immediate effects intended by
his writings on politics, science, and education.

were always readable, from the youthful *Dogood Papers*, which he persistently thrust under the door of the newspaper office for six months until they were published, to the *Bagatelles* and *Autobiography* written in old age. The message is always practical, timely, and clear.

In the library of the Historical Society of Pennsylvania is a rare pamphlet, containing Franklin's *Proposals Relating to the Education of Youth in Pensilvania*.[2] This paper, written more than a century and a half ago, stimulated the citizens of Philadelphia to establish an academy where the youth of the state "might receive the accomplishments of a regular education." It affords a perfect example of the practical aim and pure English which marked Franklin as an author. With liberal quotations from Latin and English essayists and poets—Cato, Milton, Locke, Addison, and Pope—with specific advice regarding the branches which should be taught, he closed the essay with this self-revelatory paragraph:

With the whole, should be constantly inculcated and cultivated that *Benignity* of MIND which shows itself in *searching for* and seizing every Opportunity *to serve and to oblige;* and is the Foundation of what is called GOOD BREEDING;—Ability to serve Mankind, one's Country, Friends and Family; which Ability is (with the Blessing of God) to be acquired or greatly increased by *true*

[2] Philadelphia, 1749; 32 pages and many footnotes.

*Learning;* and should indeed be the great *Aim and End* of all Learning.

Franklin did good service, during the Revolutionary period, by satiric and logical writings; but he gained his renown among his contemporaries, and is still remembered, as the foster-father of commercial thrift and literary impulse among the colonists. He was active in founding the Library Company of Philadelphia and the American Philosophical Society; he organized literary clubs and edited magazines. His travels and studies had broadened him, and given a democratic trend to his thoughts; yet he was loyal to British rule until his ideas of justice were too violently assailed. Retaining that serenity of outlook which he always urged, he became a wise supporter of American freedom, and wrote state papers and political essays in the same lucid, graceful style which had already won him a place among English authors.

The half-century from 1765 to 1815, which witnessed the birth of the new nation and its first literary expressions, may be divided into three periods, of unequal length, but of the same relative importance. There were, first, the years from occasional remonstrance against English taxation to open secession; second, those from the Declaration of Independence to the end of the Revolution; third, those from 1782 to 1815,

covering the formation of government, and its
assurance of life after the victories and treaty
of the War of 1812. The prose and verse of the
first two periods both incited and recorded the
bitter feud between two countries whose bonds
had been closely welded and were soon to be
broken. The writers of the third, or constructive, period were less bitter, but still intense in
their zeal to crush internal anarchy and to establish a prosperous, as well as a free, nation.

The earlier writings reveal fervid emotion and
strong argumentation; the later are more restrained in spirit, but the style is often crude and
bombastic. The beginnings of aesthetic culture in
the later Colonial decades seemed to have suffered
a serious interruption. The verse of the Revolution was inspired by no devotion to the fine
arts, but rather was a virile weapon for the ridicule of enemies and the encouragement of soldiers
in the wearisome conflict. In the martial odes
and satires by Philip Freneau, John Trumbull,
Timothy Dwight, and Benjamin Prime there were
occasional lyric yearnings; but they awakened
meager response. The prose of the same period,
including the early stages of the war, consisted
of formal correspondence between Tory and
Patriot leaders; heavy yet earnest state papers,
like Stephen Hopkins' *Rights of the Colonies,*
and Samuel Adams' *Appeal to the World;* and

orations from rostrum and pulpit, by statesmen like Otis, Hancock, and Patrick Henry, and preachers like Mayhew, Chauncy, and Duffield.

As the focal point of defiance was in Boston and vicinity, with open sympathy from Virginia and Pennsylvania, the most typical literary remonstrances came from those colonies. From Pennsylvania, in addition to Franklin's familiar pamphlets,[3] there issued another series of arguments that were widely read and quoted, *Letters from a Farmer in Pennsylvania to the Inhabitants of the British Colonies.*[4] The author of these *Letters*, John Dickinson, was strong in argumentation; he possessed also some literary grace. His astute mind thus framed the imminent problem of rightful taxes:

> Upon the whole, the simple question is whether the parliament can legally impose duties to be paid *by the people of these colonies only*, FOR THE SOLE PURPOSE OF RAISING A REVENUE, *on commodities which she obliges us to take from her alone,* or, in other words, whether the parliament can legally take money out of our pockets, without our consent. If they can, our boasted liberty is but *"Vox et preterea nihil."*[5]

[3] "The Causes of American Discontents" and "The Rise and Progress of the Differences between Great Britain and her American Colonies," in Bigelow's *The Complete Works of Benjamin Franklin*, Vol. IV, pp. 97-111 ; Vol. V, pp. 323-38.

[4] Boston, Philadelphia, and London, 1768.

[5] *Letters from a Farmer*, etc., Letter II, p. 14.

One minor incident of the years which preceded the war loomed large and ominous on the literary horizon—the defiant refusal to use the taxed tea. This was really symbolic of the principles involved in the later struggle; and so the prose logic contended. The verse on the theme was in forms of caustic parodies, sneering odes, and mock-heroics.[6] They shared in popularity with the *Liberty Songs,* especially that by John Dickinson, written in 1768, which was parodied by the Tories, and the parody, in turn, was re-parodied by the Patriots; the three versions were sung to the stirring melody of "Hearts of Oak." The opening stanza of Dickinson's ode reads thus:

Come, join hand and hand, brave Americans all,
Awake through the land at fair Liberty's call;
No tyrannous acts shall suppress our just claim,
Or stain with dishonour America's name.
> In freedom we're born,
> In freedom we'll live:
> Our purses are ready;
> Steady, friends, steady;

Not as slaves but as freemen our money we'll give.[7]

[6] In his *Songs and Ballads of the Revolution* (New York, 1856), Frank Moore has collected many of these droll "Ballads of Taxes and Tea."

[7] This song was first printed anonymously in the *Boston Gazette and Country Journal,* July 18, 1768. It may be found, with the parodies, in Frank Moore's *Songs and Ballads of the Revolution* (New York, 1856); pp. 36-47.

While the first period was one of political debate and mental indecision, the second period reflected vigorous action. Many of the pamphlets and verses called forth answering sneers and pleas from Loyalist wits. There was a tone of invective in the writings of the Whigs, not alone toward the English king, prime minister, and Parliament, but also against many honest Tories, whose noble characters have been honored by later generations, but whose scruples were scathingly denounced by their political opponents.

The Declaration of Independence was a signal for unbridled joy among the odists. Each futile scheme, and each defeat of the English leaders, gave occasion for satires by Freneau and Trumbull, or for a lampoon by Hopkinson. Versifiers composed rude, simple songs to cheer the Patriot army, like the variations of "Yankee Doodle;" or such fervent odes and hymns, sung in camps and churches, as "Columbia" by Timothy Dwight, "The American Hero" by Nathaniel Niles, and "Chester" by William Billings. Mistress Mercy Warren and Hugh Henry Brackenridge summoned a halting talent to dramatize *The Battle of Bunker's Hill* or to ridicule *The Group* of Loyalists in Boston who fawned upon Lord North and Governor Thomas Hutchinson, of Massachusetts. [8]

[8] *The Battle of Bunker's Hill: By a Gentleman of Maryland* (Philadelphia, 1776); *The Group* (Boston, 1775).

When the war was ended, the literature was
exultant and braggart for a few months.  This
tone was soon succeeded by one of anxiety; for
many dangers threatened the new nation.  Among
the problems to be solved were these: how to raise
money to pay the soldiers and meet the demands
of the treaties; how to secure financial and industrial confidence with depreciated paper money and
stagnant business; how to prevent recurrence of
riots and menacing conventions of various classes
in New England; how to frame a constitution, in
place of the old, futile federation of the colonies,
which would be acceptable to the states themselves; how to maintain the strong, personal
leadership of a few men, without arousing fears
of monarchical government.  The force and logic
in the spoken and written words of Jefferson,
Hamilton, Fisher Ames, Patrick Henry, and
Richard Henry Lee have given them rank among
the leaders of the age both in thought and in
diction.  More crude, but also effective, were the
lighter efforts in satire, ode, and counsel by Hopkinson and Trumbull, Humphreys, Dwight, and
Alsop.

Gradually the threatened disruption of the
country was prevented; in spite of vigorous opposition, the Constitution was adopted, the Bank
and Mint were established, treaties of commerce
were effected, the pitfall of military alliance with

France was circumvented, and the various elements were converged into an embryonic republic under Washington as president. The stages by which such union was brought out of seeming confusion, and the gradual growth of confidence in the new government among all classes, especially after the naval victories of 1812–14, are revealed, with graphic impressions, in the prose and verse of the period. The establishment of industries, and the attention to education, incited some of the writers of the time to extravagant prophecies and boastful expressions; but the leaders of the nation desired an interchange of ideas and literature with the broader schools of Europe.

The war seemed to be a serious interruption to all literary activities, in the true meaning of the phrase. On the other hand, during the half-century of aesthetic barrenness and political ferment there was developed a new vital spirit, an aspiration of freedom and valor, destined to characterize American life and writings. The first verse and prose, after the war, were less refined than some of the imitative products of the later Colonial decades, but they had a deeper earnestness and an impressive assurance. A few of the authors considered in this book lived until 1830 and after—Freneau, Trumbull, Dunlap, Theodore Dwight. They had personal acquaintance with Irving, Cooper, Bryant, and the minor authors who survived to witness and contribute to our recognized literature. The struggles and undaunted hopes of the group of earlier writers encouraged those of the generation which followed to devote their lives to literature, art, and science. Irving, Cooper, Bryant, Emerson, Hawthorne, felt the influence of these earlier impulses and were able to develop into mature artistic productions many of the seeds of promise which were germinating in the previous years of political stress.

The writings of the Revolutionary and National periods were too abundant. Those which are valuable in tracing the political and literary history of America have been submerged amid the mass of ephemerides. To all the writings we apply the term "literature"—by courtesy. Moses Coit Tyler studied the authors of the Colonial and Revolutionary eras, with patient skill, in the work which remains as his monument.[9] In a survey of this dawning literature, we must confess that it was immature as well as sincere, that the crudities of form often hide the true merit. Out of the many, a few compositions have been remembered, among them the three national songs, "Yankee Doodle," "Hail Columbia," and

[9] *History of American Literature,* "The Colonial Period: 1607-1765" (2 vols.; New York, 1879) ; *The Literary History of the American Revolution: 1763-1783* (2 vols.; New York, 1897).

"The Star-Spangled Banner." Although the
individual works of the writers of these two
periods—of war and confederation—have been
forgotten, and many of them deserve their oblivion, yet they may fittingly be recalled by students of early American history and literature,
who will thus emphasize their influence upon the
progress of national life and culture. These
scattered literary efforts, from the poignant
satires and the first impulse of poetry to the weak,
yet haunting, products of emotional drama and
fiction, were the prophetic foregleams of our
national literature.

# FRANCIS HOPKINSON: JURIST, WIT, AND DILETTANTE

From a painting by R. Pine, 1785, engraved by J. B. Longacre; reproduced from *National Portrait Gallery of Distinguished
Americans*, 1835.

## II

## FRANCIS HOPKINSON: JURIST, WIT, AND DILETTANTE

The searchlight of modern investigation, turned upon American history, has clarified many events and placed a true value upon many personalities. A few characters have thus lost some of their traditional prestige, but others have won long-deferred honor. Prominent among the wits and pamphleteers of the Revolutionary decades, and the years of crisis which immediately followed, was Francis Hopkinson. He was one of the signers of the Declaration of Independence, a noted judge, and a dilettante in music, painting, and verse-making. His efforts in art and literature seem crude to modern students, yet they indicate great ingenuity and a sincere desire to help forward the progress of America in culture. In writing, he had a cleverness in characterization comparable with that of Swift and Congreve, and in satire he well imitated Addison and Pope. Underneath the dilettantism were the principles of a patriot and a reformer, and the yearnings of an artist.

By inheritance he had a broad, penetrating mind and much nervous energy. His father,

Thomas Hopkinson, who had been trained in law and science in London, came to Philadelphia about 1731. Ten years later he succeeded Andrew Hamilton as judge of the Vice-Admiralty for Pennsylvania. His taste for science was recognized, and he became influential as a member of the American Philosophical Society, of which he was the first president. With Benjamin Franklin and Richard Peters, he brought into life the College of Philadelphia, where his son, Francis, was the first pupil enrolled upon the records, after the term "college" had been substituted for "academy." In his letters and in conversations, Franklin paid tribute to the practical ingenuity of the elder Hopkinson in scientific experiments, mentioning, especially, indebtedness to him for the suggestion of pointed, rather than blunted, instruments to attract the electric fluid—"the power of points to throw off electric fire." [1]

The taste for music, and skill in playing both harpsichord and organ, as well as the love for poetry, which characterized Francis Hopkinson, were legacies from his mother, a woman of great industry and endowed with charm of face and mind. When his father died, leaving a large family and a small income, Francis, the eldest child, was only fourteen years old. To his edu-

[1] *The Complete Works of Benjamin Franklin* (Bigelow), Vol. II, p. 211, note.

cation his mother devoted her personal efforts. Entering the College of Philadelphia at sixteen, he had some noted associates in that first class, graduated in 1757. Among them were Hugh Williamson, Jacob Duché, Paul Jackson, James Latta, and Samuel Magaw. Few men of his day were more brilliant than Duché, who married a sister of Hopkinson. As rector of St. Peter's and Christ Church in Philadelphia, Duché won distinction as orator, but his career was blighted by weakness of will.[2] When the British army entered Philadelphia, he recanted his principles of freedom, and wrote to Washington urging him to renew allegiance to the crown. Later Duché escaped with Cornwallis to London, whence he sent to Washington a pitiful appeal for permission to return to America.[3]

Choosing his father's profession as his own, Francis Hopkinson passed the years immediately after college in the law office of Benjamin Chew, the famous attorney-general of the Province of

[2] An original copy of Duché's first prayer as chaplain of the Continental Congress is in Independence Hall, Philadelphia. John Adams wrote to his wife regarding the brilliancy and promise of Duché (*Letters to His Wife* [1841], Vol. I, pp. 23, 24).

[3] This letter and other correspondence upon the subject, including letters from Francis Hopkinson to Duché and Washington, have been edited and published by Worthington C. Ford (*The Washington-Duché Letters*, Brooklyn, 1890).

Pennsylvania.  Hopkinson's first political experience was as secretary of the conference between the governor and the Indians of the Lehigh Valley.  As a youth he won some reputation by his rhymes, written in college and soon after.  One of these early efforts at versifying was "performed at the College of Philadelphia" at the commencement exercises in 1761.  It was printed as "An Exercise Containing a Dialogue and Ode Sacred to the Memory of His Late Majesty George II."  Hopkinson was accredited with both the words and music of the ode.[4]  The same year he gave expression to his zeal for scientific advancement in a poem, "Science," which was also published. [5]

Evidence that Hopkinson, as a youth, was strong in his allegiance to England is given by a "Dissertation" which he wrote for the prize medal

[4] Other early verses are to be found in manuscript in the library of the Historical Society of Pennsylvania.  Here are two sentimental reveries, "L'Allegro, Dedicated to Benjamin Chew," and "Il Penseroso, Dedicated to Rev. Dr. Smith ;" also "An Elegy Sacred to the Memory of Mrs. Ann Graeme," dated Graeme Park, July, 1765.

[5] An interesting comment upon the piratical republication of this poem, "Science," by a Philadelphia printer, and the return to its original form with the author's revision in another edition published by Hugh Gaine, of New York, may be found in the *New York Mercury,* April 19, 1762, No. 507.  This is reprinted in *The Journals of Hugh Gaine, Printer,* edited by Paul L. Ford (New York, 1902), Vol. I, p. 108.

offered by John Sargent, M.P., for the best essay
to be writen by a graduate of the College of Philadelphia upon the subject, "Reciprocal Advantages
of a Perpetual Union between Great Britain and
Her American Colonies." [6]    He hoped that he
might increase his small income from law and
music by an appointment to some colonial office.
To assist him in gaining such a position, he relied
upon the influence of two men, Franklin and the
bishop of Worcester, a kinsman of Mrs. Hopkinson and a friend of Lord North.    Some manuscript letters show the preparatory steps taken by
Hopkinson, his mother, and Franklin, to enlist
the interest of the bishop of Worcester in his
young relative, before Hopkinson went to London, in 1766, hoping thus to secure his appointment.    A letter from Franklin to James Burrow,
to be given to the bishop of Worcester, dated
Craven Street, May, 1765, is quoted first:

> Mrs. Hopkinson is greatly esteemed by the People of
> the Place, as a prudent and good woman.    Her husband,
> Thomas Hopkinson, was in repute as a Lawyer, sometime
> Judge of the Admiralty Court, and one of the Governor's
> Council.    He left her a Widow about twelve years since,
> with five young children, two Sons and three Daughters.
> These she has carefully educated, genteely but frugally,
> out of an Income of a small estate, and I believe without
> much Diminishing their Portions.

[6] *Four Dissertations on the Reciprocal Advantages of a Perpetual Union,* etc. (Philadelphia, 1766). See the Bibliography.

Her eldest son, Francis, had a College education at Philadelphia, where he took his Degrees, has since read Law under the Att'y Gen'l, but still lives with his mother, and has not entered into any material Business as yet. He is a very ingenious young man and is daily growing in Esteem for his good morals and obliging Disposition.[7]

The complement of this letter is among the Franklin manuscripts in the library of the American Philosophical Society—an appreciative letter from Mrs. Hopkinson to Franklin, after she had learned of the latter's efforts to interest her relative in her behalf.[8]   The date is October 1, 1765.

A Thousand Thanks to you for the agreeable knowledge of my Relations in England and for the Trouble yourself and your Friend Mr. Burrow have been at in obtaining it—when we consider how much Business of great importance of your own you must have to transact, how must my Gratitude and my children be heightened for the uncommon Care Regularity and Exactness you have used in tracing out my Family and for the favourable character you have been pleased to give us.   The Marks of Regard you are continually Shewing to the Family of a deceased Friend is to me a convincing proof of the Goodness of your Heart and I must declare that among all my Husbands former Friends I know of but one Gentleman besides Yourself who has been good enough to extend any of their Regard to his Wife and Children—and it is my sincere prayer that every kindness you have been pleased

[7] For a copy of this letter I am indebted to Mrs. Florence Scovel Shinn, a descendant of Hopkinson.

[8] Permission to print this and the following letter was given by the librarian of the American Philosophical Society.

to show to me and mine may be doubled in Blessings on
Yourself and Family.  Shall I beg the further Favour of
you to transmit the enclosed packet and Letters as directed.
I send you herewith an order on Messrs. Barclay and Sons
for the expense you have been at in this affair.  Your
good will and Trouble I cannot repay and must therefore remain

Your ever obliged Friend and Humble Servant,

MARY HOPKINSON

Among the letters from Hopkinson to Franklin, in the manuscript collection at the library of
the American Philosophical Society, is one supplementary, in time and message, to that just
quoted.  After thanking Franklin for his kind
recommendations, he continued in a frank manner, informing his elder friend of many matters
of personal interest:

You advised me in your last to send Mr. Burrows a
small present of Sturgeon or apples with a Letter of
Thanks for his kindness.  I did write such a Letter
before I received your advice; but was so stupid that I
never thought of the other;—I fear such a thing would
be improper now as being so late, that it will appear to be
done in Consequence of your advice & not our own free
act.  But I will write the best apology I can and will ship
some Sturgeon for him. . . . .

I visited your Family the Day before Yesterday &
put Miss Sally's Harpsichord in the best Order I could but
the Instrument, as to the Touch and all Machinery, is
entirely ruined & I think past Recovery.—I think it would
be very proper to sell this & buy her a new Harpsichd
of a more simple Construction. . . . .

> I have finished the Translation of the Psalms of David, to the great Satisfaction of the Dutch Congregation at New York & they have paid me £145 of their Currency which I intend to keep as a Body Reserve in Case I should go to England.[9]

Franklin had left England before Hopkinson arrived there. but the young man met a cordial welcome from his kinsman, and dined with Lord North, Benjamin West, and other men of note.[10] He sought in vain for a crown appointment on the Board of Commissioners of Customs for Pennsylvania. The repeal of the Stamp Act, just as he had left America, caused a bevy of Royalist office-holders to clamor for new places in the colonies, and by them the first vacant official positions were filled. His visit was not wholly fruitless, however, for two years after his return, probably through the influence of Lord North, he was appointed collector of customs at Newcastle, and was allowed a deputy for actual service. In 1774 he was appointed by the crown

[9] Copies of this translation in book form are in the libraries of the New York Historical Society and the Historical Society of Pennsylvania. An exhaustive study of Hopkinson's work as musician has been made by O. G. Sonneck, in *Francis Hopkinson and James Lyon* (Washington, 1905).

[10] Mrs. Oliver Hopkinson, of Philadelphia, has some letters which he wrote to his mother from England, with interesting details of the life at Hartleburg Castle, where he was a guest, and of the visitors there.

as a member of the Provincial Council from New Jersey.

Various influences, during the next two years, brought about a firm renunciation of Tory allegiance, and Hopkinson joined in open sympathy with the patriot leaders. One of the first and most potent influences was his marriage to Miss Ann Borden, daughter of Judge Joseph Borden and granddaughter of the founder of the town of Bordentown, in New Jersey. The Bordens were ardent Whigs, and Hopkinson began to think and write in behalf of the colonies, even while he was a nominal servitor of the king.[11] He passed a part of each year in Bordentown, and the rest of the time in Philadelphia in law practice, until 1774, when he moved his residence to Bordentown. In June, 1776, he resigned as a member of the Provincial Council and was chosen to represent New Jersey at the Continental Congress. Thus he became one of the signers of the Declaration of Independence.

The three years before the Declaration of Independence were indeed critical. The hopes of relief yielded slowly to the certainty that war must decide the issue. To break away from Eng-

[11] A graphic story of the burning of the Borden house and the patriotic defiance of Madam Borden is given in the sketch of Hopkinson by Charles R. Hildeburne, in the *Pennsylvania Magazine of History and Biography*, Vol. II, p. 319.

land was a radical thought; to suggest a possible nation from the federation of scattered colonies seemed fanatical to many conservative Whigs, as well as to pronounced Tories. The history of these years, read in the contemporary newspapers, reveals the varied influences of legislators, preachers, wits, and pamphleteers.

Among the earliest and most popular satires, which ridiculed the weakness of king and Parliament, were Francis Hopkinson's *A Pretty Story* and *A Prophecy*.[12]  The first was printed in September, 1774, when the Continental Congress was convened in Carpenter's Hall, Philadelphia. Hopkinson here portrayed existing conditions in America, "The New Farm," under oppressive treatment by the nobleman upon "The Old Farm." The king was represented as the exacting nobleman, Parliament was "the nobleman's wife, with avaricious eye," and "Jack" was the American colonist. Effective use was made of irony and argument, in reviewing the results of the

---

[12] *A Pretty Story Written in the Year of Our Lord 1774 by Peter Grievous, Esq. A.B.C.D.E. Veluti in Speculo* (Philadelphia, 1774); reprinted as *The Old Farm and The New Farm: A Political Allegory*, edited with notes by Benson J. Lossing (New York, 1857, 1864). In Hopkinson's *Miscellaneous Essays*, etc. (1792), Vol. I, pp. 92–97. Many of Hopkinson's early writings appeared in the *Pennsylvania Magazine or American Monthly Museum* (Philadelphia, 1775; edited and published by R. Aitkin).

Stamp Act, the taxed tea, and the war-vessels in Boston Harbor. The droll illustrations in the later editions emphasize the absurdity of passages, like this allegory about Lord North and Parliament:

> Now the Steward had gained an entire ascendancy over the King's Wife. She no longer deliberated what would most benefit either the Old Farm or the New but said and did whatever the Steward pleased. Nay, so much was she influenced by him that she could neither utter ay or no but as he directed. For he had cunningly persuaded her that it was very fashionable for women to wear Padlocks on their Lips and that he was sure they would become her exceedingly. He therefore fastened a Padlock to each corner of her Mouth; when the one was open she could only say ay; and when the other was loos'd could only cry no. He took care to keep the keys of these locks himself; so that her will became entirely subject to his Power.[13]

There was an abrupt and prophetic ending to this tract:

> These harsh and unconstitutional proceedings irritated "Jack" and the other inhabitants to such a degree that— COETERA DESUNT.

To encourage the sentiment of freedom and separation from England, Hopkinson wrote two clever, persuasive satires in fictional form, *Letter Written by a Foreigner on the Character of the*

[13] *A Pretty Story* (1774), pp. 65–91, in *Hopkinson's Miscellaneous Essays;* edition of 1857, in *The Old Farm and the New Farm,* p. 31.

*English Nation* and *A Prophecy*. The former
was calm and philosophical in tone: the observations of a supposed visitor in England in 1776,
who was amazed and grieved at the signs of
decadence and provincialism, and above all at
the obstinacy of the king and his ministers; for
they "have quarrelled with their loyal and bene-
ficial subjects" in America "because the latter will
not acknowledge that two and two make five."
*A Prophecy* was an answer to *Letters of Cato
to the People of Pennsylvania,* which had been
widely circulated among the Tory newspapers;
they were earnest and forceful in their counsels
against any secession of the colonies from the
motherland.[14]   This second allegory, like the first,
suggested in form Arbuthnot's *History of John
Bull,* and abounded in sentences of humor and
mock-heroic.   It was expressed in the phraseology
of an old-time prophet, who deplored the contro-
versial scenes in his vision, but declared for success to the cause of independence.

Under the imagery of a tree, fruitful for many
years, planted in a far-away country by the king
of many islands, Hopkinson described the growth

[14] These *Letters* expressed the fears and protests of Rev.
William Smith, provost of the College of Philadelphia, an
earlier friend of Hopkinson, and one of the most able and
persuasive of the Tory pamphleteers.   The *Translation of a
Letter of a Foreigner,* etc., is in Hopkinson's *Miscellaneous
Essays,* etc. (1792), Vol. I, pp. 98–110.

of the American colonies and the benefits which
they had brought to England. But, he added,
"the North Wind blasted the Tree and broke
its Branches." The prophet was introduced,
with evident reference to Franklin; "and he shall
wear spectacles upon his nose and reverence and
esteem shall rest upon his brow." Then follows
the advice of the prophet, that the old tree shall
be hewn down, and a new, vigorous, young tree
be substituted. This shall be defended against

the winds of the North by a high wall. And they shall
dress it and prune it, and cultivate it to their liking.
And the young tree shall grow and flourish and spread
its branches far abroad; and the people shall dwell under
the shadow of its branches, and shall become an exceeding
great, and powerful and happy nation.[15]

During the war Hopkinson's zeal for his
country was expressed by service on committees
for practical work, as well as by his writings. As
one of three commissioners, under direction of
the Marine Committee, he assisted in the work of
equipping the navy; he was also treasurer of the
Continental Loan Office for New Jersey. Franklin did not lose his interest in Hopkinson's career,
as is indicated by letters from France, praising
Hopkinson's "political squibs" and urging him
to write more, offering him "gim-cracks" for

[15] This *Prophecy* is in *Miscellaneous Essays*, Vol. I, pp.
92-97.

scientific use, and congratulating him on his treasury office.[16]   In return, Hopkinson both solicited and appreciated the fatherly interest of Franklin; in testimony, there is a manuscript letter, in the library of the American Philosophical Society, which contains some side-lights upon military affairs and the varied pursuits of Hopkinson:

Phila. 22d Octr. 1778

My dear Friend,

Had I consulted my own Inclinations more than your Ease, you should have frequently heard from me since you left us; but knowing your Correspondence to be extensive & your Engagements important, I have avoided offering myself to your Notice, lest I should intrude on more Weighty Concerns.   I would not, however, carry Delicacy so far as to run the Hazard of being entirely forgot by one who was my Father's Friend to the last & whom I am very proud to call mine, a continuance of your Regard will be a real Gratification to me & flatter my Vanity, as I can truly say I both love & honour you.—I have suffered much by the Invasion of the Goths & Vandals.   I was obliged to fly from my House at Borden Town with my Family & leave all my effects in *statu quo,* the Savages plundered me to their Heart's Content—but I do not repine, as I really esteem it an honour to have suffered in my Country's cause & in Support of the Rights of Human Nature & of civilized Society.   I have not abilities to assist our righteous Cause by personal Prowess & Force of Arms, but I have done it all the service I could

[16] *The Complete Works of Benjamin Franklin* (Bigelow), Vol. VI, pp. 421, 422; Vol. VII, p. 294.

with my Pen. Throwing in my wits at Times in Prose &
Verse, serious & satirical essays &c. The Congress have
been pleased to appoint me Treasurer of Loans, for the
United States with a salary of 2000 Dollars. Could our
money recover its former Value, I should think this a
handsome appointment—as it is, it is a Subsistence.

Mrs. Bache has been so good as to lend me your
portable electrical apparatus, which I have got in excellent order, & shall take great Care of; it is a great Amusement to me & I hope you will not be offended with her
& me for this Liberty. I wish to borrow also your
little Air Pump which is at present much out of Order
but I will clean it and put it to Rights if she will let me
have it. Whatever she lends me shall be punctually
restored on Demand, in good Repair. N. B. Your
Gim-cracks have suffered much by the late usurpers of
our City.

But I will not detain you longer with my Uninteresting
Chat. Sincerely wishing you a long Continuance of
Health & Ease, & all the solid Comforts which a *good
Man* enjoys in the decline of Life,

I am, dear Sir,

Your ever affectionate & unfeigned Friend,

Fras Hopkinson

Another evidence of popular esteem came to
Hopkinson when he was appointed, in 1779, as
judge of the Court of the Admiralty. He held
this position for ten years, when he was made
district judge by appointment of Washington.[17]
As lawyer and judge he was astute and liberal;

[17] Letter of appointment in possession of Mrs. Oliver
Hopkinson.

his decisions were cited with respect by later
jurists.   Apparently he was once the victim of
enmity, and was charged and impeached for accepting bribes, gifts, etc., during the first year
of his judgeship.[18]   He was acquitted, and this
forgotten episode left no stain upon his reputation for integrity and efficiency.   Four years later
Jefferson recommended him as director of the
mint, with this characterization: "a man of
genius, gentility, and great merit—as capable of
the office as any man I know and the appointment
would give general pleasure because he is generally esteemed."[19]

That the lucrative directorship did not come
to him unsought is shown by a letter from him
in the *Jefferson Papers*, in manuscript, now in
the Library of Congress.[20]   The letter was dated
Philadelphia, May 12, 1784:

It appears by your Letter that Congress have again
taken up the Idea of a public Mint. I beg leave to mention to you that I have long had it in Contemplation to
sollicit the super-Intendency of this Department should it

[18] For an account of "The Impeachment and Trial of
Francis Hopkinson, Judge of the Admiralty, November,
1780," see *Pennsylvania State Trials* (edited by Edmund
Hogan), Vol. I (Philadelphia, 1794).

[19] *The Writings of Thomas Jefferson*, edited by Paul
Leicester Ford, Vol. III, p. 495.

[20] *Jefferson Papers*, in manuscript, Series II, Vol. XL,
No. 27.

ever be established. Mr. Morris marked out this Station
for me when he first formed the Idea of striking metal
Coin for the U. States. My Gim-crack Abilities & I flatter myself my Integrity & Attention would be of Service
in the Department—but my whole Scheme would fail
unless this Mint should be carried on in or near this city.
The Business of the Admiralty Department takes up but
little of my Time, & its Emoluments (£500 per An) which
is the whole of my Income, you may easily suppose to be
insufficient for the Support & Education of so large a
Family as I have in Charge. What with the Depredations
of the enemy & my little Capital which lies entrapped (?)
in the Movement of the Public Funds—I have given up
all hope of leaving my Family anything of Importance
at my Death, but my earnest Desire is to be enabled to
leave them well educated—to do which I must procure in
some line or other, a more liberal Income than £500 per
an. This I cannot do in the way of Trade; my office as
Judge prohibits it—at least not openly—but there will be
no Inconsistence, in my holding such a Department under
Congress.

A few months before writing this letter, Hopkinson had written to Jefferson, then in Paris,
asking the privilege of correspondence with him,
that he might express his literary and scientific
fancies to one who would give appreciative response:

I shall be happy to correspond with you, if you
give me any Encouragement. My Fancy suggests a Thousand Whims which die for Want of Communication—nor
would I communicate them but to one who has Discernment to conceive my Humour, and Candour with respect

to my Faults & Peculiarities.    Such a Friend I believe you
to be.[21]

Evidently he received the wished-for encouragement, as he wrote freely to Jefferson during the next five years, of his varied inventions
and hopes for success with them. Thus, in
December, 1785, he recounts: "I have con-
trived a method of assisting a vessel in her sailing which promises great Success—it is simple,
trifling in Point of expence & demonstrable in
Theory. The Experiment has not yet been tried,
but will be before long."[22]    In April, 1787, he
wrote: "I have invented this Winter a cheap,
convenient & useful Appendage to a common
Candle-stick, which keeps the Flames from being
flared by the Wind in Summer or the Fire in
Winter."[23]    A year later he announced to Jefferson his plan to establish "a Wax Chandlery" in
Philadelphia, if he can get some gentlemen to join
in his plan.[24]    Another invention was of a musical kind: "In the course of my Experiments I
discover'd a method of drawing the Tone from
Metal Balls by Friction—to an amazing Perfec-

[21] *Jefferson Papers,* MS. (Library of Congress), Series II,
Vol. XL, No. 24.

[22] *Jefferson Papers, loc. cit.,* No. 3.    This plan was outlined in his *Miscellaneous Essays,* Vol. I, pp. 274–285.

[23] *Ibid.,* No. 40.    The model of this candle-case is in the
American Philosophical Society.

[24] *Ibid.,* No. 41.

tion.—I am getting a Set of Bells cast & expect to introduce a new musical Instrument to be called the *Bellarmonic*." [25]

Hopkinson's legal and scientific activities made far less impression upon the people of his own day than was achieved by his writings, with their peculiar cleverness and logical force. It is very difficult for us today to measure the potent influence of the writers of the Revolutionary and National periods on their contemporaries. Their products seem amusing, rather than forceful, when taken away from their context and natural environment. Many of Hopkinson's compositions were ephemeral, yet they served a purpose of more lasting importance than the issue of the hour seemed to indicate; others possess some literary merit in logical force and satire. Among the latter may be mentioned *Letter to Lord Howe,* after the devastating march of the British troops through New Jersey; *John Burgoyne's Proclamation,* and the strictures upon the Tory printers, James Rivington and Hugh Gaine.[26] Many of

[25] *Ibid.*, No. 37.

[26] *Miscellaneous Essays and Occasional Writings* (1792), Vol. I, pp. 121–26, 146–50. In *Two Letters* (Vol. I, pp. 132–45) he hurled invective against the "innumerable lies from the batteries of Rivington and Gaine." This was followed by a clever lampoon, a mock advertisement of the books, maps, etc., of Rivington, who, after the surrender of Cornwallis, found it was "convenient for the subscriber to remove to Europe" (*Miscellaneous Essays,* etc., Vol. I, pp. 159–69).

his tracts and lampoons were first published in the *Pennsylvania Packet*, under the pseudonyms of "Calamus," "Cautious," "Calumniator," "A. B.," "One of the People," and occasionally, "F.H." [27] In their original form, as read in this paper, some of the attacks are truly Rabellaisian; we easily believe the statement of his family that, in revising his writings for publication, he modified the vehemence of many phrases.[28]

His war-verses were intended to inspirit the soldiers in days of gloom; and they accomplished that purpose. Among popular odes was the "Camp Ballad," which was well adapted to a marching-song:

> To arms, then, to arms! 'Tis fair freedom invites us;
> The trumpet shrill sounding, to battle excites us;

[27] Examples of this style are as follows: "Calamus" in *Packet*, February 9, 1782: "A Parody on a Scene in Macbeth" by "Calumniator," *Packet*, April 2, 1782; a dignified remonstrance, by "A Lover of Candour," *Packet*, June 15, 1782.

[28] In manuscript volumes owned by Mrs. Florence Scovel Shinn, a descendant of Hopkinson, are some scathing satires and doggerel songs like this complaint of the Tory leaders and printers:

> Burgoyne with thousand came
> In hopes of Wealth and Fame
>   What hath he done?
> At Saratoga he
> Had the Disgrace to see
> Each soldier manfully
>   Lay down his Gun.

The banners of virtue unfurled shall wave o'er us,
Our heroes lead on, and the foe fly before us.

The single composition by Francis Hopkinson which has been generally recalled was one of his most unliterary efforts, a mere *jeu d'esprit*— "Battle of the Kegs." The incident which he has preserved in memory by his verses illustrated Yankee ingenuity, and would make a strong appeal to a man of Hopkinson's tastes and sense of humor. A device by David Bushnell of some amateur torpedoes, known as the "American turtles," was the germ of the incident and song. Several of these torpedoes were floated down the Delaware in the late autumn of 1777, to annoy the British soldiers by causing explosions among the boats. The actual facts are given in different versions, but the incident, as well as Hopkinson's verses,[29] have been mentioned in several records of the period. Without much question, the mock-heroic narrative, in prose, which was printed in the *New Jersey Gazette*, January 28, 1778, was written by Hopkinson, as a preface to

[29] Explanation of this invention is given fully in James Thacher's *Military Journal during the American Revolutionary War*, etc. (Boston, 1823), pp. 75, 76, 146–50 ; Appendix, pp. 452, 453. On p. 244, date July 10, 1780, he refers to an evening in camp when "we were delighted with the song composed by Mr. Hopkinson, called the Battle of the Kegs, sung in the best style by a number of gentlemen." For other accounts see *Pennsylvania Ledger*, February 11, 1778, *American Philosophical Transactions*, Vol. IV, p. 312.

his verses.  He thus ridiculed the effects of the
kegs upon the British soldiers:

> Some asserted that these kegs were filled with armed
> rebels, who were to issue forth, in the dead of night,
> as the Grecians did of old from the wooden horse at the
> siege of Troy and take the city by surprise; declaring that
> they had seen the points of bayonets sticking out of the
> bung-holes of the kegs.  Others said that they were filled
> with inveterate combustibles, which would set the whole
> Delaware in flames and consume all the shipping in the
> harbor.  Whilst others conjectured that they were ma-
> chines constructed by a magic, and expected to see them
> mount the wharves and roll, all flaming with infernal
> fire, through the streets of the city.

After an ironical recital of the attack upon the
kegs "by land and marine forces," the caricature
closed with this sentence of sarcasm:

> It is said His Excellency, Lord Howe, has despatched
> a swift-sailing packet, with an account of his signal
> victory to the court of London.  In short, Monday the——
> day of January, 1778, will be ever memorable in history
> for the renowned Battle of the Kegs.

This briery satire in prose was followed probably within a few months, by the rollicking
stanzas, adapted to the tune of "Moggy Lawder,"
and the jolly raillery was sung and recited
throughout the colonies.  The verses have no
true literary merit, but it cannot be denied that
they have swing and effectiveness.  The opening
stanzas are typical of the form:

From an undated ballad-broadside, in American Antiquarian Society Library.

Gallants, attend, and hear a friend
　　Trill forth harmonious ditty;
Strange things I'll tell which late befell
　　In Philadelphia city.

'Twas early day, as poets say,
　　Just when the sun was rising,
A soldier stood on a log of wood
　　And saw a thing surprising.

A sailor too, in jerkin blue,
　　This strange appearance viewing,
First rubb'd his eyes, in great surprise
　　Then said—"some mischief's brewing;

"These kegs, I'm told, the rebels hold,
　　Packed up like pickled herring;
And they've come down t' attack the town,
　　In this new way of ferrying" [30]

As an example of Hopkinson's more dignified method of writing, one may choose the tract, *A Political Catechism,* written after Washington's successful raid at Trenton and the apparent collapse of the British commanders. Contrasting the pampered Royalists with the American general, he extolled Washington in terms of hero-worship:

[30] This ballad appeared in the *Pennsylvania Packet,* March 4, 1778; its first printing was in 1779 by B. Towne, Philadelphia (see Hildeburne's *Issues of the Press of Pennsylvania,* 1885–86, Vol. II. p. 336). A broadside here photographed is in the American Antiquarian Society. The ballad is in Hopkinson's *Miscellaneous Essays,* etc., Vol. III, p. 169. An edition was printed in 1866 by the Oakwood Press.

To him the title of Excellency is applied with peculiar propriety. He is the best and greatest man the world ever knew. He retreats like a General and attacks like a Hero. Had he lived in the days of idolatry, he had been worshipped as a god. One age cannot do justice to his merit; but a grateful posterity shall, for a succession of ages, remember the great Deliverer of his country.[31]

The devotion of Hopkinson to Washington did not seem to be incited by hope of reward. It was the fervent expression of his nature, and is akin to many other tributes by ardent Federalists of that age, but in marked contrast to the anathemas heaped upon Washington and his friends by political opponents. Hopkinson considered Washington as a personal friend and patron of the arts in which he delighted. When he published a volume of his songs, with music, he dedicated the folio to Washington, in terms of intimate friendship.[32] After a reference to the sympathy between them, he said:

With respect to this little Work, which I now have the honour to present to your Notice, I can only say that it is such as a Lover, not a Master of the Arts, can furnish. I am neither a profess'd Poet nor a profess'd Musician; and yet venture to appear in those characters united; for which, I confess, the censure of Temerity may justly be brought against me. . . . . However small the

[31] *Miscellaneous Essays*, etc., Vol. I, p. 119.

[32] *Seven Songs for the Harpsichord or Forte Piano. The Words and Music composed by Francis Hopkinson* (Philadelphia, [1788]).

Reputation may be that I shall derive from this Work, I cannot, I believe, be refused the Credit of being the first Native of the United States who has produced a Musical Composition. If this attempt should not be too severely treated, others may be encouraged to enter on a path, yet untrodden in America, and the Arts in succession will take root and flourish amongst us.

In accepting the dedication and flattering letter which came with it, Washington deplored his own musical inability, but said, with kindly humor:

I can neither sing one of the songs, nor raise a single note on any instrument to convince the unbelieving. But I have, however, one argument which will prevail with persons of true taste (at least in America)—I can tell them that *it is the production of Mr. Hopkinson.*[33]

To Jefferson, or his daughter, Hopkinson sent a copy of this songbook, with special mention of the pathos of the last number and the circumstances of its writing. He explained that the songs were composed originally for his daughters,

who play and sing them well. The last Song, if play'd very slow, and sang with expression, is forcibly pathetic—at least in my Fancy. Both Words and Music were the Work of an hour in the Heighth of a Storm. But the Imagination of an Author who composes from his Heart, rather than his Head, is always more heated than he can expect his Readers to be.[34]

[33] Manuscript letter owned by Mrs. Oliver Hopkinson.

[34] *Jefferson Papers,* MS. Series II, Vol. XL, No. 43. This last, "pathetic" song is quoted in part below.

In reply, Jefferson assured his friend of appreciation, and pictured his family of daughters enjoying the music upon the harpsichord, while the youngest girl was "all in tears. I asked her if she was sick? She said, no; but the tune was so mournful." [35] Evidently this tribute was agreeable to Hopkinson, and writers of his age, as a compliment to their skill in cultivating sentimentality.

These seven songs, examined today, show limited musical skill, but they were popular far into the last century. Such songs as "With Jemmy on the Sea" and the rhythmic "Hunting-Call" are not yet forgotten by singers of the older generation. The sentimental swain, the blushing maiden, and the weeping-willow in the background, which furnish the setting for the songs, were familiar features of tales, verses, and samplers of that period. The most poetic of the verses is the seventh love-song, suggestive of Henry Vaughan or Robert Herrick in an occasional stanza. The song bore the title "My Generous Heart Disdains."

> Still uncertain is tomorrow,
>   Not quite certain is today;
> Shall I waste my time in sorrow?
>   Shall I languish life away?
> All because a cruel maid
>   Hath not Love with Love repaid?

[35] *Jefferson Papers*, MS. Series I, Vol. III, No. 280.

In the political agitation which preceded the
adoption of the Constitution by Pennsylvania,
Virginia, and New York, Hopkinson took a
prominent part through newspaper articles, urging the need of a new declaration of federation
for the states. He was one of the most urgent
Federalists, although he died before the bitter
contests of opinion between the Federalists and
Anti-Federalists after the election of Washington as president. He challenged Jefferson regarding his attitude toward the Federal party,
as is indicated by a letter from Jefferson to Hopkinson.[36] In view of the later position of Jefferson as leader of the Democratic-Republican
party, and his suspected alliance with Freneau
in editing the most aggressive Anti-Federalist
newspaper of the times,[37] this letter has a peculiar
interest to modern students. Under date of
Paris, March 13, 1789, Jefferson wrote:

You say that I have been dished up to you as an anti-
federalist and ask me if it be just,—my opinion was never
worthy enough of notice to merit citing, but since you ask
it I will give it you.

I am not a Federalist, because I never submitted the
whole system of my opinions to the creed of any party of
men whatever in religion, in philosophy, in politics, or in

[36] *Ibid.* Series I, Vol III, No. 280. Also Jefferson's
*Writings* (Ford) Vol. V, pp. 75-78.

[37] *National Gazette,* Philadelphia, October, 1791, to October, 1793.

anything else, where I was capable of thinking for myself, such an addiction is the last degredation of a free and moral agent; if I could not go to heaven but with a party, I would not go there at all, therefore I protest to you I am not of the party of the federalists, but I am much farther from that of the Antifederalists. I approved, from the first moment, of the great mass of what is in the new constitution, the consolidation of the government, the organization into Executive, legislative and judicial, . . . . the happy compromise of interests between the great and little states by the different manner of voting in the different houses, the voting by persons instead of states, the qualified negative of laws given to the Executive which however, I should have liked better if associated with the judiciary as in New York, and the power of taxation. . . . . What I disapproved from the first moment was the want of a bill of rights to guard liberty against the legislative as well as executive branches of the government. . . . . I disapproved also the perpetual reeligibility of the President.

About a year before this declaration of sentiments by Jefferson, Hopkinson had written to him frankly of the controversy, especially in Pennsylvania, over the new Constitution, and had referred to his own literary services in the movement. He announced that Philadelphia was "in a high political Fermentation about our new proposed federal Constitution," and added:

You will be surprised when I tell you that our public newspapers have announced General Washington to be a Fool influenced & led by that Knave Dr. Franklin who is a public Defaulter for Millions of Dollars, that Mr. Morris has defrauded the Public out of as many Millions as you please & that they are to cover their frauds by this new Government. . . . .

I had the Luck to discover & bring forward into public View on sufficient Testimony the writer of a Series of abominable abuse, under the Signature *Philadelphiensis,* he is an Irishman who came from Dublin about 3 years ago & got admitted as Tutor in Arithmetic in our University.[38] I am now under the Lash for this Discovery, scarce a Day's papers without my appearance in the newspaper in every scandalous Garb that scribbling Vengeance can furnish. I wrote also a piece stiled *The New Roof* which had a great Run. I would send you a copy but for the Postage. You will probably see it in some of the Papers, as it was reprinted in, I believe, every State.[39]

*The New Roof* was another clever allegory, with blended prose and verse. It was vigorous as an argument for the new Constitution versus the futile Confederation, with its defunct powers. In New York, Virginia, and Massachusetts the tract was read and quoted by Federal leaders, while it caught popular fancy by its symbolic form. In behalf of a new Constitution Hopkinson argued thus:

1. That the whole fabric was too weak. 2. That there were indeed thirteen rafters; but that these rafters were not connected by any braces or ties, so as to form a union

[38] Many articles, thus signed, were in *The Freeman's Journal,* Philadelphia, during the fall of 1787. See attack on Hopkinson as "the little Fiddler" in *The Independent Gazetteer,* March 24, 1788, *Centinel,* No. XVII.

[39] *Jefferson Papers,* MS. series II, Vol. XL, No. 41.

of strength. 3. That some of these rafters were too thick and heavy, and others too slight; and as the whole had been put together whilst the timber was yet green, some had warped outwards, and of course sustained an undue proportion of weight, while others, warping inwards, had shrunk from bearing any weight at all. 4. That the roof was so flat as to admit the most idle servants in the family, their playmates and acquaintances to trample upon and abuse it.[40]

With scathing wit, Hopkinson portrayed the leaders of the opposition to the "new roof," as the articles of agreement were generally called. He extolled James, the surveyor of the old roof —presumably James Wilson, of Pennsylvania, who had been chosen "as architect to look over the repairs;" and he caricatured such opponents as William Patterson, of New Jersey; Governor George Clinton, of New York; Robert Whitehill, and John Dickinson, of Pennsylvania. This is a typical passage of satire:

Now there was an old woman, known by the name of Margery, who had got a comfortable apartment in the mansion house. This woman was of an intriguing spirit, of a restless and inveterate temper, fond of tattle and a great mischief-maker. . . . . It so happened that in the construction of the new roof, her apartment would be considerably lessened. No Sooner, therefore, did she hear of the plan proposed by the architects, but she put on

[40] In the *Pennsylvania Packet,* December 29, 1787, is the prose part of *The New Roof,* unsigned, but prefaced by the words "For the Packet."

her old red cloak, and was day and night trudging amongst the tenants and servants and crying out against the new roof and the framers of it. Amongst these she had selected William, Jack and Robert, three of the tenants, and instigated them to oppose the plan in agitation; she caused them to be sent to the great hall on the day of debate, and furnished them with innumerable alarms and fears, cunning arguments, and specious objections.

The song which closed this allegory was effective and rhythmic:

Up! Up! with the rafters; each frame is a state:
How nobly they rise! their span, too, how great!
From the north to the south, o'er the whole they extend.
And rest on the walls whilst the walls they defend:
For our roof we will raise, and our song still shall be,
Combined in strength, yet as citizens free.[41]

If such allegorical methods seem puerile to this critical age, we must remember that their simplicity, with their wit, made them far more effective among the people of the earlier time than any more subtle method would have been. In a letter from Robert Morris to Hopkinson, dated from Williamsburg, in 1788, is a direct allusion to the general interest awakened by this argument in unique form: [42]

[41] *The Miscellaneous Essoys and Occasional Writings of Francis Hopkinson*, Vol. II, pp. 282–319. By a mistake, the date here is 1778, not 1787.

[42] From a manuscript letter owned and loaned by Mrs. Oliver Hopkinson.

I received your obliging letter before my departure from Richmond and had much pleasure not only in reading "The New Roof" but also in communicating it to others; it is greatly admired & I tell them if they could but enter into the Dramatis Personae as we do they would find it still more excellent. The character of Margery is well hit off, how does the old Lady like it? I am not surprised that they should baste you in the Freeman's Journal, it is what you must expect as long as they have anybody to Wield a Pen. I observe they will not let me alone, altho no author. It is my fate to furnish matter for reproach whether I meddle or do not meddle in Politics, my successes & my misfortunes, whichever befall me, are equally the themes for abuse. However let them indulge their spleen—if I had nothing else to disturb my repose, I should sleep much at ease.

My Wythe yesterday at Dinner introduced the New Roof as a subject and after expressing his approbation. very modestly supposed it to be one of your productions. Mr. G. Morris & myself joined in that opinion. Thus you see that whether you intend it or not, there always appear some characteristic marks in your writings that disclose the Fountain from whence they spring.

As an example of the extravagant tribute paid to Hopkinson by his friends, here is a sentence in another letter by Morris, of later date:

You are either a great Wit or Humorist, you have Superior Genius or you have great Talents or rather I shall come nearer the Truth by charging you with being the actual possessor of all these qualities.[43]

[43] From a manuscript letter owned by Mrs. Oliver Hopkinson.

This influence of Hopkinson among men of affairs was won in spite of very small stature and a weak presence. The familiar description of him, given by John Adams, has remained as a mistaken impression of his true personality.[44] After meeting him at the studio of Mr. Peale in 1776, Adams wrote to his wife:

I have a curiosity to penetrate a little deeper into the bosom of this curious gentleman, and may possibly give you some more particulars concerning him. He is one of your pretty, little, curious, ingenious men. His head is not bigger than a large apple, less than our friend Pemberton or Dr. Simon Tufts. I have not met with anything in natural history more amusing and entertaining than his personal appearance—yet he is genteel and well bred and very social.

Mingled with the delicate traits of Hopkinson were strength of mind and patience.[45] In circles of politics, education, and society his wit and geniality made him welcome. His touch was gentle, but beneath was a sting of ridicule which hurt his enemies more than the bolder satires of his contemporaries. His zeal for reform showed itself in clever essays upon education and allied

[44] *Letters of John Adams Addressed to His Wife* (Boston, 1841), Vol. I, pp. 156, 157.

[45] As illustration of his gentleness was a popular story of a mouse which came forth daily to share his meals, and a flock of tame pigeons which greeted him (Delaplaine's *Repository of the Lives and Portraits of Distinguished American Characters,* Vol. III, p. 138).

themes.   Under the favorite signature of "Calamus" he remonstrated against the scandalous
trend of journalism at the close of the war, and
contended:

Having observed with real concern, that our newspapers have for a long time past, been filled with private
calumny to the great abuse of the liberty of the press and
dishonor of the city,—I, who have ever been ambitious of
devising something for the public good, set my wits to
work to remedy this growing evil and to restore our gazettes, advertisers, journals and packets to their original
design—viz., to make them the vehicles of Intelligence
not the common sewers of scandal.

Following this statement was an outline of a
proposed plan for a "High Court of Honor" to
decide cases of scandal and calumny.[46]

On the occasion of a petty quarrel between two
bands of medical students and their respective
schools in Philadelphia, Hopkinson addressed to
the classes *An Oration,* so full of ridicule and
good sense that it silenced the wranglers.[47]   Another effective remonstrance, in satire form was,
*Dialogues of the Dead,*[48] directed against the
filth and carcasses of animals which were allowed

[46] *Miscellaneous Essays,* etc., Vol. I, pp. 151-58.

[47] *An Oration Which Might Have Been Delivered to the
Students in Anatomy on the Late Rupture between the Two
Schools in this City* (1789).

[48] *Miscellaneous Essays,* Vol. I, pp. 327-39.   This is
referred to by MacMaster in *A History of the People of the
United States* (1883), Vol. I, p. 64, note.

to putrify in the streets of Philadelphia. Among
the tributes to Hopkinson's memory were some
crude stanzas by John Swanwick, which are of
interest because they record another occasion
when Hopkinson by his pen gained a victory for
civic betterment. In apostrophe his elegist wrote:

> Sweet spring advance, and deck with flow'rets gay,
>   The tomb where Hopkinson's remains are laid:
> Ye Muses, there your constant vigils pay,
>   And guard from ills the consecrated shade.
>
> Ye city trees, protect your patron's grave;
>   He once from ruin saved your leafy charms,
> Then to his honor bid your green tops wave,
>   And fold his urn in your embracing arms.[40]

The allusion in these verses was to a plea by
Hopkinson, in the *Pennsylvania Gazette,* in 1782,
which was successful in rescinding a vote of the
city government, declaring that all the city trees
should be cut down for fear of contagion and fire.
This was entitled *A Speech of a Standing Member,
the Plea of Citizen Tree.* It was not alone
witty, but it also showed much information regarding moisture and sanitation.

When the grand federal procession was held
in Philadelphia, in July, 1788, to celebrate the
adoption of the Constitution and the confidence
of the people, Hopkinson was chairman of the

[40] *The American Museum* (Carey), Vol. IX, p. 38, Appendix
(1792).

committee of arrangements and has left a graphic account of the celebration.[50]

By such spirited attacks upon abuses of various kinds, which retarded true progress, Hopkinson often created a tide of disfavor against them. He was an earnest student of the then known sciences, and a fearless critic of the stale, scholastic methods of teaching them.  Like John Trumbull in *Progress of Dulness,* he burlesqued the formal, lifeless recitations, in a satirical essay, *Modern Learning Exemplified by a Specimen of a Collegiate Examination.*[51]  He ridiculed the stilted modes of teaching metaphysics, logic, natural philosophy, mathematics, anatomy, and "the Practice of Physic and Chemistry."  A brief portion from this burlesque on examinations of his day is the following:

Professor. "What is the salt called with respect to the box?"

Student. "It is called its Contents."

Professor. "And Why so?"

Student. "Because the cook is content, *quoad hoc,* to find plenty of salt in the box."

Professor. "You are quite right. Let us now proceed to Logic. How many parts are there in a salt-box?"

[50] The account of this celebration is in *Miscellaneous Essays,* etc., Vol. II, pp. 349–422. The gold anchor worn by Hopkinson in his hat is in the collection of federal relics in Independence Hall, Philadelphia.

[51] *American Museum,* February, 1787, pp. 142–47.

Student. "Three,—bottom, top, and sides."

Professor. "How many modes are there in a salt-box?"

Student. "Four,—the formal, the substantial, the accidental and the topsy turvy."[52]

Hopkinson had many schemes for improving the teaching of sciences. Not a few of his ideas seem only predictions of the experimental modes of today, the natural and practical way of teaching science. He had a well-trained mind, and his odd conceits showed a marked degree of ingenuity. When the British troops devastated Bordentown, Hopkinson's house was saved by an incident which attests his scholarship. The torch had been applied to the outside of the house, when the captain of the Hessians, Ewald, seeking for plunder probably, entered the library and was amazed at the books, the scientific apparatus, and the mechanical designs. As he had an interest in science, he respected such evidences of scholarship and gave command that the flames should be extinguished. Within a volume of Provost Smith's *Discourses* he wrote, beneath his own seal, "This man was one of the greatest rebels, nevertheless, if we dare to conclude from the Library and Mechanical and Mathematical instruments, he must have been a very learned man."[53]

[52] *Miscellaneous Essays,* etc., Vol. I, p. 344.

[53] *Pennsylvania Magazine of History and Biography,* Vol. II, p. 320.

Not all of Hopkinson's literary skits and essays were so purposeful and serious as those that have been cited.  He turned his wit into a merry channel when he wrote the droll impressions, in a letter from a gentleman in Philadelphia to his friend in Europe, *On Annual White-Washings*.  This custom of the past days was cleverly described and parodied, as a part of the marriage contract, giving to the young wife "the free and unmolested exercise of the rights of *white-washing,* with all its ceremonials, privileges and appurtenances."  In the same essay Hopkinson commemorated, with mingled respect and humor, another and more lasting custom of his native city:

There is also another custom peculiar to the city of Philadelphia and nearly allied to the former.  I mean that of washing the pavement before the doors every Saturday evening.  I at first took this to be a regulation of the police, but, on further enquiry, find it is a religious rite preparatory to the Sabbath and is, I believe, the only religious rite in which the numerous sectaries of this city perfectly agree.[54]

Francis Hopkinson died of apoplexy, in May, 1791, and was buried in Christ Churchyard, although the tomb cannot now be identified.[55]

[54] *American Museum,* January, 1787, pp. 48–53; *Miscellaneous Essays,* etc., Vol. II, pp. 146–60.

[55] His burial record, May 11, 1791, may be found in the *manuscript* list of burials of Christ Churchyard, to be found in the Library of the Historical Society of Pennsylvania.

Both Bordentown and Philadelphia contain
memorials of him. Much of his later life was
passed in the latter city. The Hopkinson mansion still stands in Bordentown, slightly changed
in appearance from his day. It is linked in
memory with his son, Joseph, as well as with the
elder man. Here Francis Hopkinson delighted
to return for rest and devotion to the arts. He
played the spinet with such grace that Bordentown residents would congregate before his win-
dows to listen. Here he painted many of his
sketches and portraits. One of the latter was
honored with a misplaced tribute, calling it the
work of Copley. Joseph Hopkinson inherited
his father's love for verse as well as his legal
skill, and entertained distinguished guests, among
them Joseph Bonaparte and Thomas Moore. The
only notable contribution in verse by Joseph Hopkinson which has survived is the ode, "Hail
Columbia! Happy Land!"

The death of Hopkinson followed, within a
few months, the decease of Franklin. This circumstance, and the friendship between the two
men, gave eulogists an opportunity for extravagant tribute to both. In the *Columbian Magazine*,
May, 1791, appeared a prose obituary of Hopkinson and two elegies. One contained the
refrain: "Another sage expired!" The versifier

extolled both the gentleness and courage of Hopkinson:

> The steady foe of tyranny confess'd,
> Yet with such art and gentleness reproved,
> That though some feared his *pen*, the *man* was loved.
> And be this line upon his tombstone writ—
> *The friend of virtue and the friend of wit.*

In the prose estimate of Hopkinson's qualities the writer was more restrained and forceful. With truth, he declared:

> He thought much and thought justly upon the subject of education. He often ridiculed, in conversation, the practice of teaching children the English language by means of grammar. Sometimes he employed his formidable powers of humor and satire in exposing the formalities of technical science. He was an active and useful member of three great political parties which, at different times, divided his native state—he was a Whig, a republican and a federalist and he lived to see the principles and wishes of each of those parties finally and universally successful. It only remains to add to this account of Mr. Hopkinson that the various causes which contributed to the establishment of the independent and federal government of the United States will not be *fully traced* unless much is ascribed to the irresistible influence of the *ridicule* which he poured forth from time to time upon the enemies of those great political events.

# PHILIP FRENEAU: AMERICA'S FIRST POET

PHILIP FRENEAU

From a sketch, made in his later years and finished after his
death; reproduced from 1865 edition of his *Poems*.

# III

## PHILIP FRENEAU: AMERICA'S FIRST POET

Among casual readers the name of Philip Freneau is more familiar than that of other writers of his time, but we need more information about the details of his life and work. Recent indications may be found of an awakening interest in this early poet; his poems have been republished in two large volumes, a full bibliography of his writings has been issued,[1] and bibliophiles are rivaling each other in zeal to acquire first editions of his works.

Freneau was an ardent patriot; he was even a bitter partisan. During the war his satires in verse dismayed English generals and Loyalist sympathizers; during the years of controversy over the best form of government he wrote scathing tracts and editorials against the Federalists and their marked leaders. In this primal attention to his service as satirist and political penman, too little study has been made of the frag-

---

[1] *The Poems of Philip Freneau,* edited by Fred L. Patee (Princeton, New Jersey, 1902-7; 3 vols.); *Bibliography of the Works of Philip Freneau,* compiled by Victor Hugo Paltsits (New York, 1903).

mentary, but significant, outbursts of lyrical poetry which were interspersed among his polemics and lampoons. Although the most spontaneous impulses of the lyric poet are found in his earlier stanzas, yet the martial sentiments did not wholly submerge the poetic yearnings in his later years. To Freneau, Mr. Stedman has traced "the first essential poetic spirit"[2] in America; he has included several of these poems in his anthology.[3]

As youth and man, Freneau was haunted by vague, restless desires to serve his country, and at the same time win fame for himself by his pen. His fancy and aspirations were early awakened, but, after a few ventures in poetry of the accepted mode, he realized that fate had placed him in conditions which called for other forms of literary service. There is bitterness of disappointment, but there is also determination to serve the hour, in his poem "The Author":

> An age employ'd in pointing steel,
> Can no poetic raptures feel;
>
> . . . . . . . . . . .
>
> The Muse of Love in no request,
> I'll try my fortune with the rest.
> Which of the Nine shall I engage,

[2] Edmund Clarence Stedman, *Poets of America* (Boston, 1896), p. 35.

[3] Stedman and Hutchinson, *A Library of American Literature* (1897), Vol. I.

To suit the humor of the age?
On one, alas! my choice must fall,
The least engaging of them all!
Her visage stern, severe her style,
A clouded brow, a cruel smile,
A mind on murder'd victims plac'd.
She, only she, can please the taste.[*]

It is not difficult to trace the dual traits of the
poet and the patriot in the inheritance of Freneau.
A sensitive, romantic strain of ancestry was
mingled with the sturdy Huguenot traits of thrift
and courage. The grandfather, André Fres-
neau, came to Boston in 1705. After a brief stay
there, he spent a few months in Connecticut, and
finally reached New York, where he secured a
position with the Royal West India Company.
Here he became associated with other men of
Huguenot ancestry, who clustered their homes in
the vicinity of Pine Street and the old Church of
St. Esprit.

He married the granddaughter of John Morin
Scott, thus introducing more noble blood into
the family. André died in 1725. His second
son, Pierre, was the father of the poet. By
native talents and marriage ties the family had
gained social rank in those days of old New
York when the homes of the élite were in lower

[*] *Poems Written between the Years 1768 & 1794, by
Philip Freneau of New Jersey: A New Edition, Revised and
Corrected by the Author* (Monmouth, N. J., 1795), p. 327.

Broadway and Bowling Green. A house, long standing in Frankfort Street, was the birthplace of Philip Freneau in January, 1752. The year of his birth his father bought a thousand acres of land in Monmouth County, New Jersey, building there a large mansion, to which he gave the name "Mont Pleasant," in memory of the fine estate of that name once owned by the family in France.

According to the usual narrative, the Freneau home was transferred from New York to Monmouth. Mr. Pattee thinks that Philip was left at school, in New York, when the family moved away.[5] In either case, he found the first poetic incentive of his boyhood amid the New Jersey hills, which he so often extolled in verse. His mother, Agnes Watson Freneau, encouraged all the dreamy love for nature and books which the boy revealed. She was a woman with a beautiful face and a fine mind. Her portrait, as a girl of sixteen, was long a treasured heirloom, made doubly romantic by the saber thrust through the heart, which was a reminder of vandal British soldiers. Surviving her first husband by half a century, she married James Kearny. To the end of her ninety years she was a fascinating companion.

[5] "Introduction" to *The Poems of Philip Freneau* (1902–7), Vol. I, p. xv.

After a struggle with classic textbooks at the
Latin school at Penelopen, Philip Freneau was
placed under the tutorship of Rev. William Ten-
nent, of Monmouth, and entered Nassau Hall,
Princeton.    Probably his roommate was James
Madison.    The latter was an intimate life-long
friend of the poet, and was much enamored of
Freneau's sister, Mary, when he visited at Mont
Pleasant.    Philip's brother, Pierre, generally
called Peter, was for many years identified with
the political movements in South Carolina, and
was an adviser of Jefferson and his party.    He
inherited much of the ancestral thrift and industry.    At college, Philip was a classmate of
James Madison, Aaron Burr, Aaron Ogden, and
Hugh Henry Brackenridge.    As a mere boy he
wrote verses.    Unfortunately, some of his juve-
nile and bombastic efforts, like "The Poetical
History of the Prophet Jonah," written at the
age of fourteen, have been preserved in later
editions of his poetry.    In collaboration with
Brackenridge he wrote the commencement poem
at his graduation in 1772—"The Rising Glory
of America." [6]    For some reason not explained,
both Freneau and Madison were absent, or
excused from taking part in the commencement

[6] This was published in pamphlet form, *A Poem on the
Rising Glory of America,* etc. (Philadelphia, 1772).    It is in
his *Poems* (edition of 1795), pp. 36–46.

programme, as is shown in a paragraph of record in the *History of the College of New Jersey:*[7]

> An English forensic dispute on the question, "Does ancient Poetry excel the Modern?" Mr. Freneau, the Respondent, being necessarily absent, his arguments, in favor of the Ancients, were read. . . . . Mr. James Madison was excused from taking any part in the exercises.

In the same note upon this programme we read, "A Poem on 'The Rising Glory of America' by Mr. Brackenridge, was received with great applause by the audience." Possibly this statement has led to the uncertainty regarding the real authorship of this initial, boyish poem which was afterward included in Freneau's writings. The answer seems to be conclusive, as given by a friend of Brackenridge:

> Although he courted the Muses, and in conjunction with the poet Freneau, his classmate, composed a poem on "The Rising Glory of America," he confessed that on his part it was a task of labor, while the verse of his associate flowed spontaneously.[8]

A few lines from this poem indicate both the aspiration and the zeal of its youthful authors; they seem also to prophesy the part that Freneau later was to play in commerce, as well as poetry:

[7] John MacLean, *History of the College of New Jersey: From Its Origin in 1746 to the Commencement of 1854* (Philadelphia, 1877), Vol. I, p. 312, note.

[8] *Southern Literary Messenger*, Vol. VIII, No. 1, p. 2.

Great is the praise of commerce, and the men
Deserve our praise who spread from shore to shore
The flowing sail; great are their dangers too;
Death ever present to the fearless eye
And ev'ry billow but a gaping grave;
Yet all these mighty feats to Science are
    Their rise and glory.[9]

A curious quarto manuscript may be found in the library of the Historical Society of Pennsylvania, entitled "Father Bumbo's Pilgrimage to Mecca in Arabia, Vol. II., written by H. B. and P. F., 1770." The easy translation of these letters indicates that the two friends had collaborated in poetry before they wrote the commencement poem. These earlier verses relate many adventures, and contain a few doggerel rhymes on political affairs.[10] Occasionally there is a stanza of true appreciation of nature, although expressed in stilted phrase—as this:

Sweet are the flowers that crown the Vale,
And sweet the spicy breathing Gale,
    That murmurs o'er the hills,
The hour the distant lowing throng
Thro' verdant pastures move along,
    To drink from limpid Streams and crystal Rills.

[9] *A Poem on the Rising Glory of America; Being an Exercise Delivered at the Public Commencement at Nassau Hall, September 25, 1772*, p. 18.

[10] Bound in the manuscript with this poem is a collection of tirades, probably written by Freneau and his college friends to ridicule a rival society of Tories.

Freneau taught school, for a brief period, after he left college. His first experience was in Flatbush, Long Island, but later he joined Brackenridge in Maryland, at Princess Anne Academy. The two friends made fitful attempts at the study of theology; then abandoned this for law, which became the life-profession of Brackenridge. Freneau's career as pedagogue outlasted his time spent in reading for the ministry and the bar, but he disliked the experience as teacher. His disheartening impressions were given in letters, and also in a droll poem, "The Miserable Life of a Pedagogue." To Madison he wrote of his forced acceptance of a school at Flatbush, and his disgust:

I did enter upon the business of it certain and continued in it thirteen days—but—Long Island I have bid adieu, With all its brainless, brutish crew. The youth of that detested place, Are void of reason and of grace. From Flushing hills to Flatbush plains, Deep ignorance unrivall'd reigns. I'm very poetical but excuse it.[11]

With more of humor, tinctured still by impatience, he wrote his impressions in verse-form for publication:

> A plague I say on such employment,
> Where's neither pleasure nor enjoyment;
> Whoe'er to such life is ty'd,
> Was born the day he should have dy'd;

[11] *Madison Papers*, Letters to Madison, November 2, 1772 (Library of Congress), Vol. XIII, p. 9.

Born in an hour when angry spheres
Were tearing caps or pulling ears.
And Saturn slow 'gainst swift Mercurius
Was meditating battles furious;
Or comets with their blazing train,
Decreed their life, a life of pain.[12]

During these early years Freneau did other work more worthy than the poetical efforts quoted; the latter are of interest only in tracing the story of his life, with its varied experiences. Some of his verses, written before the war, portray the customs of his age. When the war was imminent, he began his work as satirist, probably writing a parody on "Gen. Gage's Proclamation," which was widely circulated in the press and also published as a broadside, in June, 1775.[13] In the aggregate he wrote more than sixty satires, odes, and elegies on the war. One of the best lampoons of the time was "The Midnight Consultations," first issued as "A Voyage to Boston."

[12] This poem was included in a collection, printed as *The American Village; A Poem. To Which are Added Several other Original Pieces in Verse. By Philip Freneau, A.B.* (New York, 1772). Copies of this are in the Library of Congress and the John Carter Brown Library. From the latter copy a reprint has been made (1906), published by the Club for Colonial Reprints of Providence.

[13] This is so suggested by Mr. Paltsits, in his *Bibliography*, p. 27. In *The Origin of McFingal*, by J. Hammond Trumbull, it is mentioned as possibly by John Trumbull; but this seems unlikely from the internal and collateral evidence. See further explanation on p. 129.

The scene was laid in the quarters of General Gage, the night after the battle of Bunker Hill. Both Lord Percy and General Gage were ridiculed thus:

> Lord Percy seem'd to snore—O conscious Muse,
> This ill-timed snoring to the Peer excuse,
> Tir'd was the Hero of his toilsome day,
> Full fifteen miles he fled,—a tedious way—
> How should he then the dews of Somnus shun,
> Perhaps not us'd to walk, much less to run.

The moan of Gage was a familiar stanza of caricature:

> Three weeks—ye gods! nay, three long years it seems,
> Since *roast beef* I have touched except in dreams.
> In sleep, choice dishes to my view repair,—
> Waking, I gape and clamp the empty air.
> Say, is it just that I, who rule these bands,
> Should live on husks, like rakes in foreign lands.[14]

Uneven in workmanship, with less natural wit than Hopkinson and Trumbull had, Freneau was yet the acknowledged satirist of the war, who accomplished the greatest results in annoying the British and Loyalists and in cheering the patriot leaders. He was ever ready to extol the bravery of the latter, as in his alleged words of Gage, after he realized the valor of the minutemen:

[14] "A Voyage to Boston" (Philadelphia, 1775). The quotations given are in the original form, pp. 10 and 15. The whole poem is in *Poems Written between the Years 1768 & 1794* (1795), pp. 115-21.

When men like these defy my martial rule,
Good heaven! it is no time to play the fool.

During the first years of the conflict Freneau
was eager to serve his country in military hazards,
as well as by writing. He probably entered the
army as a private in 1778; possibly he was raised
to the rank of sergeant, as is reported in *Jerseymen in the Revolution*.[15] In his obituary in the
*New York Spectator* there is also reference to his
brief service under arms.[16] Whether these statements are fallacious or true—and opinions differ
—he did not serve long as a soldier. His sensitive, restless nature fretted against the delays and
reactions which preceded and followed the proclamation of independence. While waiting for the
issue to come, he carried out a long-cherished
plan and made a voyage to the West Indies.
Combining trade with pleasure, he delighted in
the sunny skies and floral beauties of Jamaica and
Santa Cruz. The impressions on his memory
and poetic imagination were expressed in such
melodic stanzas as this:

Amid the shades of yonder whispering grove,
    The green palmetoes mingle, tall and fair,
That ever murmur, and forever move,
    Fanning with wavy bough the ambient air.[17]

[15] *Jerseymen in the Revolution*, p. 465. No further information is given.

[16] *New York Spectator*, December 31, 1832.

[17] "Beauties of Santa Cruz," *Poems*, etc. (1795), p. 134.

It was under the same influences, environed by the dreamy atmosphere, that he conceived and wrote the first version of "The House of Night."[18]   This is a strange, weird vision, somewhat suggestive of Coleridge and Poe.   In some passages the uneven meters and the excess of moralizing spoil the poetic beauty, but there are bits of fine and haunting melody, not unlike that of "Ulalume."   Such is the picture of "the death of Death" at the hour of midnight:

Sweet vernal May—tho' then thy woods in bloom
  Flourish'd, yet nought of this could Fancy see;
No wild pinks bless'd the meads, no green the fields,
  And naked seemed to stand each lifeless tree.

Dark was the sky, and not one friendly star
  Shone from the zenith, or horizon clear;
Mist sate upon the plains, and darkness rode
  In her dark chariot, with her ebon spear.

And from the wilds, the late resounding note
  Issued, of the loquacious whippoorwill;
Hoarse, howling dogs, and nightly-roving wolves
  Clamour'd, from far-off cliffs invisible.[19]

[18] This poem was printed in the *United States Magazine*, edited by Brackenridge, in August, 1779, pp. 355–63. It has the subtitle "Six Hours Lodging with Death."   In the same magazine appeared, that year, other poems by Freneau, including "The Dying Elm," "King George the Third's Soliloquy," and "King George's Speech to Lord North."

[19] *Poems*, etc. (1795), p. 93.   This poem was in the first edition, 1786, pp. 101–23, as "The Vision of Night."

Certain love-sonnets, written during this voyage to southern seas, extolled a "Fair Amanda," to whom the poet paid homage. Miss Austin surmises that she was the daughter of Freneau's host in the Bermudas.[20] Such minor experiences, however, were dimmed in remembrance by his exciting adventure in 1780, as he was starting on another voyage for the Indies. His ship, "Aurora," sailing out from Delaware Bay, was pursued and captured by the British ship "The Iris." The account of this capture, and the subsequent horrors on the prison-ship to which he was transferred, afforded theme for one of his most biting satires, "The British Prison-Ship."[21]

After this dramatic experience, Freneau, weakened by fever and exposure, returned to Monmouth, where he wrote a group of deadly satires, incited by personal anger against King George, Lord Cornwallis, Sir Henry Clinton, and the Loyalist printers, Gaine and Rivington. Among the many political verses that he wrote, between 1780 and 1783, three were widely quoted, and

[20] Mary S. Austin, *Philip Freneau: The Poet of the Revolution*, edited by Helen Kearny Vreeland (New York, 1901), p. 88.

[21] From an unpublished manuscript in prose, said to have been written a few days after the release, there was printed, in 1899, *Some Account of the Capture of the Ship Aurora* (New York).

represent his versatility in form: "The Last Will and Testament of James Rivington, Printer," [22] "The Prophecy," and the elegy, "To the Memory of the Brave Americans under General Greene, who fell in the action of September 8, 1781." The last poem is better known to modern readers by its later title, "The Battle of Eutaw Springs."

"The Prophecy," characterized by bravado and personal thrusts, caught the popular fancy:

When a certain great king whose initial is G,
Shall force stamps upon paper and folks to drink tea;
When these folks burn his tea and stamped paper, like
    stubble,
You may guess that this king is then coming to trouble.
But when a petition he treads under his feet,
And sends over the ocean an army and fleet;
When that army, half starved and frantic with rage,
Shall be cooped up with a leader whose name rhymes
    to cage;
When that leader goes home, dejected and sad,
You may then be assured the king's prospects are bad.
But when B. and C. with their armies are taken,
The king will do well if he saves his own bacon.
In the year Seventeen hundred and eighty and two,
A stroke he shall get that will make him look blue;
In the years eighty-three, eighty-four, eighty-five,
You hardly shall know that the king is alive;
In the year eighty-six the affair will be over,

---

[22] *Poems,* etc. (1795), "The British Prison Ship," p. 161-75: "James Rivington's Last Will and Testament," p. 204.

And he shall eat turnips that grow in Hanover.
The face of the Lion shall then become pale,
He shall yield fifteen teeth and be sherr'd of his tail,
O king, my dear king, you shall be very sore.
The Stars and the Lily shall run you on shore,
And your Lion shall growl but never bite, more.[23]

As an evidence of the versatility of Freneau, and his skill in other forms of verse than the satire and lampoon, we recall the elegy on the soldiers who fell at the battle of Eutaw Springs. One stanza has gracious truth and deep feeling:

> Stranger, their humble graves adorn;
>   You too may fall and ask a tear:
> 'Tis not the beauty of the morn
>   That proves the evening shall be clear.

This was the poem which won praise from Walter Scott "as fine a thing of the kind as there is in the language." [24]  Critics would charge Scott with plagiarism because, admitting his knowledge of Freneau's poem, he repeated a line almost verbatim, in *Marmion:* "They took the spear, but left the shield."  More probably this was a case of coincidence or literary suggestion.

At the close of the war Freneau was a young man under thirty, with a reputation for mental alertness and wit, but without any definite pro-

---

[23] *Poems of Philip Freneau Written Chiefly during the Late War* (Philadelphia, 1786), p. 178, *Poems* (1795), p. 178.

[24] Duyckinck, *Cyclopaedia of American Literature,* Vol. I, p. 335.

gramme of life or any fixed income. For the
next six years he made frequent trips as merchant, and became known as "Captain Freneau."
Meanwhile he wrote verses of nature-love and
domestic customs, sending these often to the
*Freeman's Journal* and the *Pennsylvania Packet,*
both published in Philadelphia. From these
papers the poems were reprinted, without name,
in many other journals throughout the country.
During the year 1787 alone he gave to the
journals mentioned, without signature, such
poems as "The Almanack-Maker," "The Deserted
Farm-House" (which was also printed in the
*London Morning Herald,* July 12, 1787), "The
Hermit," "The Indian Student," and the dainty
poem, "May to April," which ranks beside his
more familiar "The Wild Honeysuckle," [25] and
contains this stanza:

> Without your showers I breed no flowers,
>   Each field a barren waste appears,
> If you don't weep, my blossoms sleep,
>   They take such pleasure in your tears.[26]

[25] *Freeman's Journal or North American Intelligencer*
(published by Francis Bailey); *Pennsylvania Packet and
Daily Advertiser;* Freneau's poems in the issues for February 14, April 2, April 18, (*Packet*), May 24, (*Packet*),
June 9 (*Packet*), June 20, November 14, etc. In these papers
appeared also an advertisement of the first collection of
Freneau's poems, in 1786 (published by Bailey).

[26] *Cf. Poems* (1795), p. 96.

Freneau had special reasons for wishing to end his roving life and gain a stable income; for he married, in 1790, Eleanor Forman, a fine woman belonging to a well-known New Jersey family. She had a taste for versifying, and the lovers corresponded "in lyric measures" for more than a year before marriage, under the names of "Ella" and "Birtha." [27] As he lacked training for any other profession, Freneau decided to try to find a place as editor, after his return to New York in 1789, from a trip to Charleston as merchant.[28] For several months he was associated, perhaps as editor, with the *New York Daily Advertiser,* published then by Childs and Swaine.[29] Here he came into friendly relations with John Pintard, who gave valuable reminiscences of Freneau after the latter's death.

Jefferson heard of Freneau as a strong Democrat in principles and a keen writer. He met him at the house of a friend, and was further

[27] These same names, "Ella" and "Birtha," were used by two other poets who contributed to Fenno's *Gazette of the United States,* 1791. See issues for February 23, April 16, May 14, etc. For these dates I am indebted to Mr. Victor H. Paltsits.

[28] For information regarding this fact and his marriage, see *Narrative of a Journey down the Ohio and Mississippi,* by Major Samuel Forman (1789-90; reprinted 1888), pp. 10-11).

[29] Hudson, *History of Journalism in the United States* (1873), p. 175.

influenced in his favor by Madison. The first direct evidence of Jefferson's interest in Freneau was his appointment of the poet, in 1791, as foreign translator for the Department of State to succeed Pintard, who did not care to leave New York when the seat of government was moved to Philadelphia. The work of this position was not heavy, and its requirements were small—"no other qualification than a moderate knowledge of French," according to Jefferson's words. The salary of $200 a year was acceptable to the young man. This appointment, held by Freneau during the two years when he was editing an Anti-Federalist paper, was widely advertised and brought upon him attacks by political opponents, who spared not Jefferson in their innuendoes. An interesting, unpublished letter has come to my notice, which bears upon this situation, in the manuscript *Pickering Papers,* at the Massachusetts Historical Society.[30] The letter was written to Timothy Pickering by George Taylor, Jr., from Philadelphia, January 23, 1809:

In order to give a full view of the circumstances under which Mr. Freneau was employed as Interpreter for the Department of State, by Mr. Jefferson, it will be requisite for me to go as far back as the year 1785.

[30] *Pickering Papers,* Vol. XXIX, No. 50. Copied by permission. The official correspondence on this appointment is in *Jefferson Papers* (Library of Congress), Series I, Vol. IV, No. 153, Vol. IX, No. 250; Series II, Vol. XXXIII, No. 48.

On the first day of January in that year several of my friends at New York, without my knowledge, having recommended me to Mr. Jay, then Secretary for foreign affairs, one of them mentioned it to me and desired me to wait upon him, which I did, when he engaged me as a Clerk in that Department. Shortly after, Mr. Jay in conversation pointed out to me the advantage of acquiring a knowledge of the French & Spanish Languages. Not being able to find a suitable Teacher of the latter, I commenced the study of the former and occasionally upon emergencies, I translated for the Department.

When in 1789 the seat of Government was about being removed from New York, finding the interpreter for the Department did not mean to go with it, I called upon Mr. Jay and mentioned the circumstance to him, at the same time intimating that, as I knew from the friendship he had evinced for me, he would not hesitate to say whether he thought me competent and that in case he did, I should esteem it a favor if he would mention me to Mr. Jefferson, as a candidate for that office. He at once said that he thought I was; that he conceived it of importance to have the secrets of the Department confined to as few a number as possible, or to those already employed in it and therefore would with pleasure call upon Mr. Jefferson on the subject. The day following Mr. Jay informed me that he had mentioned the matter to Mr. Jefferson who had declined making the appointment until he should get to Philadelphia, and advised me then to renew my application.

This I accordingly did. Mr. Jefferson told me that he did not conceive he could with propriety give me the two salaries. I observed that my salary as clerk was small, and that that of the Interpreter being only 250 Dollars no man would accept but as a secondary object, and of course the business of the office must frequently be interrupted in waiting for translations—that if I held it, I would always attend to it seasonably, without its interferring with my other official duty. He concluded by saying that he should not at present fill up the vacancy.

Some months or weeks after this, I received a letter from a friend at New York informing me that he had been told by Mr. Freneau that he was appointed Interpreter for the Department of State. I replied that it could not be correct—for that before the Government removed from that city, having the french treaties to collate, and he being in the employment of Childs & Swain, who were printing them, I asked him to assist in the collation and he declined it, alleging that he did not sufficiently understand the language, but from its affinity to the Latin, made out to read it.

However, he soon after came to this city, received the appointment and in some cases I have assisted a Dutch gentleman then an inmate of my family to translate french documents put into his hands by Mr. Freneau, which to my knowledge belonged to the Department of State. . . . . I do not recollect when he resigned but believe it was in the summer of 1793—as in the winter of 1793–1794 I translated the documents in the voluminous correspondence between the Department of State and Genet. . . .

We must recall that this letter was written by a disappointed candidate for the office given to Freneau, but it indicates the stress of feeling on the matter of this appointment. This was increased when, in October, 1791, Freneau started a newspaper, openly anti-Federalist in its principles and merciless in its attacks upon Washington and Hamilton. There is evidence that Freneau did not come to Philadelphia as an editor very willingly, for he had planned to start a democratic newspaper near his Monmouth home, and preferred to keep his residence there. Madison urged him to come to Philadelphia, but he still demurred, and Jefferson feared that he had lost his editorial ally. The former wrote to Randolph, his son-in-law, of the influence wielded by Fenno's *Gazette of the United States,* saying:

> You will have perceived that the latter (Fenno's) is a paper of pure Toryism, disseminating the doctrines of monarchy, aristocracy, and the exclusion of the people. We have been trying to get another *weekly* or *half-weekly* set up, excluding advertisements, so that it might go through the states and furnish a whig vehicle of intelligence. We hoped at one time to have persuaded Freneau to set up here, but failed.[31]

The relations between Jefferson and Freneau, in connection with the *National Gazette,* have never been fully settled. In his own age the poet was very severely arraigned on account of his editorials against the Federal leaders. Many of his friends, in later life, felt that he had been merely a tool in the hands of Jefferson. Others— and this seems the more reasonable opinion—believed in his independent advocacy of democratic principles. The sarcasms which gave spice to the

[31] *Writings of Thomas Jefferson,* Vol. V, p. 336.

editorial columns differed little from the same
form of writing in Freneau's earlier and later
works.   Jefferson was, naturally, well pleased to
have such a keen free-lance to support his views,
and he probably gave Freneau encouragement and
access to any democratic publications or criticisms on the aristocratic tendencies of the Federalists.   The detailed story of Freneau's service
as editor of this journal, and his principles at the
time, have been well studied by Dr. Samuel E.
Forman in "The Political Activities of Philip
Freneau." [32]

In the library of the Historical Society of
Pennsylvania is a manuscript letter from Freneau
to William B. Giles, dated December 2, 1793, in
which  he  announces  the  suspension  of  the
*National Gazette,* thanks his patron for his subscription, and expresses a hope that the paper
may be revived.   The paper had suspended publication on October 26; doubtless the prevalence
of yellow fever in Philadelphia affected both its
receipts and its continuance.   Jefferson openly
expressed regret that the *Gazette* was discon-
tinued, and thus emphasized its importance: "His
paper has saved our constitution which was gallop-

[32] Samuel E. Forman, "The Political Activities of Philip
Freneau," *Johns Hopkins University Studies in Historical and
Political Science,* Series XX, Nos. 9, 10, September-October,
1902.   Jefferson's explanation is in his *Writings,* Vol. VI, pp.
101–09.

ing fast into monarchy & has been checked by no means so powerfully as by that paper." [33]

A comparison of the two *Gazettes* of this time and city—those edited by Freneau and Fenno in the interests of the Democratic and the Federal parties respectively [34]—reveals many interesting paragraphs. The tone of difference was at first mild and courteous, but gradually waxed bitter and sharp. Freneau printed in his *Gazette,* throughout its existence, some of his verses of lighter vein, as "The Country Printer," "The Jug of Rum," and "The Pilot of Hatteras," as well as his more philosophical reverie "On the Sleep of Plants." [35] After Freneau's *Gazette* had been published for a few weeks, the attacks which he made, with subtle, withering ridicule, upon Hamilton and John Adams called forth answering assaults in Fenno's *Gazette.* The latter were less witty and far more virulent. The chief charge which they raised against Freneau was that he had accepted a place as interpreter in the Department of State and was guilty of treasonous censure upon the very government which he served.

[33] *Writings of Thomas Jefferson,* Vol. I, p. 231.

[34] Freneau's paper was styled the *National Gazette;* Fenno's, the *Gazette of the United States.* Files of these rival journals may be found at libraries in Philadelphia and at the Library of Congress.

[35] See *National Gazette* for November 14, and December 19, 1791; January 16, and January 23, 1792.

The most pointed attack was in Fenno's *Gazette*, in July, 1792, signed "T. L.,"[36] inquiring whether Freneau's salary was paid for translating or for publications which vilified the government which he served. With a sting, which was intended to pierce the mind of Jefferson, he added: "In common life it is thought ungrateful for a man to bite the hand that puts bread in his mouth, but if the man is hired to do it, the case is altered."

Because of insinuations like the above, Freneau was urged by Jefferson's friends to take an oath before the mayor of Philadelphia that

no negotiation was ever opened with him by Thomas Jefferson, Secretary of State, for the establishment or institution of the National Gazette; that the deponent's coming to the city of Philadelphia as a publisher of a newspaper was at no time urged, advised or influenced by the above officer, but that it was his own voluntary act;—that not a line was ever directly or indirectly written, dictated or composed for it by that officer, but that the editor had consulted his own judgment alone in the conducting of it—free, unfettered and uninfluenced.[37]

While the question of his coming to Philadelphia at the urgent wish of Jefferson would seem to be answered in the affirmative by some of the

[36] The communications thus signed have been generally assigned to Alexander Hamilton. Freneau wrote in severe satire on Hamilton's assertion that "a public debt is a public blessing."

[37] *Gazette of the United States*, August, 1792; also given in Forman, *Political Activities of Philip Freneau*, p. 56.

letters of both Freneau and Jefferson, still extant
and quoted, yet the oath was probably taken in
good faith. Freneau's enemies were not satisfied
to accept it thus. They charged him with per-
jury, and he was long suspected. In the main, he
did not reply directly in his paper to such charges,
but the pronounced inference from the paragraphs by "T. L.," just quoted, that he was a
mere hireling of a political leader, roused his
anger, and he quoted the accusation, and made
answer :[38]

The above is beneath a reply. It might be queried,
however, whether a man who receives a small stipend
for services rendered as a French translator to the department of State, and, as editor of a free newspaper
admits into his publication impartial strictures on the
proceedings of gov't, is not more likely to act an honest
and disinterested part towards the public, than a vile syco-
phant,[39] who obtaining emoluments from government far
more lucrative than the salary alluded to (by undermining
another man who was in possession of the employ)
finds his interests in attempting to poison the minds of
the people by propagating and disseminating principles
& sentiments utterly subvertive of the true republican
interests of this country, and by flattering and recommending *every* and *any* measure of government, however

[38] *National Gazette,* July 28, 1792, p. 3.

[39] John Fenno, the editor of the rival *Gazette,* was printer
to the Senate of the United States, and also for the
Treasury Department. His emoluments were declared to be
two thousand or twenty-five hundred dollars a year. See
article, signed *G,* in *National Gazette,* August 15, 1792.

pernicious & destructive its tendency might be, to the great body of people. The world is left to decide on the motives of each.

This prose statement was followed by an ode, beginning:

> Since the day we attempted the *Nation's Gazette*,
> Pomposo's dull printer does nothing but fret.
> > Now preaching
> > And screeching,
> > Then nibbling
> > And scribbling
> > Remarking
> > And barking,
> > Repining
> > And Whining,
> > And still in a pet
> From morning to night with the *Nation's Gazette*.
>
> Instead of whole columns our page to abuse,
> Your readers would rather be treated with news;
> > While wars are a-brewing,
> > And kingdoms undoing,
> > While monarchs are falling,
> > And princesses squalling,
> > While France is reforming,
> > And Irishmen storming,
> > In a glare of such splendour,
> > What nonsense to fret
> > At so humble a thing
> > As—the *Nation's Gazette*.

Freneau's criticism of Washington as President, and of his party, did not lessen his admiration for the man and the soldier. Among many

elegies upon Washington were three by Freneau,
sympathetic and loyal. In one he expressed just
resentment at the extravagant eulogies so common at the time of Washington's death; with
directness and truth he summarized the hero's
traits:

> He was no god, ye flattering knaves,
> He owned no world, he ruled no waves;
> But,—and exalt it if you can,—
> He was the upright, HONEST MAN.
>
> This was his glory, this outshone
> Those attributes you doat upon;
> On this strong ground he took his stand,
> Such virtue saved a sinking land.[40]

In further proof of the kindly personal relations which existed between Washington and
Freneau, the latter's daughter recalled a visit
which Washington made to their Monmouth
home, when he was an honored guest and devoted
himself to the children.[41]  In contrast with this
family story was another, from the same source,
which would give weight to the suggestion that
Freneau was not on very cordial terms with
Jefferson after the abandonment of the *Gazette*.
It was reported that Jefferson, when President,
would befriend Freneau, who was in financial

[40] *A Collection of Poems*, etc. (New York, 1815), Vol. I, p.
161.

[41] Mary S. Austin, *Philip Freneau: The Poet of the Revolution*, p. 170.

stress, by appointing him as postmaster, and he summoned Freneau to an audience. The poet returned a haughty answer: "Tell Thomas Jefferson that he knows where Philip Freneau lives, and if he has important business with him, let him come to Philip Freneau's house and transact it." [42]

After the failure of his *Gazette,* Freneau seemed to meet rebuffs and reverses until the end of his life—a period of forty years. As a poet, he often lost heart and was deeply depressed by the surroundings of his chequered life. In such moods he wrote some of his poems, like "To the Americans of the United States," in 1796:

> The coming age will be an age of prose:
> When sordid cares will break the Muse's dream,
> And *Common Sense* be ranked in seat supreme.

In spite of such expressions of bitterness, there were flashes of poetic impulse, and constantly recurring ambitions to try again his fate as poet-editor. After he had moved his types from Philadelphia to Monmouth, he printed there the revised edition of his poems, adding only a few new ones, but reprinting, with some corrections,

---

[42] *Loc. cit.,* p. 173. Mr. Pattee, in the "Introduction" to his edition of Freneau's *Poems,* tells the same story, but substitutes the name of Madison for that of Jefferson, with no explanation other than that of the poet's pride (Vol. I, p. lxxx).

those that had been printed by Bailey in 1786 and 1788.[43]

For a year he was editor and printer of a curious little sheet, the *Jersey Chronicle*.[44] Its eight quarto pages contained spirited comments on politics and literature, with occasional jibes at the "aggravating insults offered to Americans, notwithstanding the treaty by Mr. Jay, from which the temporizing citizens of America expected so many advantages."[45] The motto of this paper was an apt quotation from Horace: *Inter sylvas Academi quaerere verum.* In a letter to Madison he enlarged upon his plans to spend the rest of his life upon his Monmouth estate and edit "a small weekly newspaper calculated for the part of the country" in which he resided. Apparently the neighborhood failed to respond. After the abandonment of the journal, from lack of subscriptions, Freneau wrote again to Madison:

After experiencing one or two disappointments, I am now, through the kind aid of some friends here, nearly completing the project of a co-partnership with Thomas

[43] *Poems Written between the Years 1768 & 1794 by Philip Freneau of New Jersey. A New Edition, Revised and Corrected by the Author. Monmouth (N. J.). Printed at the Press of the Author: M, DCC, XCV.*

[44] *Jersey Chronicle,* Monmouth (N. J.), May 2, 1795, to April 30, 1796; file in Lenox Library.

[45] From the issue of April 2, 1796, in the American Antiquarian Society.

Greenleaf in his two Papers, The Argus, a Daily publication, and The New York Journal, twice a week: both on
a pretty respectable footing, and noted for a steady attachment to Republican principles, though open to all
decent speculations from any party if they choose to
transmit them.  In short, I would wish to revive something in the spirit of the National Gazette, if time and
circumstances allow, and with proper assistance hope to
succeed;—
    Thus,
        A Raven once an acorn took,
          From Bashan's strongest stoutest trees;
        He hid it near a murmuring brook,
          And liv'd another oak to see.[46]

Whether as a result of this project and assistance, or following another disappointment, Freneau entered upon his last journalistic venture, in
New York, in April, 1797, where for about a
year he edited a tri-weekly, the *Time-Piece and
Literary Companion.*[47]   He had two associates,
in turn, A. Menut and M. L. Davis, the latter
continuing the paper for a few months after Freneau had withdrawn for lack of financial return.
In this journal appeared some of Freneau's
poems, and his translation of "New Travels of M.
Abbe Robin in North America"—spicy prose with
satiric touches.

[46] *Madison Papers,* Freneau to Madison, December 1,
1796 (Library of Congress), Vol. XXI, p. 70.

[47] *Time-Piece and Literary Companion,* New York, April,
1797, to March, 1798.

The prose style of Freneau was, at its best, crisp and simple, in contrast with the labored pedantry of his contemporaries. Perhaps the most representative example is *Letters by Robert Slender, O. S. M.*[48] The "Advice to Young Authors," in this collection, has a sensible reminder: "Never make a present of your works to great men. If they do not think them worth purchasing, trust me they will never think them worth reading." "Robert Slender, Stocking-Weaver," became a favorite pseudonym for Freneau, used both in prose and verse. In the library of the Historical Society of Pennsylvania can be found two copies of a pamphlet, *A Laughable Poem or Robert Slender's Journey from Philadelphia to New York by Way of Burlington and South Amboy.*[49] Intended as a farce, the characters include Robert Slender, Mr. Snip, Billy O'Bluster, Snipinda, and the milliner's maid. In plot, the writing is farcical, but the tale does not appeal strongly to our conception of the "laughable." There is drollery, and a rollicking meter in some portions, as in chapter 6, "The Chapter of Vexations and Disasters," which

[48] The letters "O.S.M." meant "One of the Swinish Multitude." Many of these letters are also in Freneau's *Miscellaneous Works* (Philadelphia, 1788).

[49] This bore imprint, Philadelphia, 1809. 24 pp. A copy is also in Brown University Library. It is in his *Poems* (1795), pp. 338-50.

recalls the discomforts of that day of post-chaise
traveling:

Coop'd up in a waggon, the curtains let down,
At three in the morning, we drove out of town:
A morning more dark I ne'er saw in my life,
And the fog was so thick it would cut with a knife;
In a morning like this were the Trojans undone,
When the horse was admitted, that never could run:
It was a fit season for murders and rapes,
For drunken adventures and narrow escapes.
So, with something to think of, and little to say,
The driver drove on, looking out for the day,
Till we came to the brow of a damnable hili
Six miles on our way, when the cattle stood still;
"Are you sure you are right with the Waggon," cry'd Snip.
"I am," said the driver, and crack'd with his whip,
Then away ran the horses, but took the wrong road
And down went the waggon, with all its full load,
Down, deep in a valley,—roll'd over and over,
Fell the flying machine, with its curtains and cover,
Where shatter'd and wounded, no glimpse yet of day
A mass of perdition, together we lay!

The losses which resulted from his failures in
journalism crippled Freneau's Monmouth property, as was shown in mortgages placed upon the
estate after 1805. He sought to redeem his fortunes by a return to seafaring and trading. His
brother in South Carolina assisted him with commercial aid. From 1804 to 1809 he made several
trips as a trader to southern states; but the
journeys became irksome to him, and he longed

for retirement to his rural home. His last long cruise was to the Canary Islands in 1807, as he told Madison in a letter eight years afterward, in which he announced a new, expensive edition of his poems, to be issued by David Longworth, and to be paid for by subscription. This was the second two-volume edition which had been printed. The earlier venture, made in 1809, was an act of generosity, according to his statement to Madison, in the same letter:

That edition was published by *subscription* merely for the benefit of, and to assist Mrs. Bailey, an unfortunate but deserving widowed female, niece of General Steele, and this consideration alone induced me to pay some attention to that third edition.[50]

Freneau was keenly hurt by the lack of appreciation among his contemporaries; he yearned for some true sympathy and helpful criticism. The praise which he received was couched in the extravagant language of the day, and was irritating rather than stimulating. Such was the rough verse in which Colonel Parke heralded him, after Freneau's first collection of poems appeared, in 1786. Possibly the humor of Freneau helped him to appreciate the last line:

And when you are number'd alas! with the dead,
Your work by true wits will forever be read,

[50] *Madison Papers*, MS. (Library of Congress), January 12, 1815.

> Who, pointing the finger, shall pensively show
> The lines that were written, alas! by Freneau.[51]

Another droll tribute followed his poem, "The Pilot of Hatteras," by "Captain Freneau," in the *Freeman's Journal* three years later:

> This celebrated genius, the Peter Pindar of America, is now master of a Packet, which runs between New York, Philadelphia and Charleston. His tuneful numbers during the war did much to soften the disagreeable sensations which a state of warfare so generally occasions.[52]

With the readers of his own day Freneau's verses with a humorous tone were in greatest favor, such as "Crispin O'Connor," "Advice to the Ladies Not to Neglect the Dentist," "The Village Merchant," and "Farmer Dobbins's Complaint." There was a coarse humor, on a favorite subject of joke, in the last-named doggerel:

> Three daughters I have and as prettily made,
>   As handsome as any you'll see;
> And lovers they count,—but still I'm afraid
>   They always will hang upon me.
>
> These bucks of the town with their elegant coats
>   I'm sick of their horses and chairs.
> They plunder my hay and they pilfer my oats,—
>   Am I keeping a *tavern*, my dears?[53]

[51] *Freeman's Journal*, June 21, 1786.

[52] *Ibid.*, December 9, 1789.

[53] (*Poems.* 1795, p. 19). In the *National Gazette*, August 25, 1792, this poem appeared as "Farmer Dobbins to the Buck-Suitors," signed "Dobbins".

This song, with two others by Freneau—"The Indian Student" and "The Rights of Man"— was included in *The Columbian Songster or Jovial Companion,* a collection of popular airs published in 1797. They are ranked there with Hopkinson's "Battle of the Kegs" and "With Jemmy on the Sea."

Another favorite poem, ascribed in his own day to Freneau, and sung by school-children until recent years, was "The Death-Song of a Cherokee Indian." It is not found in any of Freneau's collected poems, and was ascribed to Mrs. Ann Hunter, of England, before 1806. There still seems justice in asking if it may not have been written or adapted by Freneau. As "original poetry" it was contributed to the *American Museum,* in January 1787, with unquestioned authorship by Freneau, thus announced:

### The Death-Song of a Cherokee Indian

#### By P. Freneau.

The sun sets at night; and the stars shun the day;
But glory remains when their lights fade away.
Begin, ye tormentors: your threats are in vain:
For the son of Alknomock will never complain.

Remember the woods where in ambush he lay,
And the scalps which he bore from his nation away,
Why do ye delay?—till I shrink from my pain?
Know the son of Alknomock can never complain.

Remember the arrows he shot from his bow:
Remember your chiefs by his hatchet laid low,
The flame rises high.  You exult in my pain:
But the son of Alknomock will never complain.

I go to the land where my father is gone:
His ghost shall exult in the fame of his son.
Death comes like a friend.  He relieves me from pain.
And thy son, O Alknomock, has scorn'd to complain.

Duyckinck, the friend of Freneau in later life, included this poem, among Freneau's, in his *Cyclopaedia of American Literature*, with a note of explanation.  Royall Tyler introduced it, with the music, into his play, *The Contrast;* [54] it seems unlikely that he would have used an English song in this first American drama, with its intense Yankeeism.  In style of writing, in sentiment and theme, it is accordant with Freneau's poetry, and with his admiration for the defiant prowess of the Indian.  In "The Indian Burying-Ground" he praised the custom of leaving the warriors, after death, in an upright posture, symbolizing immediate action and defiance to the wiles of the enemy. In "The Indian Student," one of his best poems, he awakened sympathy for his hero, yearning for the free life of the forest, when he had been taken from it and placed at college:

A little could my wants supply,—
Can wealth or honor give me more;

[54] *The Contrast* (Philadelphia, 1790).

Or, will the sylvan god deny
The humble treat he gave before?

Let seraphs reach the bright abode
And Heaven's sublimest mansions see,—
I only bow to NATURE'S GOD,
The Land of Shades will do for me.[55]

Reading with care this group of Freneau's
poems on Indian character, it seems as if the song
in question might be his rendering. It was written after the first edition of his poems was
printed, in 1786. The second edition, his *Miscellaneous Works*,[56] in 1788, was compiled while he
was away at sea, by the printer Bailey, and Freneau regretted that he was not consulted in its
preparation. He had an opportunity to place this
poem in his Monmouth reprint, in 1795, but before
the edition of 1809 appeared, the poem had been
ascribed to Mrs. Hunter. Possibly Freneau was
content to have it recognized as his in America,
and would not openly dispute its authorship.
On the other hand, it must be confessed that
Freneau seldom omitted to claim as his own
all his verses that had appeared in magazines or

[55] *Poems Written between the Years 1768 & 1794* (Mon
mouth, 1795), p. 80. When this poem appeared in the
*Pennsylvania Packet*, June 9, 1787, unsigned, Freneau explained a reference to "Harvard's Hall," with accurate details, as at Cambridge, Mass.

[56] *The Miscellaneous Writings of Mr. Philip Freneau*
(Philadelphia, 1788).

newspapers, and were adapted for inclusion in his collected poems.

The last thirty years of Freneau's life were full of memories and fading hopes rather than much active service. He wrote occasional essays and poems for the newspapers, often unsigned; many of them may be found in Bache's *Aurora,* a Philadelphia journal of democratic trend. The War of 1812 called forth from him several patriotic odes, celebrating the victories of Hull, Decatur, and their crews. Belonging to this period of composition was his "Ode to Liberty," beginning, "God save the Rights of Man," which was sung for many years to the tune of England's national hymn—the same which was later chosen for Dr. Smith's national hymn of America. Because of the interest which seemed to be revived in Freneau by his celebrant poems written during and after the second war with England, Longworth decided to issue his poems in a two-volume edition. This was done in 1815,[57] and such recognition nourished a feeling of grateful pride in the poet's heart. To Madison he wrote:

I found last winter that an edition would soon be going on at all events, and in contradiction to my wishes, as I had left these old scribblings to float quietly down the stream of oblivion to their destined element, the ocean of forgetfulness. . . . . I do not know that the Verses are of

[57] *A Collection of Poems,* etc. (2 vols.; New York, 1815).

any superior or very unusual merit, but he tells me the Town will have them, and of course, have them they will, and must, it seems.[58]

It is pathetic to follow, in letters, Freneau's rising hopes as a poet, gradually sinking into feigned indifference, then into periods of silence from wounded pride. Although he spoke slightingly of his verses, they were very precious to him, and he grieved at each new sign of neglect by the public. Such a temperament, however, will feed upon its own food of fancy and hope; his imaginative delights were confessed in one of his most dainty odes, "Apostrophe to Fancy":

> Wakeful, vagrant, restless thing,
> Ever wandering on the wing,
> Who thy wondrous source can find,
> FANCY, regent of the mind!
> . . . . . . . . . . . . .
> FANCY, to thy power I owe
> Half my happiness below;
> By thee Elysian groves were made,
> Thine were the notes that Orpheus play'd;
> By thee was Pluto charm'd so well
> While rapture seized the sons of hell;
> Come, O come, perceiv'd by none,
> You and I will walk alone.[59]

[58] *Madison Papers,* Vol. XXXV, p. 17; letter dated January 12, 1815.

[59] "Ode to Fancy," *Poems Written between the Years 1768 & 1794* (1795), p. 31.

During the last years of his life Freneau was often seen in New York, where he would come from Monmouth to visit his friends—Governor Clinton, Dr. John Francis, and other men of note and letters. He persistently refused to sit for a portrait, but, on one of these visits to New York, his face was sketched; after his death the drawing was enlarged, and is the only likeness which we possess. The eyes, there pictured, represent the tender heart which could not endure the sacrifice of a chicken or the killing of a fly, and which prompted him to manumit all the slaves on his estate and support the old servants from an income which was insufficient for all his own needs. He had collected one of the best private libraries in his neighborhood; this, with many other treasured heirlooms, was destroyed by fire in 1818. After the loss of his home, he passed the rest of his days at the former home of Mrs. Freneau's father, in the vicinity. He had four daughters, but no son. His second daughter, Agnes Freneau Leadbeater, was a beautiful, witty woman. Her son perpetuated the family name by changing the order of his surnames. She was often her father's companion on his visits to New York; she also inherited some of his poetic gifts and wrote graceful rhymes of domestic life.

Like many men of his age, Freneau delighted to mix a "glass of flip" for convivial occasions, although in his verses he advises against the excessive use of tobacco and "the jug of rum." One of his most spontaneous lyrics was the poem of friendship, "The Parting Glass," with its closing stanza:

> With him who loves a pot of ale,
> Who holds to all an even scale;
> Who hates a knave in each disguise,
> And fears him not whate'er his size,—
> With him, well pleased my days to pass,
> May Heaven forbid THE PARTING GLASS.[60]

Freneau was found frozen to death in a bog-meadow after a severe snowstorm, in December, 1831. He was returning, in the evening, from a call upon a friend a short distance from his home and, at his advanced age, was not able to battle against one of the most turbulent storms of the winter.[61] Local and New York newspapers published brief obituaries of the poet whom his countrymen had seemed to forget. Side by side, in a field near his former home, are the graves of Freneau and his wife. His resting-place was beneath a tree where he frequently sat and mused. Near by flows the little stream which inspired one of his sprightly poems, "The Brook of the Valley":

[60] *Poems Written between the Years 1768 & 1794* (1795), p. 85.

[61] Newspapers of the time mention this storm as unusually severe.

When the shower of waters fell,
How you raged, and what a swell!
All your banks you overflow'd
Scarcely knew your own abode!

How you battled with the rock!
Gave my willow such a shock
As to menace by its fall
Underbrush and bushes, all!

Muddy now and limpid next,
Now with icy shackles vext,—
What a likeness here we find!
What a picture of mankind! [62]

There were winsome traits in the personality of this elder poet. He was impractical in business and aggressive in political feelings, but he left some tuneful, hopeful messages of devotion to nature and sane living.[63] He was not so far removed from our pioneer writers of repute, as we might surmise. When he died, Irving and his Knickerbocker friends had written, not alone the *Salmagundi Papers* and the *Knickerbocker History of New York,* but also *The Sketch Book* and *Bracebridge Hall.* Emerson, at twenty-nine, already gave promise of becoming a force in American letters. Bryant had written *Thanatopsis* fifteen years before, and was in the full maturity of his development. Longfellow and

[62] *The Poems of Philip Freneau* (1815), Vol. II, p. 83.

[63] It is fitting that on his tombstone should be read "A Poet's Grave."

Whittier had sounded the primal notes of their poetry. During the last years of Freneau's life a wave of interest in American authors began to spread over the land. He was not included in the generous plaudits of reviewers—possibly because the stigma of his political virulence against Washington's administration was not forgotten. To claim that he was the most gifted poet of American literature, prior to the nineteenth century, is not extravagant tribute, for the attempts at verse were crude imitations of Pope and Gray. Many of such imitators, who gained more renown in their time than did Freneau, are now wholly forgotten, while his work is gaining attention. The true distinction that he merits is as the first poet of indigenous themes, with a fearless strength and a true promise. In his poems are hints of later, more familiar verses; his lyric "To a Caty-did" seems suggestive, both in fancy and form, of Dr. Holmes's "To an Insect":[64]

> Tell me, what did Caty do?
> Did she mean to trouble you?
> Why was Caty not forbid
> To trouble little Caty-did?
> Wrong indeed, at you to fling,
> Hurting no one while you sing
> "Caty-did! Caty-did! Caty-did!"
>
> Why continue to complain?
> Caty tells me she again

[64] *A Collection of Poems,* etc. (1815), Vol. II, pp. 84–86.

Will not give you plague or pain:—
Caty says you may be hid,
Caty will not go to bed
While you sing us "Caty-did!
Caty-did! Caty-did! Caty-did!"

Freneau's poems reveal his blended traits
—playfulness mingled with intense zeal, affability
with possible rancor, delight in mystic fancy with
vital interest in true democracy. In his satires and
essays he showed his knowledge of the best
English models; his sharp war-poems were often
reflections of the Latin satirists. His lyrics of
greatest skill were adaptations of Gray and
Cowper, with unmistakable signs of originality in
thought. Although he retained traits of French
parentage, he was a true American, who shared
fully in his country's struggles and rejoiced in its
progress.

# JOHN TRUMBULL: SATIRIST AND SCHOLAR

JOHN TRUMBULL

Judge and author.  From a portrait painted by John Trumbull,
artist, and engraved by Durand.

## IV

## JOHN TRUMBULL: SATIRIST AND SCHOLAR

According to a romantic tradition, a yeoman, in the time of an early English king, risked his own life in saving his majesty from an attack by an angry bull. In return for this service he was knighted as Turn-bull, with three bulls' heads for insignia and a bull's head for a crest. A descendant of this hero married a wealthy woman, and the remembrance of the knight's courage could not atone to her and her husband for the unpleasant name. He requested that, for his branch, the letters might be transferred; hence the name was called Trumbull or Trumble. The American progenitor of this family settled at Ipswich, in 1645, and had three sons—John, Jonathan, and Benoni —from whom were descended the two Governors Jonathan, the portrait-painter John, and the satirist of the same name.

The little parish of Westbury, Connecticut, now a part of Waterbury, called as pastor of its village church, in 1729, a young man of athletic build, John Trumble. His muscularity seemed to make the first deep impression, according to a story often repeated. A band of competitive wrestlers, known as "Town Spotters," were accustomed to meet at a "half-way house" in the neighborhood, to decide the championship of the town. On one occasion, when the last wrestler had won the contest, a masked stranger appeared, caught the champion by the foot, and threw him on the open fire. The stranger disappeared suddenly but was soon after recognized as the young minister, Mr. Trumble.

In the first church of the adjacent town of Waterbury there ministered a Mr. Leavensworth. Chancing to meet his Westbury colleague soon after the wrestling, he rebuked him for two sins —levity, and rashness in tossing the wrestler so near the fire, at the risk of fatal injury. With a wit which was as bold as his courage, the younger clergyman accepted the rebuke for levity, but declared: "As for the scorching, I thought it might be my duty to give your parishioners a foretaste of what they might expect after sitting under your preaching." [1]

This Rev. John Trumble was a man of unusual traits, and became the father of a remarkable scholar. His second son, John, is the

[1] This story is told fully in *The Town and City of Waterbury, Connecticut, from the Aboriginal Period to the Year Eighteen Hundred and Ninety-Five*, edited by Joseph Anderson, D.D. (New Haven, 1896), Vol. I, p. 326, 327.

subject of this chapter. In those days before preparatory schools, the local minister, if a good classical scholar, was often chosen as tutor to fit boys for college. Among the students whom Mr. Trumble was instructing in the mysteries of Corderius, Tully, and other classic texts, was William Southmayd, seventeen years old. The task seems to have been laborious for both teacher and pupil, but persistence won success. While this youth was struggling with his classic enemies, a little boy of six or seven years played about in the minister's study and, perhaps unconsciously, acquired the Latin words which daunted the olde pupil.

If we can believe the family journals—and there seems to be no good reason for distrusting them—little John Trumble [2] was the great American prodigy. At two years he recited all *The New England Primer* and Watts's *Divine Songs for Children.* At two and a half he could read, and at four or five he made his first reading-excursion through the Bible and Watts's *Lyrics.* At the same age he composed rhymes in the form of his venerable model, and "lay awake some nights" to get the correct prosody. By some unexplained lapse, he was unable to write until he

[2] The name was spelt Trumble in records until about 1768.

was five; so he preserved his hymnal compositions in printed letters.[3]

After such a life-record of five years, one is not surprised to read that from five to seven he mastered many of the Greek and Latin texts required for entrance to college. When two candidates were presented at Yale, in 1757, by Rev. Mr. Trumble, the older pupil was nineteen and the younger, his son, was seven years and five months. Dr. E. A. Park, in his *Sketch of Nathaniel Emmons,* states that the latter had the honor of "holding on his knee" young Trumble, as he was examined in the specified Latin, Greek, and mathematics.[4] Newspapers at this early date seldom gave personal items, except marriage and death notices, but this incident was mentioned in the *Connecticut Gazette,* September 24, 1757; numbered among the candidates for admission was "the Son of Rev'd Mr. Trumble of Waterbury, who passed a good Examination, altho but little more than seven years of age; but on account of his Youth his father does not intend he shall at present continue at College."

One would expect better judgment from the

---

[3] *The Poetical Works of John Trumbull, LL.D.* (Hartford, 1820), Memoir, p. 10; extracts from Trumbull manuscripts in *Tyler's Literary History of the Revolution,* Vol. I, pp. 190–94.

[4] *Works of Nathaniel Emmons,* Vol. I, p. clxviii.

ex-wrestler, but he allowed his son to spend the
next six years reading the classics usually read at
college, instead of roaming about care-free in the
fields and woods, to counteract the mental
excesses of earlier years. When the boy entered
Yale at thirteen, he was so perfected in Greek
and Latin that he devoted himself to mathematics,
astronomy, and the few volumes of English essay
and poetry then in the library. He had previously
made acquaintance with Milton, Addison, and
Thomson, in his father's study, and thus laid the
foundations for his own literary expressions.
After graduating, he remained as "Dean's
scholar" for three years, until he won his master's
degree at twenty years of age.

The curriculum and educational modes at Yale
were passing through a transition period. For
more than a decade advocates of a broader spirit
had sought to introduce oratory, sciences, and
English literature, as Harvard had already done.
But Yale, more conservative in both educational
and theological tenets, lost ground among the progressive men of the later Colonial period. President Daggett and his venerable advisers were convinced that "solid learning alone" was necessary,
and that the new branches, in contrast with the
classic texts, and logic and theology, represented
"folly, nonsense and an idle waste of time." The
crisis came in 1771, when three of the conserva-

tive professors resigned, and Timothy Dwight
and John Trumbull were chosen as tutors.[5]

In the library at Yale University may be read
the first argument in serious prose by John Trumbull in behalf of the cultivation of literary tastes
of college students. It was entitled *An Essay on
the Use and Advantages of the Fine Arts.*[6] The
paper revealed a broad scholarship for that day.
In a few words, Trumbull characterized sciences,
literature, and art as educative agencies. He con-
trasted the culture of the heathen nations with
that of Greece and Rome, and summarized each
classic writer of special note in a few, cogent
sentences. Then followed a review of English
history and literature, from the reign of Elizabeth to the time of Pope and Thomson. Brought
thus down to contemporary times, he urged upon
Americans the need of culture, especially along
the lines of the fine arts. A few sentences will
illustrate the clearness and earnestness of thought:

America hath a fair prospect in a few centuries of
ruling both in arts and arms. It is universally allowed

[5] W. L. Kingsley, *A Sketch of the History of Yale College,* Vol. I, pp. 95–97.

[6] *An Essay on the Use and Advantages of the Fine Arts:
Delivered at the Public Commencement in New Haven, Sept.
12, 1770* (New Haven, 1770; 16 pages, 8vo). Copies of this
may be found at Yale University, Watkinson Library of Hartford, Library of Congress, and Massachusetts Historical
Society.

that we very much excel in the force of natural genius:
and although but few among us are able to devote their
whole lives to study, perhaps there is no nation in which
a larger portion of learning is diffused through all ranks
of people. For as we generally possess the middle station
of life, neither sunk to vassalage, nor raised to independance, we avoid the sordid ignorance of peasants, and the
unthinking dissipation of the great.

The sentences which follow are significant, for
they indicate the political conditions of the time
and predict the part soon to be played by Trumbull as patriot-satirist:

Happy, in this respect, have been our late struggles for
liberty! They have awakened the spirit of freedom; they
have rectified the manners of the times; they have made us
acquainted with the rights of mankind; recalled to our
minds the glowing independance of former ages, fired us
with the views of fame, and by filling our thoughts with
contempt of the imported articles of luxury, have raised an
opposition not only to the illegal power, but to the effemi-
nate manners of Britain. . . . . Our late writers in the
cause of liberty have gained the applause of Europe.
Many elegant essays have been produced in the style of
wit and humour; nor hath Poetry been entirely unculti-
vated among us!

In witness of the last statement, and in accord-
ance with the custom of the times, Trumbull
closed his peroration with lines of prophecy upon
America's future bards. This attempt at verse is
weak and bombastic, in contrast with the simpler,
fluent prose. One stanza, often quoted at the

time, arouses a smile today because of the allied
names of the popular poets in that day:

> This land her Steele and Addison shall view,
> The former glories equall'd by the new;
> Some future Shakespeare charm the rising age,
> And hold in magic charm the listening stage;
> Another Watts shall string the heavenly lyre,
> And other muses other bards inspire.[7]

In spite of many flaws and some puerility, this
essay was remarkable for its purity and directness
of diction, in contrast with the cumbrous, pedantic
form of many contemporary writers. That it
attracted more than usual interest, at the time it
was read, is attested by a notice in the *Connecticut Journal,* September 30, 1770.[8] After com-
menting on the essay as the chief feature of the
commencement programme, the editor eulogized
its author, but chose, unfortunately, his verse
rather than his prose for special praise:

> Immortal Pope! thy son immortal see;
> He treads the steps that once were trod by thee;
> All that for future times he bids us hope,
> We see in him as England saw in POPE.

This essay was not the first venture in Addi-
sonian prose by Trumbull. He had written
anonymously in favor of a study of modern literature, as a means of creating a progressive spirit

[7] *Loc. cit.,* p. 15.

[8] Not November 30, as cited by Tyler, *Literary History of
the Revolution,* Vol. I, p. 210.

at the colleges. With earnestness, lightened by
mild ridicule, he wrote several editorials,
signed "The Meddler," for the *Boston Chronicle,*
from September, 1769, to January, 1770. The
errors of the day in educational ideas and in social
standards, as well as the religious narrowness, all
came under his censure. To relieve heaviness,
he introduced a few satiric sketches, like that of
Jack Dapperwit, who had later companions in *The
Progress of Dulness.*[9] "Wit; True and False,"
and the abuses of newspaper writing, were treated
with frankness.[10] Some of the articles were
signed "The Schemer," an ally of "The Meddler." All had the same aim, announced with
the confidence of youth—"assistance, (however
trifling soever it may be) towards instructing the
ignorant, diverting and improving the learned,
rectifying the taste and manners of the times, and
cultivating the fine arts of the land."

The first essay by "The Meddler"[11] struck the
keynote of the series in a remonstrance against
the shams and veneer of life, versus its realities.
As an example, he cited the fashion of publication

[9] *Progress of Dulness,* etc. (1772) ; see later pages of this
chapter.

[10] "The Meddler," II, *Boston Chronicle,* September 14-18,
1769. Some of these papers were probably written by
Timothy Dwight and other friends of Trumbull, but his ideas
and style are recognized in many.

[11] *Boston Chronicle,* September 4-7, 1769.

then in vogue, with a caricature of the author's entrance in a grand "equipage" and heralded by a pompous preface. With ridicule he concluded:

> And sometimes for our further information, a curious frontispiece is engraved, containing an elegant portrait of the Author, surrounded with antique symbols, and allegorical devices; such as Minerva, Apollo or some other of their Godships, standing by him with a label of *"Hic est meus"* or something familiar hanging out at their mouths.

Again, he was ironical regarding the so-called "gentlemanly qualifications"—extravagant manners and dress, dancing, complimenting, cursing, drinking, gaming, etc.[12] In contrast was the attitude of the day toward the cultivation of a love for letters:

> Poetry is indeed much neglected in this age, being looked upon as the lowest qualification of a gentleman. Under this head, as I am an advocate for the moderns, I will make use of the best arguments I can in their favour. It is a well-known maxim that every poet is a fool: if this be true, I believe that no one, who has read thus far, can doubt of our qualification for that office.

Such an anticlimax was often used by Trumbull, with humorous effect.

"The Schemer" delighted to satirize the artfulness of the young ladies, who resorted to silly schemes to captivate the men. Behind clever parody was an earnest remonstrance against the mere "accomplishments" which formed the usual

---

[12] "The Schemer," *ibid.*, December 18, 1769.

education of women of that period, leaving their minds vacant and fickle.  In burlesque, appeared the following "Advertisement":

> To Be Sold at Public Vendue,
> The Whole Estate of
> Isabelle Sprightly, Toast and Coquette,
> (Now retiring from business)

This announcement was followed by a detailed list of her "Tools and Utensils"—darts, arrows, patches, cosmetics, caps, Cupids, and other adornments, "very proper to be stationed on a ruby lip, a diamond eye, or a roseate cheek." [13]

These newspaper essays, written while Trumbull was still a student at Yale studying for his second degree, were followed by others of similar tone in the *Connecticut Journal,* during the spring of 1770, under the signature of "The Correspondent." The authors treated many of the same topics as before, but wrote with more boldness and conviction upon certain other interests of the day, as second-sight, palmistry, the morality of dancing, and the promotion of the slave-trade by "so-called Christians."

Such ventures in authorship, and the liberal, fearless ideas there advocated, called popular attention to the young man, who had amazed New

---

[13] *Boston Chronicle,* October 23–26, 1769, signed "B." This cannot be proved to be Trumbull's, but bears close relationship to his later satires.

Haven professors by his brilliant scholarship as a boy. With wisdom, as was proved in his mature life, he chose to study law, since devotion to letters would bring meager return as a life-profession. For this purpose he went to Wethersfield for a year; but the reading of law was somewhat interrupted, for he was called back to Yale as tutor. He continued his studies for the profession, however, and became a successful lawyer and judge.

Meantime the progressive spirit at Yale, advocated by the younger graduates, had gained the ascendency. The autumn of 1771 found three young tutors at the college, men of reforming zeal and popularity—Joseph Howe, Timothy Dwight, and John Trumbull. The beauty of Howe's character called forth tributes from his parishioners in Boston, where he preached for a brief while before his death in 1775. With less alertness and confidence than Trumbull and Dwight, Howe was a very popular teacher at Yale and awakened noble ambition in the souls of his pupils. The effect of his benign personality upon Trumbull was expressed in the closing lines of the latter's "Ode to Sleep":

Teach me, like thee, to feel and know
Our humble station in this vale of woe,
Twilight of life, illumed with feeble ray,
The infant dawning of eternal day;

With heart expansive through this scene improve
The social soul of harmony and love.[14]

. . . . . . . . . . . .

During Trumbull's two years of teaching at
Yale he devoted himself to both law and literature. His capacity for mental work was phe-
nomenal throughout his life. By the students he
was considered a man of marvelous brain-power;
but he was also a social favorite. Among the
boys he was familiarly called "Trum." In a
romance which reveals truthfully the life at Yale
during the years just prior to the war, James
Eugene Farmer has devoted one chapter to "An
Evening with Trumbull."[15] There are also vivid
glimpses in this story of popular students like
Nathan Hale and David Humphreys. In this
fictional narrative the students are listening with
delight to Trumbull's reading from two incom-
plete satires. One of these was *The Advertisement of a Coquette,* already quoted, and the other
was the first part of *The Progress of Dulness.*

The question has been asked, by Tyler and
other critics, whether satire was a natural or an
accidental form of literary expression on the part
of Trumbull. He once asserted that his native

[14] *The Poetical Works of John Trumbull* (1820), Vol. II,
p. 120.

[15] James Eugene Farmer, *Brinton Eliot; from Yale to Yorktown,* (New York, 1902), part I, chap. 7.

taste was imaginative rather than satirical, and that the latter trend came from the political conditions which confronted and stirred him. Evidence from his literary efforts of varied types, and also from reading some of his keen, satiric pleas and letters, seems to indicate that satire was a legitimate expression of his witty, penetrating mind. Doubtless it was fostered both by the political conflict, and also by his devotion to the English essayists of satirical form. Before the patriotic impulse had awakened within him, he had chosen to write in burlesque and satire. Unlike Freneau, he showed no proof of a poetic temperament, before or after the stress of war and national federation. His work that has lived in memory has been that of the satirist and scholar. His only attempts at verse of lyrical kind were labored and stilted.

Among his burlesques, *The Progress of Dulness* will take rank as inventive and forceful.[16] This was conceived when the leaders of pro-

---

[16] The title-page of the first part of *The Progress of Dulness* is unique and interesting: "Part First: or the Rare Adventures of Tom Brainless; shewing What his Father and Mother said of him; how he went to College, and what he learned there; how he took his Degree, and went to keeping School; how afterwards he became a great man and wore a wig; and how any body else may do the same. The like never before published. Very proper to be kept in all Families." (1772.)

gressive methods in education, among whom was
Trumbull, were trying to overthrow prejudices
and false standards at Yale. The satire was in
octosyllabic meter, in three parts, published at
intervals of a few months. The first issue told of
the career of Tom Brainless, a dull lad who had
been sent to college to fritter time away upon
stilted, uninspiring texts. He succeeded in "hood-
winking" professors, so that he was passed
through college and entered the school of theology. With the same spiritless, droning routine,
he became a minister. In his pulpit he is thus
portrayed:

> In awkward tones, nor said nor sung,
> Slow rumbling o'er the faltering tongue,
> Two hours his drawling speech holds on,
> And names it preaching when 'tis done.

The type of the teacher unworthy the name was
also satirized:

> Then throned aloft in elbow chair,
> With solemn face and awful air,
> He tries, with ease and unconcern,
> To teach what ne'er himself could learn;
> Gives law and punishment alone,
> Judge, jury, bailiff all in one;
> Holds all good learning must depend
> Upon his rod's extremest end,
> Whose great electric virtue's such
> Each genius brightens at the touch;
> With threats and blows, incitements pressing,

> Drives on his lads to learn each lesson,
> Thinks flogging cures all moral ills
> And breaks their heads to break their wills.

Beside this dull master of the rod is the teacher who was long known as "the book-worm," thus portrayed with justice as well as wit:

> Read ancient authors o'er in vain,
> Nor taste one beauty they contain,
> And plodding on in one dull tone,
> Gain ancient tongues and lose their own.[17]

The first part of this burlesque was reprinted, in a corrected edition, the year after its appearance. In a preface note, Trumbull explained its purport thus:

> The subject is the state of the times in regard to literature and religion. The author was prompted to write by a hope that it might be of use to point out, in a clear, concise, and striking manner, those general errors, that hinder the advantages of education, and the growth of piety. The subject is inexhaustible; nor is my design yet completed.[18]

As proof of the last sentence, he published this same year, 1773, the second part of the burlesque. Here the character ridiculed was Dick Hairbrain, antitype of the first dull collegian, but equally familiar then and today. His foppish airs, his

[17] *The Poetical Works of John Trumbull* (1820), Vol. II, p. 17.

[18] *The Progress of Dulness*, etc., *Reprinted in the Year MDCC, LXXIII*, Preface, p. 2.

feather brain, his swagger and swearing, his
skeptical opinions exploited after a hasty reading
of Hume and Voltaire—such qualities were de-
lineated with keen, biting sarcasm.  The style in
this part was more earnest than in the earlier
issue.  There were lines of moral teaching,
mingled with the portrayal of the rakish student:

> More oaths than words Dick learned to speak,
> And studied knavery more than Greek.

The career of this young man abroad, his excesses
and failures to win respect or success, are told
with vividness, until

> In lonely age he sinks forlorn,
> Of all, and even himself, the scorn.[19]

To complete the trilogy of characters, mis-
guided and educated according to wrong standards, Trumbull introduced in the third part Miss
Harriet Simper, a vain coquette.  In a preface
the author affirmed "that the foibles we discover
in the fair sex arise principally from the neglect
of their education, and the mistaken notions they
imbibe in their early youth."  The same thought
was thus expressed in ironical verse:

> And why should girls be learn'd or wise?
> Books only serve to spoil their eyes.
> The studious eye but faintly twinkles,
> And reading paves the way to wrinkles.

[19] *The Progress of Dulness,* Part II, "Life and Character
of Dick Hairbrain" (New Haven, 1773), p. 38.

To give a touch of romantic unity, Trumbull depicted his coquette in various flirtations; she is scorned by Dick Hairbrain and marries Tom Brainless, to escape the "stigma of being an old maid." [20]

This burlesque was popular as a production of wit, and it exerted no little influence as a rebuke to the conditions of the time which fostered such drones, fops, and coquettes. The pages contain some pictures of society and epigrams which are relevant today, as:

> Follies be multiplied with quickness,
> And whims keep up the family likeness.
>
> Good sense, like fruit, is rais'd by toil,
> But follies sprout in every soil. [21]

After two years as teacher at Yale, Trumbull passed his law examinations. Possibly in order that he might have a wider contact with men of affairs, he went to Boston, in November, 1773, to

[20] In the complete poem the third part reads: "Sometimes called The Progress of Coquetry, or the Adventures of Miss Harriet Simper, of the Colony of Connecticut." In the preface the author expresses his desire "to laugh at with good humor, and to expose without malevolence." Of the young lady's mother he writes:
> From whom her faults that never vary,
> May come by right hereditary.
*The Progress of Dulness, or the Rare Adventures of Tom Brainless. By the celebrated author of McFINGAL. Printed at Exeter. 3 parts. MDCCXCIV. 72 pages; 16mo.*

[21] *The Progress of Dulness* (1794), pp. 49, 53.

the law office of John Adams. This year gave
new impulse to his interests and literary activities.
He had taken a mild part in urging freedom of
expression in America and had praised the tendency toward resistance. Now he came into personal contact with statesmen who had already
shown their radical opposition to the Stamp Act
and other measures of injustice. Soon after he
reached Boston, the affair of the tea-ships took
place, and the military discipline directed against
Boston increased the political ferment. All these
steps, tending toward independence and war, must
have impressed a young man so keen and zealous
for reform as Trumbull was. His legal chief,
John Adams, was recognized as one of the leaders among the patriots and was sent to Philadelphia to attend the Continental Congress of
1774 while Trumbull was in his office.

The influence of these agitations, and the
political principles involved, may be read in the
literary work of Trumbull during this year and
the following. His first writing in verse, "The
Destruction of Babylon" [22] was probably only the
completion of an earlier effort. With the exception of a few lines, which might be applied to the

[22] This paraphrase of the thirteenth and fourteenth chapters in Isaiah and the eighteenth in Revelations was included
in *The Poetical Works of John Trumbull* (1820), Vol. II,
pp. 195-201.

situation in Boston and the incipient thought of
freedom, the poem showed no distinct marks of
its author's environment. At about the same time
he wrote certain light fables in verse, as "The
Owl and the Sparrow" and "To a Young Lady
Who Requested the Author to draw Her
Character." These are merely occasional verses,
with bits of covert sarcasm.

Quite a new spirit permeates "An Elegy on
the Times," which was first printed at Boston,
September, 1774.[23] The author said that it was
written soon after the Boston Port Bill. It had
a tone of sadness as well as of courage, as if
Trumbull still hoped that the worst might be
averted, but, if necessary, he would defend his
country's rights with his pen. A few stanzas
show the deepening zeal of this awakened patriot:

> In vain we hope from ministerial pride
>   A hand to save us or a heart to bless:
> 'Tis strength, our own, must stem the rushing tide,
>   'Tis our own virtue must command success.
>
> . . . . . . . . . . . . . . . . .
>
> Then, tell us, NORTH, for thou art sure to know,
>   For have not kings and fortunes made thee great;
> Or lurks not wisdom in th' ennobled brow,
>   And dwells no prescience in the robes of state?
>
> And tell how rapt by freedom's sacred flame
>   And fost'ring influence of propitious skies,

[23] Published in Boston, 1774; in New Haven, 1775.

This western world, the last recess of fame,
   Sees in her wilds a new-born empire rise,—

A new-born empire whose ascendant hour
   Defies its foes, assembled to destroy,
And like Alcides, with its infant power
   Shall crush those serpents, who its rest annoy.[24]

These stanzas seem faulty judged by poetical canons, but they were superior to the majority of verses of these years. Philip Freneau's best satires began to appear within a few months, but Trumbull preceded in literary evidence of patriotism, combined with keen wit. By his contemporaries he was called "the finest satirical lance of the age," and was urged to write yet other poems for the cause of freedom. He had come into friendly relations with James Otis, John Hancock, John Adams, and Thomas Cushing. The influence of these patriots doubtless incited Trumbull to the burlesque stanzas which were afterward expanded into his masterpiece of satire, "M'Fingal." To the Marquis de Chastelleux, after *M'Fingal* had become known in Europe as well as in America, Trumbull wrote that "it was written merely with a political view, at the instigation of some of the leading members of the first Congress who urged me to compose a

[24] *The Poetical Works* (1820), Vol. II, pp. 208-17.

satirical poem upon the events of the campaign of 1775." [25]

Parts of this satire were written during the latter part of 1774 and at intervals in 1775. Although the first edition bears the date of publication 1775, it was really issued in January, 1776. The bravado of General Gage had weakened somewhat after the evidence of bravery, as well as defiance, on the part of the beleaguered Bostonians. To quell their patriotic zeal and still protect himself, he began issuing proclamations, some intimidating, others with a patronizing note that was almost insulting. These may be found in all the leading newspapers of the time. They gave incentive to the first political lampoons and satires by both Trumbull and Freneau. The former contributed to the *Connecticut Courant,* August, 7 and 14, 1775, an unsigned parody upon Gage's proclamations, that contains lines almost identical with his later passage in the second canto of *M'Fingal:*

> The annals of his first great year;
> While wearing out the Tories' patience,
> He spent his breath in proclamation;
> While all his mighty noise and vapour
> Was used in wrangling upon paper.

[25] J. Hammond Trumbull, "The Origin of M'Fingal," *Historical Magazine,* January, 1868; see also letter by Trumbull on subject to Silas Deane, *Deane Papers,* Vol. II, pp. 88–9, New York Historical Society Collections.

J. Hammond Trumbull, in his study of "The
Origin of M'Fingal," has suggested that possibly
Trumbull wrote the parody upon Gage's procla-
mation beginning,

TOM  GAGE'S  PROCLAMATION,
Or blustering Denunciation,

which appeared in the *Connecticut Courant,* July
17, 1775. As has been stated in the chapter on
Freneau, the weight of evidence, as given by Mr.
Paltsits, both in his bibliography of Freneau and
in a private letter, would seem to disprove the
possibility that this was Trumbull's, for it had
appeared in Philadelphia and New York papers
before it was printed in those of Connecticut.

The first canto of *M'Fingal,* published in Philadelphia, was soon circulated through the newspapers and reprinted in several editions. It was
viewed with dismay by the British leaders, for it
was too popular to be counteracted by any Tory
satire.[26]  The second canto came within the year
1776, but the third part was deferred until 1782.

M'Fingal, the Loyalist, is a well-conceived and
sustained character. His introduction was preceded by a few lines of general ridicule:

When Yankees, skill'd in martial rule,
First put the British troops to school;

[26] The effect of this satire was cumulative. It appeared
near the time of Hopkinson's *A Pretty Story* and *A Prophecy,*
and Thomas Paine's *Common Sense.*

Instructed them in warlike trade,
And new manoevres of parade,
The true war-dance of Yankee reels,
And *manual exercise* of heels;
Made them give up, like saints complete,
The arm of flesh, and trust the feet.
And work like Christians undissembling,
Salvation out by fear and trembling;
Taught Percy fashionable races
And modern modes of Chevy-Chases;
From Boston, in his best array,
Great Squire M'Fingal took his way,
And grac'd with ensigns of renown,
Steer'd homeward to his native town.

.   .   .   .   .   .   .   .   .   .   .   .   .   .

His fathers flourished in the Highlands
Of Scotia's fog-benighted islands;
Whence gained our Squire two gifts by right,
Rebellion and the Second-sight.[27]

In contrast with *M'Fingal* was the character
of *Honorius,* the staunch Whig, generally considered a portrait of John Adams.   In the scene
of the town-meeting, which has its forenoon and
afternoon sessions respectively in Cantos I and
II, Honorius speaks boldly regarding the arro-
gance and injustice of England and her decline
in power.   Gage had explained to various colonial
officers, among them Governor Trumbull of Connecticut, that he sent his troops to Concord merely
"to prevent a civil war."   This statement was

[27] *M'Fingal:   A Modern Epic Poem,* Canto I, p. 4.

# M'FINGAL:

## A MODERN

# EPIC POEM.

## CANTO FIRST,

### OR

## THE TOWN-MEETING.

PHILADELPHIA:

Printed and Sold by WILLIAM and THOMAS BRAD-
FORD, at the London Coffee-House, 1775.

Title-page of first edition of *M'Fingal;* from copy in Watkinson Library, Hartford, Conn.

used with caustic effect in the speech of Honorius,
in Canto II:

> There, when the war he chose to wage,
> Shone the benevolence of Gage;
> Sent troops to that ill-omen'd place,
> On errands mere of special grace;
> And all the work he chose them for,
> Was to *prevent a civil war.*
> For which kind purpose he projected
> The truly certain way t' effect it,
> To seize your powder, shot and arms,
> And all your means of doing harms;
> As prudent folks take knives away,
> Lest children cut themselves at play.
> And yet, when this was all his scheme,
> The war you still will charge on him;
> And tho' he oft has sworn and said it,
> Stick close to facts and give no credit.

In a fractious temper, M'Fingal tries to respond, taunting the Whigs with both cowardice
and foolishness. Interrupted by sharp questions
and sarcasms from Honorius, he pleads in vain
the cause of British justice. At last, recognizing
that he is losing ground, he passes into a trance
of second-sight, and depicts his vision of the
grand rewards assured to the Tories who will
stand by their king in the conflict. In the great
day of British victory—

> Whigs subdued, in slavish awe,
> Our wood shall hew, our water draw,

And bless that mildness, when past hope,
Which sav'd their necks from noose of rope.[28]

By this speech of M'Fingal, Honorius has
gained a point—exposure of the greed and dis-
loyalty of the Tories—and he breaks forth into
an eloquent plea for patriotism. M'Fingal and
his friends find their only resource in stirring up a
riot by hisses; and thus ends the town-meeting.[29]

When this satire, of fifteen hundred lines, was
reprinted in Hartford, London, Boston, and
elsewhere, it attracted universal attention. In
England there was much speculation as to its
authorship. It was accredited to Butler and other
wits. Some affirmed that it was the work of a
British officer who had been superseded in command, and who chose this method of venting his
wrath. In the "Memoir" to his *Poetical Works*,
Trumbull referred to the various surmises regarding the authorship of "M'Fingal," and said that
there were ascribed to him

Jests he ne'er uttered, deeds he ne'er atchiev'd,
Rhymes he ne'er wrote, and lives (thank heaven) he never
lived.[30]

[28] *M'Fingal, a Modern Epic Poem*, Canto II, p. 41. The
name was from *Fingal*, an epic poem by Ossian, published by
MacPherson.

[29] It was stated that forty editions of the first two cantos
were printed. One of the best collections of editions is in the
Watkinson Library of Hartford. Several are also found in
the Library of Congress, Brown University, and elsewhere.

[30] *The Poetical Works of John Trumbull*, "Memoir," p. 8.

The fact that Trumbull was the author of this satire was known, however, long before the third canto was written. This came in response to a popular demand. There he depicted his Scottish orator as seized by a mob and tried by a hastily convened court at the foot of a Liberty Pole; he was convicted of Toryism, and condemned to a coat of tar and feathers. The illustration of this scene in later editions was rude, but vigorous. In the last canto the once vain-glorious leader of the Loyalists had assembled his anxious, dwindling followers to cheer them with another vision. Meanwhile, the entrance of the Whig forces scattered the company, and the frightened M'Fingal escaped to Boston.

The last portion of the satire was weak, in contrast with the earlier, spirited cantos, although there were two passages of clever construction. The first was the famous scene of the tar-and-feather process, once so popular as a means of punishment. This description by Trumbull was long a favorite "piece" for recital by schoolboy orators:

> So from the high-raised urn the torrents
> Spread down his sides their various currents:
> His flowing wig, as next the brim,
> First met and drank the sable stream;
> Adown his visage stern and grave
> Roll'd and adhered the viscid wave;

With arms depending as he stood,
Each cuff capacious holds the flood:
From nose and chin's remotest end
The tarry icicles descend;
Till, all o'erspread, with colors gay,
He glittered to the Western ray
Like sleet-bound trees in wintry skies,
Or Lapland idol carved in ice.
And now the feather-bag display'd
Is waved in triumph o'er his head,
And clouds him o'er with feathers missive
And, down upon the tar adhesive:
Not Maia's son, with wings for ears,
Such plumage round his visage wears;
Not Milton's six-wing'd angel gathers
Such superfluity of feathers.[31]

There is more wit and ease in the second familiar portion, where M'Fingal makes his recantation, to escape from the taunts of the patriots:

I here renounce the Pope, the Turks,
The King, the Devil and all their works;
And will, set me but once again at ease,
Turn Whig or Christian, what you please.[32]

This satire, as a whole, may be censured for many offenses against literary taste and many examples of strained meter. It must be regarded, however, not as a finished poem, like Butler's "Hudibras" or Churchill's "The Ghost," although

[31] *M'Fingal*, Canto III, pp. 61, 62.
[32] *Ibid.*, p. 59.

it resembles these in form. It was a hastily written weapon of warfare. Its purpose was utilitarian and its effect upon the contending parties cannot be overstated. It represented progressive patriotism against reactionary fears. Few writings of that day reached such a wide circulation. It was reprinted in piratical editions until, we are told, it brought about, in 1783, the passage of an "Act for the Encouragement of Literature and Genius," by the General Assembly of Connecticut, which secured to authors their copyrights within the state.[33]

While we recognize the specific aim of this burlesque and its immediate service to patriotism, we still find, within its lines, atmosphere and silhouettes of characters of the past which are well worth remembrance, apart from its purpose. Not alone external pictures of the times are here, but also a clear presentation of the mental processes of Whig and Tory, in the period which preceded secession. If the humor is broad and the words often uncouth, such were the traits of the classes which were represented—the sturdy, uneducated farmers, the rude soldiers, the blacksmiths, storekeepers, and other characters of early village life in America.

[33] This assertion is made by J. Hammond Trumbull in *The Memorial History of Hartford County* (1886), note to p. 157, Vol. I.

Donald G. Mitchell has said, with unique appreciation of this satire:

> It has a sportive, easy, rollicking flow. There's no dreaming in it; there's no swashy sentiment; it does not stay to moralize; it goes on its rhythmic and satiric beat— as steady and sure and effective as a patent threshing-machine. For an American it should make more piquant reading than Butler's "Hudibras." [34]

Although it bore such a close resemblance to "Hudibras" that, before its authorship was determined, some couplets were confidently asserted to be Butler's, yet it has a strong individuality. Regarding the method of writing, Trumbull explained, in a letter to the Marquis de Chastelleux:

> I determined to describe every subject in the manner it struck my own imagination, and without confining myself to a perpetual effort at wit, drollery and humour, indulge every variety of manner, as my subject varied, and insert all ridicule, satire, sense, sprightliness and elevation, of which I was master." [35]

John Trumbull was only twenty-five when the best part of *M'Fingal* was written, and he lived

[34] D. G. Mitchell, *American Lands and Letters*, Vol. I, pp. 158, 159. Mr. Mitchell recalls the popularity of this burlesque in the days of his boyhood.

[35] J. Hammond Trumbull, "The Origin of M'Fingal," *Historical Magazine*, January, 1868. "Time has a little blunted the edge of McFingal, yet it remains the best of American political satires in verse, with the possible exception of The Biglow Papers"—so says J. Hammond Trumbull in *The Memorial History of Hartford County*, Vol. I, p. 158.

past eighty years; yet he is known to history as
the author of that satire. The later events of his
life were personal in the main, and only indirectly
associated with political history. That he had a
prominent part in the writings of "the Hartford
wits," in behalf of internal harmony and federalism, will be indicated in the next chapter. However, this service was done in collaboration, and
his special writings have only been partially identified. "The Genius of America," an ode of thirteen stanzas, written in 1777 after the capture of
Burgoyne, was included in Trumbull's *Poetical
Works,* but it has slight value either as a historical record or as poetry. His earlier fame,
nevertheless, clung to him among his Connecticut
friends, and he was generally considered the
leader of the patriot-wits of Hartford. With extravagant tribute, Timothy Dwight testified to
this leadership, in his "Epistle to Col. Humphreys," in 1785:

> Hence, too, when Trumbull leads the ardent throng,
> Ascending bards begin the immortal song:
> Let glowing friendship wake the cheerful lyre,
> Blest to commend, and pleas'd to catch the fire.[36]

In spite of such excursions into literature,
Trumbull's mature success was achieved in law.
After his return from Boston in 1776, and his
marriage to Sarah, daughter of Leverett Hub-

[36] *American Poems, Selected and Original* (1793), p. 83.

bard, of New Haven, he practiced law in New Haven and Waterbury. The next few years must have been full of trial, for he was frequently ill, largely from excess of nervous activity. In 1780 he was considered fatally sick, but he recovered and moved to Hartford for his future home. Here he held positions of honor. He was attorney for the County of Hartford, member of the state legislature, and, in 1808, was appointed judge of the Supreme Court of Errors and served until 1819.

The judicial appointment of Trumbull and his highly-rated literary cleverness aroused some envy among the less fortunate of his political opponents. Evidence of this is found in a pamphlet entitled "Federalism Triumphant in the Steady Habits of Connecticut Alone, or, the Turnpike Road to a Fortune." This was called "A Comic Opera, or Political Farce in Six Acts, as performed at the Theatres Royal and Aristocratic at Hartford and New Haven, October, 1801." It was printed the next year. One of the leading characters is "John M'Fingal, a Poet,—late Student with J. Adams." With sarcasm, the author of this farce depicts Trumbull seeking in every way to gain influence with political leaders, especially with "Jonathan," easily recognized as Governor Jonathan Trumbull, that the judiciary may be increased and his place secured. In soliloquy, he is represented as saying (pp. 17, 18) "I must not dip my pen, until I've got through that judiciary bill,—suppress my wit & satire till that bill is passed, and get the appointment, and then and not till then may my vein of humour be indulged."

A note supplies the somewhat sneering information that, "It's universally known that John Trumbull wrote M'Fingal and sundry other poetic pieces of merit, obtained a law for a patent, for books, maps, charts, etc., has piddled occasionally at Hartford in the New Year addresses of the boys who carries (*sic*) the papers, and that when elected member for Hartford he assisted Noah in the answer to Hamilton's development of Adams' imbecility.  He supposed himself cunning in all writings."

This reference to the assistance given by Trumbull to Noah Webster, in the latter's writing, is verified by a statement frequently made that Trumbull was of great value to Webster in the compilation of the latter's Dictionary.  These facts and reminiscences have been given by Trumbull's grandson (Mr. Dudley Bradstreet Woodbridge, of Groose Pointe Farms, Michigan, to whom I am much indebted).  Webster and Trumbull were good friends and the latter's classical education amazed Webster, so he called upon his friend to revise almost every sheet of the Dictionary, as it came from the printer, especially relying upon his knowledge of derivations.

Another friend of Trumbull, who won fame, was Mrs. Lydia Huntley Sigourney. Trumbull's grandson has recalled that Mrs. Sigourney was the daughter of a Revolutionary soldier, who lived in a cottage adjoining Trumbull's estate. The little girl, Lydia, interested the judge and scholar, and he taught her many things from nature and books: "seeing she had a natural talent for poetry he bent her mind in that direction. She would write little rhymes and he would correct them for her, and point out all the errors, until she became fascinated with the writing of verse." After the death of Trumbull, Mrs. Sigourney sent to his daughter, Mrs. Woodbridge, a tribute in prose and verse from which the following is an extract, given by Mr. Woodbridge: the poem is a vision of Trumbull in his later years at Detroit.

"To the memory of the Hon. John Trumbull, Author of M'Fingal, and other poems; a native of Connecticut: who died at Detroit, Michigan: a tribute to the memory of one who was no less the pride of his native State than of his Country; the patriotic bard, who having left among his native hills the thrilling Harp which had animated every camp, and enlivened every cottage, till its notes resounded across the Atlantic."

This was he
Whose shaft of wit had touch'd the epic strain
With poignant power.   The Father of the Harp
In his own native vales.   He seems to muse
As if those loved retreats did spread themselves
Again before his eye.   The sighing wind
Through the long branches of those ancient trees
When first his boyhood lisp'd the love of Song
Doth lull his soul.   There brighter visions gleam,
A sound of music rises.   'Tis thy voice Connecticut
As when by vernal rains
Surcharged, it swells in tuneful murmurs round
The vine-clad mansion where his children grew.
But the hoarse clangor of yon mighty Lakes
Holding high conflict with the winged Storm
      Doth quell its melody.
      And is it so
That in the feebleness of four-score years
Thou with unshrinking hand didst pitch thy tent
Near the broad billows of the Michigan
And mark in that far land young life start forth
In beauty and in vigor and in power
Where erst the Indian, and the Panther dwelt
Sole lords.   It was a bold emprize
To change the robe of science and of mistrelsy
Worn from thy cradle onward
For the staff of the strong emigrant.
.   .   .   .   .   .   .   .   .   .   .   .   .   .   .
Master and friend; until this feeble lyre
In silence moulders, till my heart forgets
The thrill of gratitude, the love of song,
The praise of knowledge, shall thine image dwell
Bright with the beauty of benignant age
      In my soul's temple-shrine!

In spite of his vivacity and power of accomplishment, Trumbull was compelled to do his work with ill-health constantly against him. He visited mineral springs and gained temporary relief. After such respite from suffering he would work with marvelous energy, and thus compensate for lost time. Among the manuscript letters in the Oliver Wolcott, Jr., papers, at the Connecticut Historical Society, is one from Dr. Lemuel Hopkins to Wolcott, written in June, 1795, which contains an interesting reference to Trumbull and his physical condition :[37]

Trumbull will, I fear, within a year or two, quit "the visible diurnal sphere." What, then, O Hartford, hast thou for me? Pleasant indeed shalt thou remain, but chiefly for the joys that are past.

Another letter, in the same collection, from Trumbull to Wolcott, has been printed, but, as it is one of the few extant letters by Trumbull, it is valuable as a revelation of his personality.[38] Under date of December 9, 1789, from Hartford, Trumbull wrote :

[37] Dr. Hopkins was one of the collaborators with Trumbull and his friends, mentioned in the next chapter. The date of this letter was June 28, 1795. It is printed by permission of the Connecticut Historical Society.

[38] Printed in *Memoirs of the Administrations of Washington and John Adams, Edited from the Papers of Oliver Wolcott, Secretary of the Treasury* (1840), Vol. I, pp. 25, 26.

I received yours by Dr. Coggswell, who appears a sensible, agreeable young man, & I am glad that he proposes to settle in Hartford. Indeed our circle of friends wants new recruits. Humphreys, Barlow and you are lost to us.—Dr Hopkins has an itch of running away to New York, but I trust his indolence will prevent him. However, if you should catch him in your City, I desire you to take him up & return him or secure him so that we may have him again, for which you shall have sixpence reward, & all charges. . . . . .

I cannot conceive what Barlow is doing—After being eighteen months abroad, you tell me he has got so far as to see favorable prospects. If he should not affect something to the purpose soon, I would advise him to write "The Vision of Barlow," as a sequel to those of Columbus and M'Fingal.

When Trumbull was seventy-five years old, and had survived nearly all of his associates in Connecticut, he left Hartford to spend his last years in Detroit, which then seemed on the borderland of the far West. Here he lived with his daughter, Mrs William Woodbridge, until his death in 1831. This experience gave him an opportunity to realize the growth of the nation which he had served in its infancy, and he rejoiced in all marks of progress. When he passed through New York, on his way to Detroit, a banquet was given in his honor by lawyers and men of letters. At the same time his poems, in two volumes, were printed by his friend, S. G. Goodrich, better known to his own day as "Peter

Parley." In his *Recollections of a Lifetime,* Mr. Goodrich thus commented upon this publication:

About this time I published an edition of Trumbull's poems, in two volumes octavo, and paid him a thousand dollars and a hundred copies of the work for the copyright. I was seriously counselled against this by several book-sellers—in fact, Trumbull had sought a publisher in vain, for several years previous. There was an association of designers and engravers at Hartford, called the Graphic Company, and as I desired to patronize the liberal arts there, I employed them to execute the embellishments. For so considerable an enterprise I took the precaution to get a subscription, in which I was tolerably successful. The work was at last produced, but it did not come up to the public expectation, or the patriotic zeal had cooled, and more than half the subscribers declined taking the work. I did not press it, but putting a good face upon the affair, I let it pass and—while the public supposed I had made money by my enterprise, and even the author looked askance at me in the jealous apprehension that I had made too good a bargain out of him—I quietly pocketed a loss of about a thousand dollars.[39]

We must make some allowance for the usual exploitation of his own merits by "Peter Parley." He was, however, a good friend to the satirist and would-be poet, Trumbull, who sought vainly (after his young manhood) for literary success. The general influence of Trumbull, among his friends of patriotic impulses and literary tastes, must be admitted as his greatest claim to recog-

[39] *Recollections of a Lifetime,* Vol. II, pp. 111, 112.

nition, beyond the success which he won as author of a single clever burlesque. The face of this writer and judge was painted from life by his kinsman, John Trumbull. In accord with the features there seen, and the traits suggested, is this description of him given by Mr. Goodrich:

His features were finely cut, and he must have been handsome in his younger days. His eye was keen and bright, his nose slightly aquiline, his mouth arching downwards at the corners, expressive of sarcastic humor. There was something about him that at once bespoke the man of letters, the poet, and the satirist.[40]

[40] *Ibid.*, pp. 114, 115.

# A GROUP OF HARTFORD WITS

# V

## A GROUP OF HARTFORD WITS

Classification is a common substitute for literary criticism. Often a relative convenience, it has sometimes only obscured the distinct traits of an author. Occasionally an individual daunts the cataloguer and stands in comparative isolation —like Dante, Carlyle, Thoreau, or Tolstoy. Classification is often based upon the governing motif of the writers—as the "Transcendentalists," the "Pre-Raphaelites," and the "Decadents." The more common allotment is by eras and localities; the "Augustan age," the "Elizabeth dramatists," the "Victorian novelists," are phrases as familiar as the "Oxford Movement," the "Lake Poets," the "Knickerbocker Group," or the "Hartford Wits."

After the middle of the eighteenth century the center of literary activity in America was transferred from the vicinity of Boston, where it had been for many years inspired by Harvard College, to the environment of the younger colleges, Nassau Hall, or the College of New Jersey, which later became Princeton, and the College of Philadelphia, which formed the nucleus of the University of Pennsylvania. Graduates of these

institutions became progressive leaders in political
and literary zeal.   At Yale College, also, victory
for modern educational methods had been gained,
at about the same time that the first notes were
sounded against British tyranny and in behalf of
independence.   John Trumbull was the leader
among the Connecticut reformers and satirists,
but his life reflected his association with a few
companions, often called the "Hartford Wits."
While the burlesques and satires that gave fame
to Trumbull were written during the early years
of the war, many of his later efforts in satire and
reform were in collaboration with some patriot-
comrades who realized the dangers which im-
periled the new nation.

Although independence had been won, anarchy
was menacing; government, finance, and commerce were unstable.   Such affairs formed subjects for grave discussion, varied by witty verse,
at the gatherings of a "Friendly Club" in Hartford.   Among the nine names mentioned of those
who formed the original membership of this club,
there is a major and a minor list: familiar to
our ears are the names of John Trumbull,
Timothy Dwight, Joel Barlow, and David
Humphreys; seldom recalled are their associates,
Theodore Dwight, Richard Alsop, and the three
physicians, Elihu Smith, Mason Cogswell, and
Lemuel Hopkins.   Other men, possibly allied

with this coterie, were Congressman Uriah
Tracey, Judge Tappan Reeve, and Zephaniah
Smith.[1]  The series of publications assigned to
this first group of wits dated from 1785 to 1807.

Seventy-five years seems to us an incredibly
long period to elapse between the appearance of
some literary work in a journal and its first publication in book-form.  On the title-page of *The
Anarchiad,* dated 1861, is this editor's note,
"Now first published in book form."  Research
shows that the twelve satiric papers constituting
*The Anarchiad* were printed first in the *New
Haven Gazette,* beginning October 26, 1786, and
continuing, at intervals, until September 13, 1787.
They were copied in Federalist journals throughout many of the states of the Union.  In this
first, belated edition of *The Anarchiad,* its
editor, Luther G. Riggs, expresses an assurance
"that he is in performance of a duty—that he
becomes, as it were, an instrument of justice, a
justice delayed for more than half a century, to
the genius and loyalty of its authors, who were

[1] At the library of the Connecticut Historical Society in
Hartford are several unique pamphlets, generally assigned to
a later group of "Hartford wits," between 1819 and 1830.
This group is probably the same mentioned by Goodrich in
*Recollections of a Lifetime,* Vol. I, pp. 92–98.  The same
phrase, "Hartford wits," has been passed on to another
group, of our own day, "Mark Twain," Charles Dudley War-
ner, Harriet Beecher Stowe, and Rev. Joseph Twitchell.

among the noblest and most talented sons of the
Revolution." We would exchange his term
"genius" for "wit," but we cannot question the
quality of patriotism and the influence of these
satires in subduing threatened anarchy, and in
arousing higher ideals during the crucial years
after the war, while feeling was strong regarding
the Constitution and the basis of political and
financial security.

The name, borrowed from Miltonic Anarch,
suggested the purpose, which was further explained in the sub-title, "A Poem on the Restoration of Chaos and Substantial Night." The
wits wished to show, with forceful satire, the
warfare waged against the stability of the new
nation by the promoters of local rebellion, paper
money, and selfish greed. Although the papers
were sent unsigned to the newspaper, and the
various portions have never been perfectly
identified, the series was undoubtedly the work
of four men who had shown earlier evidence of
their patriotism either by service in the army
or by their writings—John Trumbull, David
Humphreys, Joel Barlow, and Dr. Lemuel Hopkins.

To Colonel Humphreys belonged the credit
for suggesting this unique literary plan. While
abroad, serving on the commission for treaties
with foreign powers, he had shared in the popu-

lar curiosity over an anonymous English satire, *The Rolliad*. Returning to America, he saw with dismay the signs of insurrection in Shay's Rebellion and other dangers. He suggested the use of satire in verse, akin to the form of *The Rolliad* and Pope's *The Dunciad,* to arouse public curiosity and also to teach lessons of patriotism.

The prose "Introduction" to the first paper mystified the readers and entertained them. It is an interesting commentary upon the credulity and emotional ferment of the period. The supposed archaeologist thus addressed the publishers of the *New Haven Gazette:*

I have the felicity to belong to a society of critics and antiquarians, who have made it their business and delight for some years past, to investigate the ancient as well as natural history of America. The success of their researches in such an unlimited field, pregnant with such wonderful and inexhaustible materials, has been equal to their most sanguine expectations. One of our worthy associates has favored the public with a minute and accurate description of the monstrous, new-invented animal which had, till its elaborate lucubration, escaped the notice of every zoologist. . . . . Others have spared no pains to feast the public curiosity with an ample supply of great bones from the Wabash, and, at the same time, to quench the thirst for novelty from the burning spring on the Ohio.

It has happily fallen to my lot to communicate through the medium of your paper, a recent discovery still more valuable to the republic of letters. I need scarcely premise that the ruins of fortifications yet visible, and other vestiges of art, in the west country, had sufficiently demonstrated that this delightful region had once been occupied by a civilized people. Had not this hypothesis been previously established, the fact I am about to relate would have placed it beyond the possibility of doubt. For upon digging into the ruins of one of the most considerable of these fortifications, the labourers were surprised to find a casement, a magazine, and a cistern almost entire. Pursuing their subterranean progress, near the north-east corner of the bastion, they found a great number of utensils, more curious and elegant than those of Palmyra and Herculaneum. But what rendered their good fortune complete, was the discovery of a great number of papers, manuscripts, etc., whose preservation, through such a lapse of years, amid such marks of hostility and devastation, must be deemed marvellous indeed, perhaps little short of miraculous. This affords a reflection, that such extraordinary circumstances could scarcely have taken place to answer only vulgar purposes.

Happening myself to come upon the spot, immediately after this treasure had been discovered, I was permitted to take possession of it, in the name and for the use of our society. Amongst these relics of antiquity, I was rejoiced to find a folio manuscript which appeared to contain an epic poem, complete; and, as I am passionately fond of poetry, ancient as well modern, I set myself instantly to cleanse it from the extraneous concretions with which it was in some parts enveloped, defaced and rendered illegible. By means of a chemic preparation, which is made use of for restoring oil paintings, I soon accomplished the desirable object. It was then I found it was called "The Anarchiad, A Poem on the Restoration of Chaos and Substantial Night," in twenty-four books.

While public curiosity was thus assailed, the second, and ulterior, motive of patriotism was emphasized by some interwoven verses. Choosing Shay's Rebellion as a pivotal example of anarchy, the vision of its "mob-compelling," destructive course was outlined by the supposed prophet:

> Thy constitution, Chaos, is restor'd,
> Law sinks before thy uncreating word;
> Thy hand unbars th' unfathomed gulf of fate,
> And deep in darkness whelms the new-born state.[2]

In addition to the insurrections against martial laws and state organizations, there was another lurking evil, especially in New England —the futile paper money, and the consequent depreciation and instability of all industries. Rhode Island was suffering much from this cause, and seemed to be in the power of wary, selfish schemers. In the second and third numbers of "American Antiquities," as the *Anarchiad* series was called, mock-heroics in verse were mingled with serious advice, in prose, from Connecticut to her oppressed neighbor state. With direct truth it was asserted:

> For it will scarcely be denied in any part of the United States, that paper money, in an unfunded and depreciating condition, is happily calculated to introduce the long-expected scenes of misrule, dishonesty, and perdition.

[2] *The Anarchiad* (New Haven, 1861), p. 6.

The fourth and fifth papers in the series appealed for a revival of national pride and progress. Hesper, the promise of Dawn, confronts Anarch, god of Night, and by the contention seeks to arouse loyalty among the people:

> Teach ere too late, their blood-bought rights to prize,
> Bid other Greenes and Washingtons arise!
> Teach those who suffer'd for their country's good,
> Who strove for freedom and who toil'd in blood,
> Once more in arms to make the glorious stand;
> And bravely die or save their natal land![3]

In the fifth article of the series was an ode, "Genius of America"—a favorite title of the day. In offering it, the authors expressed a hope that, "should the taste of their countrymen in general be uncorrupted, as they flatter themselves it is, they expect this song will be introduced into most of the polite circles of the United States." The author of this ode was Humphreys; for it was included later among his poems. He must have rejoiced—for he sought appreciation—when the song was "introduced" and reprinted. Sung to the tune of "The watery god, great Neptune, lay," it won much popularity; but in thought and meter it ranks among the most inferior portions of *The Anarchiad*. A single stanza will indicate both form and theme—the dangers which threatened to destroy America's glory:

[3] *Loc. cit.*, p. 13.

> Shall steed to steed, and man to man,
> With discord thundering in the van,
>     Again destroy the bliss!
> Enough my mystic words reveal;
> The rest the shades of night conceal,
>     In fate's profound abyss![4]

The dialogue between Anarch and his pupil Wrongheads, in the sixth and seventh portions, extorted a confession from the demagogue that his aim was selfish greed, and the enemies whom he most feared were the friends of law, justice, and education.

One of the objects of special censure by the Democrats, who feared the tendencies toward monarchy and militarism, was the Society of the Cincinnati. In eastern Connecticut there lived William Williams, a prominent lawyer, who had ventured to question the wisdom of continuing the Cincinnati as a banded society. Williams was a fine scholar, and had proved himself a staunch patriot during the war, by giving lavishly of his money and service in town offices. Later he became judge of Windham County, and married the daughter of Governor Trumbull. His criticisms of the Cincinnati, however, had aroused Barlow and Humphreys, who were prominent among its members and orators, and they found an opportunity to retaliate. In April,

[4] *Ibid.*, pp. 26–28.

1786, Williams was a candidate for election, as a Democrat, to the State Assembly. To Joseph Hopkins he sent a letter and an "Address," urging his friend to guard carefully the contents of the letter until the right time for use. In transmission the letter was lost—or purloined—and was published soon after. The result was the so-called "Wimble War," which was waged in the *Connecticut Courant* during the autumn of 1786.[5]

This intercepted letter, and its author, furnished material for a caustic burlesque in the eighth number of the "American Antiquities." The newspaper stanzas of lampoon letters by "William Wimble" and "Joseph Copper," suggest to us the wit of Trumbull:

> Hoping to see you in October,
> With face full long, and cant full sober;
> So pray be cautious, sly and nimble,
> Your loving servant, William Wimble.[6]

After this personal digression, the authors of *The Anarchiad* returned to more general themes and uttered a strong plea for federalism. With biting sarcasm, they decried Congress, indiffer-

[5] In idea and form these papers of retort were modeled somewhat after the "Wimble Papers" in the *Spectator*.

[6] *The Anarchiad*, Appendix, p. 109. First in the *Connecticut Courant*, October 9, 1786.

ent to "Hamilton's unshaken soul" and his wise
counsel:

> My band of mutes, in dire confusion throng,
> Convinc'd of right, yet obstinate in wrong.[7]

"The Speech of Hesper to the Sages and
Counsellors at Philadelphia" was probably the
work of Dr. Lemuel Hopkins. With details of
sufferings and scars, he recounted the grief of the
war veterans because of political inertia and
anarchical tendencies. The last stanzas made a
strong appeal for a centralized government:

> But know, ye favor'd race, one potent head
> Must rule your States, and strike your foes with dread,
> The finance regulate, the trade control,
> Live through the empire, and accord the whole.
>
> Ere death invades, and night's deep curtain falls,
> Through ruined realms the voice of UNION calls;
> On you she calls! Attend the warning cry:
> YE LIVE UNITED, OR DIVIDED DIE!

The last two numbers of this strange, in-
choate "epic" represented a journey through
"The Land of Annihilation" and "The Region
of Preexistent Spirits." Various critics of the
new nation and its poets mingled here with
enemies of national unity. Notable among the
critics chosen for special mention were Raynal,
Mirabeau, and Robertson. Abbé Raynal's open

[7] *Ibid.*, p. 53. See also J. C. Hamilton, *History of the Republic as Traced in the Writings of Alexander Hamilton,* etc.
(1859), Vol. III, p. 228.

denial that "America had produced a Man of Genius in one single Art or one single Science" seemed anathema to these versifiers, who considered each other men of genius. They poured forth their wrath also against fictitious narratives about America by foreign writers, especially the false and maligning stories of Washington's *amours,* as told by D'Aubertcul. Perhaps it was Humphreys who hurled that last shaft of invective, to redeem the honor of his commander:

> In wit's light robe shall gaudy fiction shine,
> And all be lies, as in a work of thine.[8]

*The Anarchiad* was essentially a literary curiosity, although it had immediate influence upon the policies of Connecticut and more distant states. It is uneven in merit, and often anticlimactic. Probably it was written without any perfected plan, or expectation of publication in sequential form; later numbers were intended by the authors, if circumstances should call them forth. The series corresponded to the more didactic and aggressive columns of arguments in behalf of federalism which were contributed at the same time to newspapers in Massachusetts, New York, Pennsylvania, and other states where there was contest over the adoption of the new

[8]*The Anarchiad*, p. 82. *The Revolution of America*, by the Abbé Raynal, Salem, MDCCLXXXII. *History of America*, by William Robertson, D.D., Dublin, 1777. New York, 1798.

Title-page of *The Echo* (1807); from copy in Connecticut Historical Society Library.

Constitution, in place of the old Articles of Confederation.

*The Echo* was, in a way, a continuation of these satiric papers, although the members of the Hartford coterie had changed somewhat, and the subjects chosen for ridicule or remonstrance were more varied. *The Echo* had less significance in the politico-literary history of the age, yet here were satires of strong feeling directed against political evils, and lampoons upon democratic publications. A secondary motive of the writers was to caricature the excesses of literary style found in many publications of the time. Of the group who had written *The Anarchiad* in collaboration, Humphreys and Barlow were abroad when *The Echo* series appeared, and Trumbull's part has been questioned. Dr. Lemuel Hopkins, alone of the earlier coterie, was assuredly a contributor to the later series. Associated with him were Theodore Dwight, Richard Alsop, Dr. Elihu Smith, and Dr. Mason Cogswell.

That Trumbull had a vital interest in these papers written by his friends, and was informed regarding many matters there suggested, is shown by a copy of *The Echo* which belonged to him and bears his name, to be found now at the Connecticut Historical Society. His notes, in ink, assist one in deciding the authorship of certain

portions.  In the preface to the collected papers
the explanation was given that the idea of these
word-cartoons came

of a moment of literary sportiveness at a time when pedantry, affectation and bombast pervaded most of the
pieces published in the gazettes, . . . . thus to check the
progress of false taste in American literature, the authors
conceived that ridicule would prove a powerful corrective,
and that the mode employed in *The Echo* was the best
suited to this purpose.

The political evils were also emphasized and the
plan of the authors to scathe and correct

that hideous morality of revolutionary madness, which
levelled the boundaries of virtue and vice, . . . . that destructive torrent which threatened to overwhelm everything
good and estimable in private life, everything venerable
and excellent in political society.[9]

The first "Echo" appeared August 8, 1791, in
the *American Mercury*—a weekly newspaper
started in 1784 by Joel Barlow and Elisha Babcock.  It was a parody upon a florid report in a
Boston newspaper.  The latter, in recording a
thunderstorm, had used such language as this:
"uncorking the bottles of Heaven, revealing livid
flame, disploding thunders, amid the brilliance

[9] *The Echo, with Other Poems.  Printed at the Porcupine
Press by Pasquin Petronius* (New York, 1807; 8vo).  The
droll illustrations were conceived by Elkanah Tisdale, a face-
tious miniature-painter.  The book was really issued by Isaac
Riley, brother-in-law of Theodore Dwight and Alsop.  (Goodrich, *Recollections of a Lifetime*, Vol. II, p. 109, note.)

of this irradiated arch!"   The wits thus parodied
the prose:

> Even the last drop of hope, which dripping skies,
> Gave for a moment to our straining eyes,
> Like *Boston Rum,* from heaven's *junk bottles* broke,
> Lost all the corks and vanished into smoke.
>
> .  .  .  .  .  .  .  .  .  .  .  .  .  .  .
>
> The sons of Boston, the elect of Heaven,
> Presented Mercy's Angel, smiling fair,
> Irradiate splendors frizzled in his hair,
> Uncorking demi-johns, and pouring down
> Heaven's liquid blessings on the gaping town.

The ornate phrases of Hugh Henry Brackenridge and Governor John Hancock, John Adams,
striving to please both aristocrats and democrats,
certain demagogues of Jacobin type, a Philadelphia "Mirabeau" who ventured to attack the
politics and literary abilities of the Hartford
group—such were some of the individuals
singled out for special ridicule by the authors
of *The Echo.*   Many of the numbers appeared
first in the *American Mercury,* and were reprinted
in other newspapers, from 1791 to 1800.   In the
years that intervened before they were collected
and published in book-form, in 1807, some
of them appeared as broadsides or pamphlets,
generally soon after they were written.   Often
the papers were intended as New Year's verses.

One of the most representative of the satires,
which won popular reading among the Federalists

and was printed in pamphlet form, was by Dr. Hopkins, "The Democratiad: A Poem in Retaliation, for the Philadelphia Jockey Club. By a Gentleman of Connecticut. 1795." This passed into at least two editions; it is No. XVIII in *The Echo*. The *Philadelphia Jockey Club*,[10] the publication which had roused the wrath of the Wits, gave the example of the Hartford writers and William Cobbett, or "Peter Porcupine," whom they echoed, as an excuse for its attacks upon individuals of prominence among Federalists. Thus, the Philadelphia satirists declared their course of personal attack was "authorized by the precedent of the infamous PETER PORCUPINE and the literary out-law Snub, whose political squabbles have involved the characters of many respectables." In his answering satire, Hopkins attacked the Democrats and Jacobins, leveling his shafts of abuse especially against Benjamin Franklin Bache, the editor of the *Aurora*, and a grandson of Franklin:

Thou great descendant of that wondrous man,
Whose genius wild through all creation ran—
That man who walk'd the world of science o'er,
From ink and types to where the thunders roar,—
To thee, friend Bache, these lines I now address,

[10] *The Philadelphia Jockey Club; or Mercantile Influence Weighed consisting of Select Characters taken from the Club of Addressers. By Timothy Tickler, 1795. Philadelphia. Printed for the Purchasers.* (16 pages.)

Prepar'd on purpose for thy hallow'd press,
I've pick'd thee out because I highly prize,
Thy grandsire's memory and thy knack at lies.[11]

After further invective against the leaders of the Jacobinical faction, the author said in apostrophe to Washington:

ILLUSTRIOUS MAN! thy indignation shew,
And plunge them headlong where they ought to go,
Then turn thine eye, this mighty realm survey,
See Federal Virtue bless thy glorious sway.

The next year Dr. Hopkins was again chosen to write the New Year's verses in *The Echo* series,—"The Guillotina; or, A Democratic Dirge: A Poem. By the Author of Democratiad." They first appeared in the *Connecticut Courant,* January 1, 1796, and were afterward published as a pamphlet, possibly also as a broadside.[12] The bald witticisms are recognized as those of Hopkins, as in the stanza:

Come sing again! since Ninety-Five,
Has left some *Antis* still alive,
Some Jacobins as pert as ever,
Tho' much was hoped from Yellow-fever.

[11] Copies of *The Philadelphia Jockey Club* and *The Democratiad* are in the Connecticut Historical Society, the Historical Societies of New York and Pennsylvania, and the Library of Congress. Both were issued in Philadelphia.

[12] Another "Guillotina for 1797" was issued as a broadside (Hudson & Goodwin, Hartford). It is unsigned and was not printed in *The Echo.*

"The Political Green-House for 1798" was another widely quoted composition by this group. According to the record by Trumbull, in his copy of *The Echo*, this was written by Lemuel Hopkins, Richard Alsop, and Theodore Dwight.[13] With earnest patriotism and wit blended, the verses began:

> Oft has the NEW YEAR'S Muse essay'd,
> To quit the annual rhyming trade,
> Oft has she hop'd the period nigh,
> When fools would cease, and knaves would die,
> But each succeeding year has tax'd her
> With "more last words of Mr. Baxter."
> And most of all has Ninety-Eight
> Outstripp'd the years of former date,
> And while a Jacobin remains,
> While Frenchmen live and Faction reigns,
> Her voice, array'd in awful rhyme,
> Shall thunder down the steep of Time.

With unexpected details, the authors of this New Year's message gave specific directions how to avoid contagion from yellow fever, which was the scourge of that year in New York. There was a reason for these references, since one of the wits had fallen victim to the fever and died, Dr. Elihu Smith. He made the first large compilation of American poetry during the summer of

[13] *The Political Green-House for the Year 1798. Addressed to the Readers of the Connecticut Courant, January 1st, 1799.* (Hartford, no date; small 8vo), *The Echo*, pp. 233–59.

1793, while he was resting at his home in Litchfield, Connecticut. He thus preserved many
scattered verses by his friends and other writers,
which would otherwise have remained unknown.
Although associated somewhat with the Hartford
Wits, he was more closely linked with the early
writers of fiction and drama in New York.
Further mention of his life, therefore, will be
deferred until the later chapters of this book.
According to a note by Trumbull, Dr. Smith was
the author of one paper in *The Echo* series,
"Extracts from Democracy by Aquiline Nimblechops." [14]  He probably assisted in collaborating
others.

Burlesque and satire characterize the pages of
*The Echo,* but there are also lines of earnestness,
as these in *The Guillotina*:

> Spread knowledge then; *this only Hope*
> Can make each eye a *telescope,*
> Frame it by microscopic art;
> To scan the hypocritic heart.

One poem, assuredly assigned as the composition of Theodore Dwight, was a feigned
rejoicing at the election of Jefferson. It was
entitled "The Triumph of Democracy," [15] and re-

[14] An answering satire to the pamphlet *Democracy* by
Henry Brockholst Livingston, who wrote over the above
pseudonym.

[15] Written for the *Connecticut Courant,* January 1, 1801 ;
in *The Echo,* pp. 268-82.

vealed the feeling of bitterness on the part of the
Federalists against Jefferson, with scornful
innuendo against Aaron Burr, in the closing lines:

> Let every voice with triumph sing—
> JEFFERSON is chosen king!
> Ring every bell in every steeple,
> T' announce the "Monarch of the People!"
> Stop,—ere your civic feasts begin,
> Wait till the votes are all come in;
> Perchance, amid this mighty stir,
> Your Monarch may be Col. BURR!
> Who, if he mounts the sovereign seat,
> Like BONAPARTE will *make you sweat,*
> Your Idol then must quaking dwell,
> Mid Mammoth's bones at *Monticelle,*
> His country's barque from anchors free,
> On *"Liberty's tempestuous sea,"*
> While all the Democrats will sing—
> THE DEVIL TAKE THE PEOPLE'S KING!

While we acknowledge only occasional literary
merit in the work of the Hartford Wits—and a
large part of it has political rather than literary
interest—it must be confessed by one who
examines their writings in detail that they reflect
strong, unique personalities. They have received
far less attention than their predecessors in
political and social progress, yet they bore a part
in the development of an upright and sane Americanism. If Trumbull was considered the leader,
as we have said, he had companions in fame,
among his contemporaries,—Timothy Dwight,

Joel Barlow, and David Humphreys. These Connecticut men formed a mutual-admiration society seldom equaled in extravagant tribute, which reads like a farce today. Thus Alsop praised

> Majestic Dwight, sublime in epic strain,
> Paints the fierce horrors of the crimson plain,
> And in Virgilian Barlow's tuneful lines
> With added splendour great Columbus shines.[16]

In the eighth book of *The Columbiad*, Joel Barlow became effusive over the poetic gifts of the Connecticut poets, especially Trumbull, Timothy Dwight, and Humphreys:

See TRUMBULL lead the train. His skilful hand
Hurls the keen darts of satire round the land.
Pride, knavery, dulness feel his mortal stings,
And listening virtue triumphs while he sings.
Britain's foil'd sons, victorious now no more,
In guilt retiring from the wasted shore,
Strive their curst cruelties to hide in vain,
The world resounds them in his deathless strain.

. . . . . . . . . . . . . . .

See HUMPHREYS glorious from the field retire,
Sheathe the glad sword and string the soothing lyre;
His country's wrongs, her duties, dangers, praise,
Fire his full soul and animate his lays:
Wisdom and War with equal joy shall own
So fond a votary and so brave a son.

. . . . . . . . . . . . . . .

For DWIGHT'S high harp the epic Muse sublime,
Hails her new empire in the western clime.

[16] *The Charms of Fancy* (New York, 1856), Book II.

The lines just quoted will suffice to indicate the exuberance of phrases, and the triteness of thought, which seem to have been the chief characteristics of the once famous Joel Barlow. Of all the Hartford group he was the most prominent in the earlier years. He was a chaplain in the war, was agent in Paris of the Scioto Land Company of Ohio, and served abroad on commissions for treaties with the Barbary tribes and other peoples. In spite of the popular verdict of his own day upon his voluminous "Vision of Columbus," "Conspiracy of Kings," and "The Columbiad," he will be remembered, if at all, by the simple rhyme of "Hasty-Pudding," written during an hour of loneliness on foreign soil.[17]

Barlow's published writings of varied sorts— poetry, addresses, "Advice"—are found at many libraries, and his life has been more often studied than that of contemporary writers and friends.[18] In the Pequot Library at Southport, Connecticut, is a rare collection of manuscript letters, written by Barlow, only a few of which have been printed. The letters to his wife, which form the large part, are interesting revelations of the per-

[17] *Hasty Pudding: A Poem, in Three Cantos. Written in Chambery, in Savoy, January 1, 1793,* (New Haven, 1796).

[18] Charles Burr Todd, *Life and Letters of Joel Barlow, LL.D., Poet, Statesman, Philosopher* (New York, 1886). Moses Coit Tyler, *Three Men of Letters* (New York, 1895.)

sonality of this man who promised so much and achieved so little, in diplomacy, business, and literature. In the letters to his wife from Paris, in 1789, he describes the Revolution as he has witnessed it, and feels that it is "no small satisfaction to have seen two complete revolutions in favor of Liberty." With frequent apologies for remaining abroad, he explains that his "affairs are still in a degree of uncertainty." The chief faults which his friends deplored were vacillation and a proneness to speculate with money, both his own and that of others. Manuscript poems in embryo, especially inspired by his acquaintance in Paris with Robert Fulton, are found among these letters.[19]

After Barlow's return to America, and the publication of his long poems, he expected wide recognition among his countrymen; but he was embittered by indifference on some sides, and criticisms from other sources upon his political vacillation and seeming infidelity. Two of his letters, unpublished and here given by permission, indicate his sensitiveness, and they also show his foresight regarding national evils. The first was addressed to Gideon Granger, postmaster-general, and urged the appointment of a friend to office, emphasizing his scholarship and mental abilities:

[19] "The Canal: A Poem on the Application of Physical Science to Political Economy" etc. (manuscript).

It is really discouraging to all liberal pursuits, & proves that the government is accessory to the great national sin of the country, which I fear will overturn its liberties,—I mean the inordinate & universal pursuit of wealth as a means of distinction.

For example, if I find that writing the Columbiad,[20] with all its moral qualities, literature, & science which that work supposes, will not place me on a footing with John Tayloe, who is rich, why then (God damn you) I'll be rich too. I'll dispise my literary labors (which tend to build up our system of free government) & I'll boast of my bank shares (which tend to pull it down) because *these* & not *those,* procure me the distinction which we all desire.

I will teach my nephews by precept & all the rising generation by example that merit consists in oppressing mankind & not in serving them.[21]

Another significant letter was written by Barlow to Jonathan Law, a prominent citizen of Hartford, with political influence in answer to charges brought against the would-be poet "by the malicious hypocrisy of such men as Dwight, & Parke & Coleman":

I know as well as they do that all they say against me is false. All they mean or ever did mean by calling me an antichristian is that I am a republican. This latter appellation they don't like to quarrel with openly, & for that reason they disguise it under the other. . . . . But I shall probably never condescend to give my calum-

[20] See *Critical Observations on the Columbiad*, etc., in the Bibliography.

[21] The Letters were dated Kalorama, near Washington City, May 3, October 24, 1809.

niators any sort of answer. I ask nothing from them, not even to let me alone. Poor fellows, they must live. Parke says individuals & nations have a right to get their bread in any manner they can. And these men slander me to get their bread.

I remember to have seen a song in praise of the guillotine in one of Cobbett's pamphlets about a dozen years ago, which he said was written by me. It might have served the purpose of the faction at the time to lay it to me; whatever might be their motive it was a forgery.[22]

Timothy Dwight was deeply interested in the publications of this band of Hartford wits, but he did not contribute directly to their writings. He was included in their effusive praises of each other, and his ambitious "Conquest of Canaan" and "Greenfield Hill" were considered works of lasting renown.[23]  These voluminous poems are seldom read today, but the reposeful, hymnal

[22] This is given in "A Bone to Gnaw for the Democrats, or Observations on a Pamphlet, entitled 'The Political Progress of Britain,' " p. 16, 3d ed., Philadelphia, 1795. In a note it is stated that the song was sung at the Fourth of July celebration at Hamburg, written by "the celebrated Mr. Barlow who was then at that place." The first stanza will indicate the radical character of the song:

> God save the Guillotine,
> Till England's King and Queen,
>   Her power shall prove ;
> Till each appointed knob
> Affords a clipping job
> Let no vile halter rob
>   The Guillotine.

[23] "The Conquest of Caanan" 1785 (eleven books). "Greenfield Hill," 1794 (seven parts).

lines by Dr. Dwight, and his strong influence upon young men in behalf of better citizenship, have won for him a revered name in American history. He was an ardent patriot and a great admirer of Washington. A letter to Oliver Wolcott, Jr., written after Dwight's visit to Philadelphia, in 1793, denounced Freneau and his paper for its attacks upon Washington. It was evident that Dwight considered Freneau's *Gazette* as a Jeffersonian organ:

> The late very impertinent and shameless attacks on the first Magistrate are viewed with a general and marked indignation. *Freneau* your printer, Linguist, &c., is regarded here as a mere incendiary, or rather as a despicable tool of bigger incendiaries; and his paper as a public nuisance.

A few miles from New Haven is the hill-town of Derby. Here is an active chapter of the Daughters of the American Revolution—the Sarah Riggs Humphreys chapter—that has preserved many relics which pertain to the life-history of David Humphreys.[24] As a young captain in the army under Colonel Meigs, and later as aide-de-camp to Generals Putnam, Greene, and Washington, Humphreys showed his alertness of mind, his courage, and his zeal for American

[24] See *Chapter Sketches, Daughters of American Revolution* (Connecticut, 1900) ; also *Seymour: Past and Present* (1902). For editors, etc., see the Bibliography.

progress. After the war he was with Jefferson, for a time, at Paris on the commission for treaties with foreign powers, and also served as diplomat at Lisbon and at Madrid. With these manlier traits he blended gallantry and cleverness, which made him a social favorite in foreign circles of society, but which called forth censure from some court-despising Americans. After he had returned to America, he was invited to visit at Mount Vernon, and Washington offered him aid in pursuing a literary plan [25] which he had mentioned in his letters, namely, to write a history of the Revolution. At first thought, it may seem unfortunate that this plan was abandoned by Humphreys because of its magnitude. His tastes and effusive style, however, would not have produced a history of permanent value. His biographic essays on Israel Putnam were subjected to severe censure, but they gave the materials for later historians to utilize with better results.[26]

In letters and poetic ventures, Humphreys left a vivid impression of Washington's life at Mount Vernon, in the years between the close of the war and his presidency. He pictured him as super-

[25] *The Writings of Washington,* edited by W. C. Ford, Vol. X, pp. 473, 474.

[26] *An Essay on the Life of the Honourable Major-General Israel Putnam* (Hartford, 1788; Philadelphia, 1798). See more fully in the Bibliography.

vising his eight hundred acres of wheat and
seven hundred acres of corn, and giving his personal attention to the task of navigating the
Potomac, and extending the settlement of the
western boundaries of the country. Humphreys
was very proud of his friendship with Washington, and often referred to the latter with deep
admiration, marred sometimes by such lines of
egotism as in this. stanza :

> Let others sing his deeds in arms,
> A nation saved and conquest's charms
>     Posterity shall hear.
> 'Twas mine, return'd from Europe's courts,
> To share his thoughts, partake his sports,
>     And soothe his partial ear.[27]

This soldier-versifier was vain and aspiring to
literary fame, but he showed sturdier qualities
when occasion called them forth. He took command of a band of men to guard the arsenal at
Springfield, when it was threatened in Shay's
Rebellion; he served in the state assembly during
the years when he was collaborating with his
friends in the series of papers of *The Anarchiad*.
His "Poem Addressed to the Armies of the
United States of America," first published in
1780, was reprinted in Paris six years later; this

---

[27] Ode "Mount Vernon" *Connecticut Courant,* October 9,
1786; *Miscellaneous Works of David Humphreys,* p. 68.

sign of appreciation gave him much delight.[28]
While abroad he lived in a style which attracted
attention for its luxury, but which he seemed to
defend in a manuscript letter to Timothy Pickering, which I am permitted to print here.[29]    It
was written soon after his appointment as
minister at Madrid; he explained the necessary
expenses involved in moving his effects from
Lisbon to Madrid:

I do not wish to make any unnecessary display, foreign
to the dignified simplicity so becoming, in every character,
but more particularly in that of a Republican Minister; or
to live in any respect in an ostentatious manner; but I desire to be able to live in a decent style (as other ministers
are accustomed to do) without being under the necessity of
incurring debts. . . . . I hope & believe I shall never affect
a style of hauteur; and whenever I cannot live abroad
without embarrassment or meanness, I shall think it time
to retire from public life—for sometimes the embarrassed
conduct of a Diplomatic Agent extends beyond his individual Character and leaves an unfavorable impression
of the Character of his Nation on the Minds of for-
eigners. . . . . The transportation of my Carriages (of
which I shall be obliged to carry four) Baggage, and
necessaries will certainly, in the augmented price of for-
age, etc. cost me a good sum of money—for besides taking

[28] *Discours en vers, addressé aux officiers et aux soldats
des differentes armées americaines* (Paris, 1786). Humphreys
presented several libraries in America with copies of this
poem.

[29] *Pickering Papers*, Vol. XXI, No. 1 (Massachusetts Historical Society). Lisbon, January 1, 1797.

with me my own horses, I must order six or seven Mules
to be sent from Madrid, and moreover employ a considerable number of common Carriers.

In spite of such indications of coxcombry in
Humphreys, shown also in his delight to introduce foreign forms into the President's levees in
New York,[30] he was a true patriot in his impulses and aims. At forty-five, while abroad, he
married the daughter of an English banker, but
he was unwilling to live abroad, after his diplomatic missions were ended. As he had shared in
gaining the liberty of America, so he wished to
help in fostering her industries and arts. While
at Lisbon he had written "A Poem on Industry,"
which ranked with his poem to the armies in its
patriotism, as well as its verbosity; Humphreys
could not write in simple English.[31] The poem,
however, and his practical success in manufac-
turing homespun cloths, entitle him to credit for
noble motives. He brought with him from Spain,
in 1802, one hundred and fifty merino sheep, as a
nucleus for his enterprise. Near his Derby home
he established a number of mills which made the
settlement, at first called Chusetown and later

[30] See *Jefferson's Writings,* edited by Paul L. Ford, Vol.
I, p. 216, 233.

[31] *A Poem on Industry: addressed to the Citizens of the
United States of America. By Col. David Humphreys, Minister
Resident at the Court of Lisbon* (Philadelphia, 1794).

Humphreysville, a flourishing village.[32]  The
fulling-mill, cotton-mill, and paper-mill were
opened in turn, and employment was given to
scores of artisans.  He brought several boys from
the New York almshouses as apprentices.  From
England came master-workmen to superintend
the manufacture of cloth, which was worn by
Jefferson and other statesmen, and which encouraged the growth of American industries.[33]

Humphreys was not alone a patriotic manu-
facturer, but he was also a pioneer social settler.
In his village he sought to produce fine manhood
as well as fine cloth.  He furnished a library and
recreation-room for his operatives, led his boys in
military drills, took part with them in games, and
coached them in rehearsals of various plays and
"pieces" of his own composition.  One of these,
*The Yankey in England*, was acted in 1815, and
printed.  In studying the life of Humphreys, we
always find many evidences of his besetting
sin, literary vanity.  He won respect as a soldier
and a promoter of industry, but he sought for
rank in letters.  This he obtained among his
friends, and often he was highly praised in
journals of the day.[34]  He cultivated his inferior

[32] See *Seymour: Past and Present* (1902).

[33] *Jefferson's Writings*, Vol. IX, p. 225.

[34] In the *Literary Magazine and American Register* for
1805 is a so-called "review" of his *Miscellaneous Works* which
is absurd in praise.

talents too ardently, forgetting the moral in "The Monkey Fable," probably finished by Trumbull:

> Who cannot write, yet handle pens,
> Are apt to hurt themselves and friends.[35]

In contrast with the admiration which Humphreys craved, and often gained in America, was the frank disgust of Southey. He had met Humphreys at Lisbon, and wrote later to a friend:

> Timothy Dwight, an American, published in 1785 an heroic poem on the Conquest of Canaan. I had heard of it, and long wished to read it, in vain; but now the American Minister (a good-natured man, whose poetry is worse than anything except his criticism) has lent me the book. There certainly is some merit in the poem; but when Col. Humphreys speaks of it, he will not allow me to put in a word in defense of John Milton.[36]

His writings were prefaced by long notes of explanation and tribute.

The poems which are least effusive and offensive in form, among those included in his *Miscellaneous Works*, were the odes descriptive of the burning of Fairfield by the British, in 1779, and

---

[35] *The Miscellaneous Works of David Humphreys, Late Minister Plenipotentiary from the United States of America to the Court of Madrid* (New York, 1804), p. 228. An earlier edition of poems and essay on Putnam, 1790. See the Bibliography.

[36] *Life and Correspondence of Robert Southey,* Vol. I, p. 269.

that on the "Happiness of America." [37]    The
stanza in the latter which portrays the interior
scene of a humble American home in winter may
be fittingly recalled:

> The cattle fed—the fuel pil'd within—
> At setting day the blissful hours begin;
> 'Tis then, sole owner of his little cot;
> The farmer feels his independent lot;
> Hears with the crackling blaze that lights the wall,
> The voice of gladness and of nature call;
> Beholds his children play, their mother smile,
> And tastes with them the fruit of summer's toil.

During the War of 1812, Humphreys was
general of a company of war veterans for home
protection, and he wrote, with rejoicing, of his
country's victories on the sea.   His monument,
erected soon after his death in 1818, stands near
the entrance to the old cemetery at New Haven,
close to Yale University buildings.   Its verbose
Latin epitaph was written by his friend John
Trumbull.

Associated with the men of greater renown
in their own day—Timothy Dwight, Trumbull,
Barlow, and Humphreys—were three collaborators of less familiar but influential lives—
Theodore Dwight, Richard Alsop, and Dr.
Lemuel Hopkins.   Theodore Dwight, the elder,
and brother of Timothy, was a lawyer, and was

[37] The former poem was written "on the spot" soon after
the burning of the town, where lived his sister, who barely
escaped (*Works*, p. 112).

editor of the *Connecticut Mirror* from 1809 until
1815. For two years previously, 1806–7, he was
a member of Congress. The latter part of his
life was passed in New York, where he conducted the *New York Daily Advertiser* from
1817 to 1835.[38] He wrote a partisan study of
Jefferson's character, a fervent hymn on Washington, some strong orations and an etymolog-
ical dictionary. To him we owe the preservation
of the long poem by Richard Alsop, *The Charms
of Fancy,* and many interesting revelations of the
poet, who was not alone Dwight's friend, but
also his brother-in-law.[39]

Alsop was probably the editor of the papers
known as *The Echo,* when they were first printed.
A letter, in manuscript, from him to Dr. Mason
Cogswell is in the copy of *The Echo* owned by
John Trumbull, now at the Connecticut Historical
Society. Alsop mentioned some errata and con-
tinued, regarding the tone of the papers:

I should be very sorry to have The Echo considered
as a party production, as it must considerably lessen its
reputation, & any alterations which will take off from that
appearance without injury to the object in view, in my
opinion will be best.

[38] Facts about Dwight and Alsop are in J. Hammond
Trumbull, *The Memorial History of Hartford County,* Vol. I,
pp. 157–60. See also the Bibliography.

[39] A review of Dwight's character and works were published in the New York Historical Society *Proceedings,*
1846, p. 13.

Born in Middletown, Connecticut, Alsop prepared for college, but continued his studies at
home, becoming a fine translator of Runic
poetry, Homer, Ossian, and Molina's *History
of Chili*. For a time he had a bookstore in Hartford, where he lived with his sister. In an address, *To the Freemen of Connecticut,* (which is
classified as his by an ink ascription in a copy at
the Massachusetts Historical Society, dated Middletown, September 12, 1803,) he expressed confidence that God would protect "the Vine of this
state" against "the rude shocks of democratic
violence, nor will He suffer its ripened clusters
to be trampled in the dust." [40]

In William Dunlap's manuscript journal, 1797,
he mentions a visit to Alsop at Middletown, "to
shoot ducks;" later he accompanied Alsop "in a
chaise to Hartford where lived, at that time, Miss
Fanny Alsop."

In the "Memoir" of Alsop which prefaced his
visionary poem, *The Charms of Fancy*, we learn
of his scholarship and scientific interests which
blended with his poetic tastes. His sister said:
"He seemed to know every variety of birds, and
I might almost say, every feather." In boxes of
his own design he kept his natural-history specimens—a large collection. His long, ambitious

*To the Freemen of the State of Connecticut*, p. 16 (no
place), 1803.

poem on fancy, and its inspiration for poet, painter, and musician, has a few fine lines, and reveals his wide reading and patriotic zeal for America's progress in the arts. The poem by Alsop which seems to me the most worthy, however, was not printed in permanent form, except in collections of poetry, but it suggests, as a forerunner, Bryant's "To a Waterfowl." Alsop's poem was entitled "Verses to a Shearwater on the Morning after a Storm at Sea":[41]

> . . . . . . . . . . . .
> On the fiery tossing wave,
>   Calmly cradled dost thou sleep,
> When the midnight tempests rave,
>   Lonely wanderer of the deep!
>
> . . . . . . . . . .
> Far from earth's remotest trace,
>   What impels thee thus to roam?
> What hast thou to mark the place,
>   When thou seek'st thy distant home?
>
> Without star or magnet's aid,
>   Thou thy faithful course dost keep;
> Sportive still, still undismay'd,
>   Lonely wanderer of the deep!

Alsop spent the last years of his life in the vicinity of New York. He died at Flatbush in 1815. In his lifetime he was generally known as author of one of the most widely quoted elegies

[41] Kettell, in *Specimens of American Poetry,* Vol. II, p. 60.

on Washington, and was honored for his translations from the *Eddas,* and from Spanish and Italian.[42]

The sharpest wit among the Hartford writers was Lemuel Hopkins. He used travesties and imagery which defied all poetic standards. As a physician he ranked among the progressive leaders of his day; in his memory the Hopkins Medical Society was formed in 1826.[43]   Born at Hopkins Hill, in Waterbury, in 1750, he served as a soldier for a time, but lost no opportunity to study for the profession of medicine, which he had chosen in youth as a goal.   After gaining some experience with two noted men of his day and state—Dr. Seth Bird, of Litchfield, and Dr. Jared Potter, of Wallingford—he settled in Hartford, in 1784, where he remained until his death sixteen years later.   By success in his profession, and by his courageous advocacy of inoculation for small-pox, use of anaesthetics, and radical remedies for yellow fever, he gained repute outside his state and was often called into consultation. Yale conferred an honorary degree upon him.

[42] *A Poem Sacred to the Memory of George Washington,* etc., by Richard Alsop (Hartford, 1800 ; 23 pages, 8vo).   For Alsop's translations, see the Bibliography.

[43] A good account of Dr. Hopkins is in *American Medical Biography; or, Memoirs of Eminent Physicians Who Have Flourished in America,* by James Thacher, M.D. (Boston, 1828), Vol. I, pp. 298-306.

Many traditions and local stories cluster about his personality. He was nervous, brusque, with keen eyes, and a peculiar, awkward gait. One story illustrates his brusqueness combined with faithfulness. On a stormy night he rode four miles to assure himself that a certain remedy was accomplishing the desired results. Arriving at the house, he entered, made a silent examination, refused to speak to any of the inmates, and rode away. He was a dreaded enemy of impostors and quacks. Another anecdote indicates this trait. With Dr. Cogswell, he was attending a patient who was dying of tubercular disease. The sister of the sick girl unreasonably besought the doctors to use some "fever powders," which she had bought from a peripatetic quack. Dr. Hopkins asked her to bring the powders, announced that one and a half was recorded as the largest dose which it was safe to take, calmly mixed twelve of the powders in molasses, and swallowed them, remarking to his colleague: "Cogswell, I am going to Coventry today. If I die from this, you must write on my tombstone: 'Here lies Hopkins, killed by Grimes.' "[44] In indignation against a "cancer doctor" who had troubled the neigh-

[44] This anecdote, with others, may be found in Charles W. Everest, *The Poets of Connecticut* (Hartford, 1843). Here are also several of Hopkins' poems (pp. 51–58): "Poland" (1775); "On Gen. Ethan Allen," "Robespierre," "Gen. Wayne and the West," "Lines on the Yellow Fever," etc.

borhood, he wrote the rugged verse, "On a
Patient Killed by a Cancer Quack":

> Here lies a fool, flat on his back,
> The victim of a cancer quack;
> Who lost his money and his life,
> By plaister, caustic and by knife.

More dignified were the ironical stanzas, "The
Hypocrite's Hope":

> He tones like Pharisee sublime,
>     Two lengthy prayers a day,
> The same that he from early prime,
>     Has heard his father say.
>
> . . . . . . . . . . . .
>
> Good works he careth nought about,
>     But faith alone will seek,
> While Sunday's pieties blot out,
>     The knaveries of the week.[45]

A few letters from Dr. Lemuel Hopkins to
his friend Oliver Wolcott, Jr., are in manuscript
at the Connecticut Historical Society; I have been
given the privilege of quoting from them.   One
written in October, 1783, reveals Hopkins' wit
and his interest in political affairs:

I thank you for your inteligence & thoughts on
politicks; but have not time to tell you my own.   But
I lament with you the ill aspect of our affairs, and am
afraid to think much of the next scene for of late, when
I have indulg'd such thoughts, the Ghost of a certain text

<hr />

[45] *American Poems,* Litchfield, (1793)., p. 139; Samuel Kettell, *Specimens of American Poetry,* Vol. I, p. 282.

has grinn'd *horrible* at me *a ghastly smile,*—'tis this—
"Wo unto thee oh land when thy king is a fool."

In a letter from Hartford, after his removal
there from Litchfield, he refers to the *American
Antiquities* (*The Anarchiad*) as having "given a
considerable check to a certain kind of popular
intrigue in this state."

During the prevalence of small-pox in the summer of 1793, he wrote to Mr. Wolcott regarding inoculation, which he practiced freely:

> This business is much like that of the Treasury De-
> partment in regard to existing jealousies, raising party
> spirit &c., yet, from certain causes, my particular mode
> of conducting it, in case of any suspicion of wrong meas-
> ures, does not admit of so unanswerable a justification.

There are some philosophic sentences in the
same letter regarding the influences of city and
village life, which are interesting today:

> The more a man is among all sorts of people, the
> more fully will he learn the unmeasured difference there is
> between the sentiments of newspapers, replete with local
> politics, and the opinions of an enlighten'd people in
> the peaceable and successful pursuit of wealth & happi-
> ness.—I find more & more that a busy set of wrong-
> heads can at pleasure stir up, for a time, any sentiments
> they please in cities—and that there is a great aptitude in
> most men to consider *cities* as *worlds,* or at least as the
> manufactories of sentiments for whole countries—and
> much of this may be true in the old world; but in N.
> England the contrary is, and ever will be true, as long
> as our schools, presses & Town-corporations last.

With his shrewd insight into the diseases of individuals and of the nation, with his urgent desire for progress through education, Dr. Hopkins was a good type of his time, and especially of this group of Connecticut writers. They were earnest, as well as witty; they sought to use their talents for the advance of industry and political sanity. Their writings mirrored many of the aspirations and fears of the period which followed the war and was concerned with the establishment of stable government.

# JOSEPH DENNIE: "THE LAY PREACHER"

JOSEPH DENNIE
From portrait owned by his family; reproduced from Clapp's
*Sketch of Dennie*, 1880.

## VI

## JOSEPH DENNIE: "THE LAY PREACHER"

Journalism is an altar on which have perished the hopes and fortunes of many. Today our libraries and homes are crowded with magazines of all degrees of merit and ranges of topics. Publishers announce extraordinary figures of circulation of many of these journals; others, of more intrinsic value, perish after a brief existence. The latter fate was the common lot of many interesting ventures in journalism during the earlier decades of American literature. The student who follows the lives of our pioneer authors, from Franklin to Charles Brockden Brown, will be impressed by the many fitful, short-lived journals by which these writers sought to promote literary culture and progress in art and science.

Freneau ventured and lost, both hopes and funds, in his later newspapers, which combined literature with politics. Brown devoted his mature years to experiments in reviews, intended to educate the middle classes and make them acquainted with the best foreign authors, far too unfamiliar to many Americans during the first quarter of the nineteenth century.

One of the most prominent and successful of early American journalists was Joseph Dennie, known in his own day as "the Lay Preacher," or often as "the American Addison." He was born in Boston, August 30, 1768, but during his boyhood his family moved to Lexington. He is associated in literature with New Hampshire and Philadelphia. After studying at a commercial school in Boston, and at Samuel West's school at Needham, he entered Harvard in the sophomore class, in 1787. As a boy he wrote ambitious verses. His mother declared, with farcical pride:

> He wrote poetry in early life after the manner of Horace and various other modes but never pleased himself. . . . . His father persuaded him to quit a pursuit where he would kill himself with his own sword.[1]

At college, Dennie was a favorite with the students. Genial and merry, he was also impetuous and ready to combat any injustice. Once he was absent from college because of illness. On his return, he was reprimanded by someone

[1] Sketch of Dennie in *The Philadelphia Souvenir* by John E. Hall (Philadelphia, 1826). Mr. Hall told here also of Dennie's hatred of arithmetic throughout his life. In mature years he spent more than a day puzzling over his landlady's problem of the cost of seven and three-fourths pounds of mutton at five and one fourth cents a pound and finally assured the lady that "the butcher was doubtless honest and she might safely pay her bill."

who did not know the circumstances.  Serious
differences arose between him and his tutors.  He
declaimed, with emphasis and vocal insult, one of
Lord Chatham's speeches which could be con-
strued as a direct affront to his tutors, and he was
suspended for six months.  He passed the time
pleasantly in the home of a clergyman, Mr. Chap-
lin, of Groton, who combined tutoring with moral
influence.  In one of his *Lay Sermons*,[2] Dennie
referred to this episode in his college life, saying:
"I lost my tutors and found a friend.  It was
like the exchange of armour between Glaucus and
Diomede; it was brass for gold."  He cherished
his hurt pride, however, declaring that the action
of the faculty had awakened in him "a prejudice
which no time shall destroy."  He was restored
to membership in the college and his class by
making a written appeal for pardon and rein-
statement, and suffering a public reprimand before the college.  He did not forget the severe
treatment, although he made no open defiance.

His mother seemed to sympathize with his
sensitive, fractious nature.  She was the daughter
of Bartholomew Green, Jr., who had been associated with his father as printer of the early newspaper, the *Boston News Letter*.  Dennie was
devoted to his mother.  In tribute to her influence
he wrote: "During the course of my pilgrimage

[2] "Interment of Saul," *The Lay Preacher*, 1817.

I have found many friends but only one mother. For two and twenty years you have been uniformly my guide and patroness." His father was less sympathetic and more thrifty, as was recalled by the son in his sermon "Of Precipitation":

> In my boyhood, I remember that a parent would sometimes repeat lessons of economy as I sat upon his knees, and then lift me in his arms, that I might look at Hogarth's plates of Industry and Idleness. On youthful fancy the picture was more impressed than the precept.

After leaving college, Dennie decided to study law. His first inclination had been toward the ministry, but he said he gave up that because of "its starchedness of thinking and behaviour." He read law in the office of Mr. West, of Charlestown, New Hampshire, and thus began association with the vicinity where he was to gain his experience in journalism and his unique pseudonym. With an impressive voice and manner, he was chosen to read the liturgy and lay sermons during a season of pastoral vacancy at the Episcopal church in Charlestown. So well did he please the people that he was given a contract "for four months as a Reader at the rate of 24s per Sunday."

At first he read sermons by noted preachers. Later he interpolated original sentences; and finally he began to preach an occasional lay sermon of his own writing. This youthful service he recalled in after years, in one of his published *Sermons:*

> Many years ago I stood in a rustic pulpit, and was wont to address myself to the few villagers who thought my sermons worth listening to. It was literally the "voice of one crying in the wilderness," for the forest was frequently my study and my principal hearers a gurgling brook, a silent valley or an aged tree. I had but few of the fathers to consult and perused the best of books, not with Poole's, but my own commentary.[1]

He was urged to give up law and study theology. He could then be ordained as minister of the Charlestown church; the parish was willing to wait for him to take a theological course. It is evident, from chance references in his letters, that he considered the subject carefully before he decided in the negative. Moreover, he was much annoyed by the criticism passed upon him by some Boston friends regarding the propriety of his serving as a lay preacher. That a lawyer should officiate in a pulpit seemed to some a questionable practice. Even his honesty of religious belief and expression was assailed, and his first *Lay Sermons,* as published in local newspapers, were called indecorous, if not irreligious.

---

[1] "Design of the Preacher," text from Solomon, 3:2 (*The Lay Preacher, collected and arranged by John E. Hall, Esq., Counsellor at Law* [Philadelphia, 1817]). See earlier editions of *The Lay Preacher* in the Bibliography.

Such slanders increased his resentment against Boston, although he returned there for a brief journalistic venture.

While he defied these critics, he wished to vindicate his action to his parents. He wrote to them frankly:

A casual glance on the ecclesiastical etiquette of Great Britain, which the Episcopalians here servilely copy, discovers to *you*, that a mere Readership does not in the least militate with my secular & lay employments, that it demands not hypocrisy of heart or face but *decency* of life & such a mode of reading as your kindness, the instructions of *Dame Rogers*, and the *boyhood* perusal of your little library have inspired.

With a characteristic touch of egotism he adds:

You know that my natural fluency is such that, when I have a stock of ideas, words of course will follow.[4]

The last sentence seems to have been true, for he was fecund in words, both spoken and written, in the pulpit, in journals, and at the bar. His readiness with flowery language once brought ridicule upon him in the courtroom. The story has passed down in literary anecdote and may suggest a reason for his retirement from law.[5] The case on trial involved a promissory note and its requital. In a style acquired by devotion to

[4] W. W. Clapp, *Sketch of [Joseph] Dennie* (Cambridge, 1880).

[5] This story was told by Royall Tyler in the *New England Galaxy*, July 24, 1818; it is also given, with expansions, in *The Philadelphia Souvenir*, 1826.

Pope and Swift, the young attorney pictured, with artificial pathos, a home-scene in humble life. The panorama was vivid and glowing: "the taper's solitary ray glimmered," while the "children ran to lisp their sire's return." Then came the bailiff, "down whose hard, unmeaning face ne'er stole the pitying tear." Through "the pelting, pitiless storm the father was dragged to a loathsome prison." As Dennie grew more florid in his harangue, the farmer-judge was mystified, and confessed:

I am in rather a kind o' a quandary; I profess I am somewhat dubus; I can't say that I know for sartain what the young gentleman would be at.

When some fellow-lawyer explained that Dennie wished to have the case postponed, the judge exclaimed:

Ay, now I believe I understand,—the young man wants the case to be hung up for the next term, duz he? Well, well, if that's all he wants, why couldn't he say so in a few words pat to the purpose, without all this *larry cum lurry.*

Dennie had a keen sense of humor, and he was compelled to join in the general laugh at his expense; but he was disgusted with law in the rural districts and declared that he would make no further attempts "to batter down a mud wall with roses." [6]

[6] J. T. Buckingham, *Anecdotes, Personal Memoirs and Biographies of Literary Men* (Boston, 1852), Vol. II, p. 175.

He had evidently saved some money from his lay-reading and his practice of law, although the latter was not very lucrative nor long continued; for he wrote to his mother, while still in Charlestown:

I am now worth 416 dollars, clear and unencumbered. I enjoy a high station on the rock of independence, unscared, as Pope says, by the spectre of poverty, and I hope I shall be able to walk through life without a crutch.[7]

He had already begun to contribute a column of witty essays, "The Farrago," to the *New Hampshire Journal* and *Farmer's Weekly Museum* of Walpole, New Hampshire, which was started, in 1793, by David Carlisle, Jr., a native of the town and a "freed apprentice" of Isaiah Thomas, of Worcester, who had a printing-shop and bookstore in Walpole. On the last page of this little newspaper was "The Dessert," to which Dennie contributed.

Some of these sketches by Dennie were reprinted in the *Boston Centinel,* and he was encouraged to return to Boston for a journalistic venture. This was the *Tablet,* a twelve by eight sheet, whose issues as long as life lasted, from May 19 to August 11, 1795, may be found at the

---

[7] J. E. Hall, *The Philadelphia Souvenir: A Collection of Fugitive Pieces from the Philadelphia Press, with Biographical and Explanatory Notes* (Philadelphia, 1826).

Boston Public Library.[8] "The Farrago" was its
leading feature, although current events in literature, politics, and society were recorded. Here
also appeared verses "From the Shop of Colon
and Spondee." The chief writer of this doggerel was Royall Tyler, who was associated with
Dennie under a similar pseudonym in the *Farmer's Museum* and *The Portfolio.* Tyler's name is
more closely related to the beginnings of drama
through his play *The Contrast,* which is discussed
in the next chapter.

Tyler was practicing law at Brattleboro, Vermont, and became a warm friend to Dennie when
the latter returned from Boston to Walpole.
Dennie was a great admirer of his friend, who
was ten years older. Together they planned literary schemes and read classic authors. Dennie was
more adroit and polished than Tyler. The latter's
humor was puerile, and his stanzas were weak
and too alliterative, as "From Fond Frederic to
Fanny False Fair." He could write more worthy
odes, like one for the Fourth of July, 1799.[9] The
two friends were marked contrasts in looks and
mental traits. Tyler, with his plain, stolid face,

[8] Files of this journal are also at the Lenox Library and
the Historical Society of Pennsylvania. It was "Dedicated
to the Belles-Lettres," and published by William Spotswood,
of Marlborough Street.

[9] Kettell, *Specimens of American Poetry,* Vol. II, p. 48.

high forehead, and hair unadorned, was quite different from handsome Dennie, with "befrizzled ear-locks," pea-green coat, silk stockings, shoes with huge buckles and generous bows.[10]

Dennie was gay and dilatory; Tyler was prompt and careful. Dennie often wrote his best under pressure. The printing-shop of Walpole was next to the Crafts Tavern, and Tyler recalls an incident when Dennie was forced to finish his "Lay Sermon" in great haste. He was playing cards at the tavern, when the printer's boy came in with a demand for the copy which Dennie had promised. The latter ignored the summons as long as he could, but was compelled at last to yield his "hand" to a neighbor while "he gave the devil his due."

The year after Dennie had failed with *The Tablet* in Boston, he undertook the editorship of the *Farmer's Weekly Museum*.[11] He was inventive and introduced several features which gave popularity to the journal for a few months. There were political lampoons by "Simon Spunkey," or F. T. G. Fessenden, sketches by "The Meddler," and "The Hermit," and jocose

[10] J. T. Buckingham, *op. cit.,* Vol. II, pp. 195–202.

[11] The full name of this paper was *The New Hampshire and Vermont Journal; or Farmer's Weekly Museum.* A complete file is at the American Antiquarian Society. A Summary of its contents is in *The Spirit of the Farmer's Museum and Lay Preacher's Gazette* (Walpole, 1801).

verse and prose from "The Shop of Colon and Spondee." Several men in the neighborhood formed a literary club and contributed at times to Dennie's paper. Among the members, beside Tyler, were Jeremiah Mason, Major Bullard, Samuel Hunt, and Royal Vose, the last two afterward members of Congress.[12]

The metrical announcement of the journal emphasized its aims. Its motto was: "Ho, every one that thirsteth for novelty, Come!"

> To greet each good and letter'd man,
> A Journal form'd on generous plan,
> None of your dull, mechanic Dutch things,
> But fraught with poetry and such things;
> With politicians, wise as Solon,
> With PREACHER, HERMIT, SPONDEE, COLON,
> With pointed, pithy, pretty PETER,
> Whom ladies called the charming creature.[13]

In adition to the bagatelles and squibs, there were serious essays of educational and literary kinds—biographical studies of contemporary American authors, among them Trumbull and Barlow, and of statesmen, like John Adams and Oliver Wolcott. Extracts from English authors, with comments, were given freely; there was also

[12] George Aldrich, *Walpole as It Was and as It Is* (Claremont, 1880), pp. 74-82.

[13] This last contributor was Isaac Story, known as "Peter Quince," rival and cousin of "Peter Pindar."

a summary of foreign news. There was an occasional stanza of wit, as—

> Women were born, so fate declares,
> To smoothe our linen and our cares;
> And 'tis but just, for by my troth,
> They're very apt to ruffle both.

The climax of popularity under Dennie's editorship seemed to be in December, 1797, when the editor wrote:

> The constant swell of our subscription book suggests a theme to our gratitude, and a motive to our industry. The Farmer's Museum is read by more than *two thousand* individuals and has its patrons in Georgia and on the banks of the Ohio.[14]

In spite of such bright prospects, and the fact that the paper kept a neutral attitude in politics until 1800, when it became Federal, the journal was constantly threatened with financial disaster, and Isaiah Thomas bore the losses from three failures within a few years. Dennie, as editor, soon began to make appeals for "punctual payment," adding of the rights of the editor: "Like every other industrious workman, he has a right to *bread*, and sometimes, to write all cheerily, he ought to have wine."

Perhaps too much of Dennie's time and money went for this tonic to merry writing. At least so

[14] *Farmer's Museum,* December 4, 1797; quoted also by Aldrich, *op. cit.,* p. 80.

the veteran newspaper worker, J. T. Buckingham, relates in citing his experiences as a boy in the office of the *Farmer's Museum.*[15] Here he was an apprentice at sixteen years, but found that he was expected "to treat" soon after he entered the office. He was "nagged" for a few days, until he conformed to what seemed to be the custom of the place. He said: "I spent more than half the small amount of money I possessed for brandy, wine, sugar, eggs and crackers."

Throughout his life Dennie was accused of overindulgence in light wines, but his best friends defended him from the charge of being an inebriate in any sense. In this connection we recall a story told by Griswold[16] about Dennie and Timothy Dwight. It occurred some years after Dennie had left Walpole and was editing *The Portfolio* in Philadelphia. In the days of limited stage and hotel accommodations, Timothy Dwight, then president of Yale, arrived at a New Jersey inn one evening and was able to secure a comfortable room. Soon afterward Dennie reached the same tavern, but was told that all the rooms were occupied, and nearly all the guests "paired" except the college president. The host was unwilling to disturb so illustrious a man by offering

[15] Buckingham, *op. cit.,* Vol. I, p. 25.

[16] *Curiosities of [American] Literature* (New York, 1848), p. 51, 52.

him a roommate, but Dennie begged to be allowed
to plead his case with Dr. Dwight, saying: "Although I am a stranger to the reverend doctor
perhaps I can bargain with him for my lodgings."
President Dwight received his caller with dignified grace, and the two men were soon discussing
statesmen and authors of the day, although Dennie did not reveal his identity. After a time
Dwight mentioned, among the promising writers,
"Joseph Dennie, the editor of *The Portfolio*, the
Addison of the United States, and the father of
American Belles-Lettres." Praising his writings,
he said: "But is it not astonishing, that a man
of such genius, fancy and feeling, should aban-
don himself to the inebriating bowl and to Bac-
chanalian revels?" "Sir," said Dennie, "you are
mistaken. I have been intimately acquainted with
Dennie for several years and I never knew or saw
him intoxicated." "Sir," said Dr. Dwight, "you
err; I have my information from a particular
friend. I am confident that I am right and that
you are wrong." Dropping the subject, Dennie led
the conversation to educational topics and spoke
of Dr. Dwight, of Yale, as "the most learned
theologian, first logician and greatest poet
America had ever produced. But there are traits
in his character unworthy so great and wise a
man—of the most detestable description—he is
the greatest *bigot* and *dogmatist* of the age."

"Sir," said Dr. Dwight, with anger, "you are grossly mistaken.    I am intimately acquainted with Dr. Dwight and I know to the contrary." "Sir," said Dennie, "you are mistaken.   I have it from an intimate acquaintance of his, who I am confident would not tell an untruth."  Rising, with dismissal in his manner, Dr. Dwight said: "No more slander; I am Dr. Dwight of whom you speak."  "And I," exclaimed Dennie, merrily, "am Mr. Dennie of whom you spoke."

The *Farmer's Museum* survived its financial crisis in the spring of 1797 and recovered to a new season of favor, as we have shown; but Dennie evidently left the paper in charge of a new manager, Alexander Thomas, and went to Boston for a few weeks.   Two letters to Hon. Jeremiah Mason, written by Dennie from Boston in August, 1797, are of interest and value in placing his absence from Walpole, and also as indicating his social tastes.[17]  The first letter was dated Boston, August 6, 1797:

From the *ennui* which you apprehended I should experience in a counting-room I was relieved, the day you left town, by the company of Jos. Barrell and a Mr. Morewood, a youthful Englishman of some promise.   But greater things were reserved for me.   For at five o'clock I found myself, by Barrell's civility, at his chateau and by his daughter's side.   Be assured I was very eloquent

[17] *Massachusetts Historical Society Proceedings*, March, 1880, Vol. XVII, pp. 362–65.

on this joyful occasion. . . . . But among the many great events which agitate this puddle called Boston, the arrival of John Adams is one. People here tell me it is wise to make my rustic bow to the great man, and I must dine with the king tomorrow and drink some two dozen such perplexed toasts as the bungling creatures here give.

From the tone of this and the following letter it is evident that Dennie was still resentful toward his native town. The second letter was written August 25 of the same year:

I have had the honor of making two bows to the President and receiving three. About three hundred guests were bidden to the feast, and I am sorry to say that the toasts were followed by clamorous hootings and applause quite in the French style. All this is suited to the taste of the Bostonians, who are unquestionably the merest boys at all kinds of play.

I find strong sense, urban manners, and *Elsworth's* energy in Cabot. He amuses me by his political zeal, and instructs me by his worldly wisdom. Moreover, he giveth good dinners, and, sinner that I am, I think partridge at least as palatable as politics.

There is here a kind of would-be literary club. It meets each Wednesday, and consists of certain lawyers, divines, quacks, and merchants. . . . . They are all lazy; and reversing the ancient rule of the symposium, they convene rather to *eat,* than *talk,* together.

On his return to Walpole and the journal, Dennie wrote for its columns one of his cheerful sermons from the text, "Here am I, for thou

didst call me." [18]  Emphasizing the good results
of his sojourn amid the fashions and culture of
the city, he said:

While I was mingling with the crowd on 'change,
lounging in the book-seller's shops, arguing in a coffee-
house, or chatting with sensible women round a supper-
table, I was in fact composing Lay Preachers. The
process, though invisible, still continued. I entered hints
in my note-book, though I did not expand them in the
Museum and kept for future use the fruit of my observations, as my prudent and tender mother used to
store for me autumnal russetings to bless my infant
palate in the scarce and spring time.

A pointed appeal for subscriptions and payment of the same, in the *Farmer's Museum* for
February 11, 1799, showed that another struggle
for existence was upon the journal. As a venture it appeared in a more ornate and expanded
form, April 1, 1799. For this issue Dennie wrote
a clever remonstrance against the silly tricks of
"All Fools' Day," then so commonly played. He
inquired: "Why mankind are so anxious to form
fools when the business seems to be fully done?"
With evidence of his own love of nature, he
advised:

This day should indeed be a festal one but not dedicated to "idiot laughter" and the petty tricks of childhood. It should be a kind of vernal thanksgiving. The
goddess, Flora, rather than Folly, should have our vows.

[18] He used the same text for a later sermon while editing
*The Portfolio.*

In spite of the discouragements and financial losses which Dennie shared with his partners in the vacillating fortunes of this journal, he gained some returns in fame and money from publishing at the same press, in 1796, the first volume of *The Lay Preacher*.[19] In a sentimental preface to these collected "sermons" he outlined his aim and his literary hopes:

To instruct the villager, was his primary object. Hence, an easy and obvious stile was indispensable. To rise to the gorgeous phrase of BOLINGBROKE would have been absurd, to sink to the vulgarity of L'ESTRANGE would have been ignominious. The familiarity of FRANKLIN'S manner, and the simplicity of STERNE'S proved most auxiliary to his design. He therefore, adventured their union. Diffident of success, and prepared for censure, he will not be surprised at a harsh sentence from the critical tribunal. The vanity of authorship has already caused him to prove the negligence of his NATAL TOWN; the same passion now urges him to try suffrages of his COUNTRY. Should this, like the former attempts, slide rapidly down the slope of oblivion, it will add the last item to the catalogue of literary disappointments and CURE THE AUTHOR.

Through the circulation of this volume, and of the journals where his contributions had appeared, Dennie had won considerable reputation for mental alertness and a fluent style, according to the tastes of that day. He was offered positions

[19] *The Lay Preacher; or, Short Sermons for Idle Readers* (Walpole, 1796; 132 pages, 16mo); Preface, pp. iii, iv.

in journalism in New York and Philadelphia, and possibly elsewhere. He hoped to go from New Hampshire to Congress, but failed to win in the election. While he was debating with himself which place he should choose as editor, another opportunity came, which combined a larger, assured salary with a good opportunity to wield both political and literary influence. This was an offer to become private secretary to Timothy Pickering, then secretary of state. The correspondence which led to the acceptance of this position by Dennie, affording revelations of his egotism and flowery language, is still extant, and is printed by permission.[20]

The first letter was from Dennie to Lewis R. Morris, from Walpole, February 10, 1799. After thanking his friend for recommending him to the Department of State, he explains his unfitness for any other departments:

My talents are not *warlike*, and Mr. McHenry would find me a miserable tactician. The meanest clerk in the office of Wolcott,[21] would detect and deride my fiscal inability; and I am too much of a *landsman* to comprehend the nautical lore of Stoddert. . . . . If I enter into

[20] These letters are in the Massachusetts Historical Society; the *Pickering Papers*, Vol. X, No. 644; Vol. XXIV, Nos. 45, 275, 287; Vol. XIII, No, 557.

[21] References here are to the secretaries of war, the treasury, and the navy at that time. *Pickering Papers*, Vol. XXIV, No. 45.

the service of government I expect that *exertion* will be required, and I am willing to make it. Considering this as a stepping-stone to views more enlarged and ambitious, I am abundantly sensible that these will never be gratified, without a satisfactory fulfilment of my initial tasks.

With characteristic vanity, he asks to be called "confidential secretary," saying:

The term *clerk* is hardly soothing enough to *my* pride; it might disgust that of my family; and you, in your noble spirit of candour, will forgive, what only wears the *appearance* of dictation, and results from my well-known love to whatever has *gloss,* and *some sort of high colouring* about it.

The second letter in the series is from Timothy Pickering to Lewis R. Morris, Esq., dated Philadelphia, April 29, 1799:

I have just received your letter of the 21st respecting Mr. Dennie. I have room for him in my office and shall now be glad to employ him. If with his genius and taste, he can in a sufficient degree relinquish the pursuits of literature, and submit to the drudgery of business, it will give me much pleasure to have been in any degree instrumental in availing the public of the benefit of his talents. His compensation may be eight hundred, or a thousand dollars a year, according to the time his health (which I understood you was delicate) may permit him to apply to the public service.

It seems as if Dennie was very dilatory after receiving the first letter from Pickering, just quoted, both in his answer and also in arrangements for moving to Philadelphia. His reasons

were almost hidden under the verbiage of the two
letters which he wrote to Pickering, May 26,
1799, and June 1, 1799.  In the first he accepts
the position with effusion and announces that he
will go "expeditiously," but adds, in apparent contradiction of the last word:

But, as my health is not confirmed, and as I cannot
definitely ascertain the number of days, business here
and a parent's tenderness, at home, may detain me, you
will permit me, Sir, to apprize you, by no very distant
post, of the time, when I shall have the pleasure of
hearing and obeying your official commands.

In the second letter he asks for further extension
of time, because he feels that he must give three
months' notice to the printers of the *Farmer's
Museum*, saying: "Good faith obliges me to
comply entirely with the spirit of my promise."

The result of Dennie's service in the office of
Pickering may be best revealed in a letter from
the latter to John Marshall, about a year after the
above correspondence.[22]   One is not surprised to
read here the criticisms on Dennie's efficiency as a
clerk:

Mr. Dennie will have the honor to present to you
this letter.  Desirous of being at the seat of government,
and to be relieved from the drudgery of editing a newspaper for a very inadequate compensation, his friend
Gen'l Morris recommended him for a place in the de-

[22] Letter dated June 27, 1800 (*Pickering Papers*, Vol.
XIII, No. 557).

partment of State. But I cannot, because I ought not, to conceal from you, that Mr. Dennie's habits and literary turn—I should rather say, his insatiable appetite for knowledge, useful as well as ornamental, render his service as a clerk less productive than the labours of many dull men.

He still wishes, however, to renew his attendance in the department of State, to make a fresh essay to serve his country, provide for his own support, and promote his ultimate views of rendering, in another line, more important benefits to his fellow citizens and to mankind. He therefore, being a perfect Stranger to you, has asked of me a letter of introduction. You will be gratified by the proofs he will give you of an enlightened mind, and with his admirable manners; and I am sure you will be inclined to the most liberal indulgence of his laudable proposition.

After reading this last letter, one can better understand why, in the latter part of 1800, Dennie again turned to journalism for his income, establishing in December of that year a new journal in Philadelphia, *The Portfolio*. He was joined in this enterprise by Asbury Dickens. He had continued his contributions of occasional sermons to the *Farmer's Museum,* and had written editorials for Fenno's *Gazette of the United States,* the Federal organ which had survived and gained in favor, after its experience as a rival of Freneau's *National Gazette.* Dennie modeled his new paper after *The Tablet,* the early Boston venture, but *The Portfolio* was long-lived and existed,

in varied forms, from 1801 to 1827.[23]  The
motto, chosen from Cowper, might well apply to
all journalistic efforts of that age:

> Various,—that the mind
> Of desultory man, studious of change,
> And pleas'd with novelty, may be indulg'd.

A large sheet of "Announcement" accompanied the first number:

A YOUNG MAN, once known among village-readers,
as the humble historian of the hour, the conductor of a
*Farmers Museum* and a *Lay Preacher's Gazette,*
again offers himself to the public as a volunteer editor.
Having, as he conceives, a right to vary, at pleasure, his
*fictitious* name he now, for higher reasons than any
fickle humour might dictate, assumes the appelation of
OLD SCHOOL. Fond of this title, indicative of his
moral, political and literary creed, he proposes publishing
every Saturday, on a super-royal quarto sheet

A NEW WEEKLY PAPER to be called
THE PORT FOLIO
by Oliver Oldschool, Esq.

He commented on the Lilliputian page as an
experiment, like that of "a saving grocer, who
gives of his goods only a small sample," and declared his purpose to offer "something tolerable

---

[23] From 1801 to 1808 the *Portfolio* was a weekly; from
1809 to 1818 it was a monthly; in later years its publication was generally as a monthly or a quarterly.  Files of this
journal are found at many libraries throughout the country;
perfect files are in Philadelphia and New York.  Nicholas
Biddle succeeded Dennie as editor.

on political, literary, and transient topics and
something auxiliary to sound principles which,
*after church*, 'retired leisure' may read on Sunday."

Although this journal was essentially designed
as a literary organ, it was strongly Federalist, and
was disliked and parodied by Jefferson's friends
as the "Portable Foolery." [24] During the first
two years Dennie criticized Jefferson freely and
indulged in strictures even upon the Declaration
of Independence. For such fearless politics he
was arrested and charged, in 1804, with being the
editor of "a seditious publication against the government." He was acquitted, but the tone of his
journal henceforth was less virulent. He was a
pronounced Federalist or Republican from his
youth, anu would not listen to any enticing offers
to edit Democratic newspapers. He was once
offered a large salary to edit the *Independent
Chronicle* of Boston, but refused, expressing his
convictions in extravagant language, thus:

If he had offered me $120,000,000 annually to conduct a
Democratic paper, I must have refused the offer. It
would have belied my feelings, my habits, my principles,
my conscience. I should have been an infinite apostate.[25]

Dennie was a social favorite in Philadelphia

[24] See Scharf and Westcott, *History of Philadelphia* (Philadelphia, 1884), Vol. I, pp. 508, 509.

[25] W. W. Clapp, *Sketch of Dennie*, 1882.

from the first days there. He was instrumental
in forming the Tuesday Club, a social organization with literary aims. He was a fine story-
teller, and was in demand for convivial occasions
wherever he might be. One of the vivid pictures of Dennie, as a companion, is given by
Josiah Quincy, of Boston,[26] who was a college
classmate of Dennie and a friend throughout life.
Speaking of Dennie's mental equipment, as compared with that of other classmates, this friend
said:

> The most talented, taking light literature as the
> standard, was Joseph Dennie, whose acquaintance with the
> best English classics was uncommon at that period. His
> imagination was vivid, and he wrote with great ease and
> felicity. . . . . While at college he might unquestionably
> have taken the highest rank in his class, for he had great
> happiness both in writing and elocution; but he was negli-
> gent in his studies and not faithful to the genius with
> which nature had endowed him.

In reminiscence of his father's conversations
regarding Dennie, Edmund Quincy wrote:

> Mr. Dennie was a most charming companion, brilliant
> in conversation, fertile in allusion and quotation, abound-
> ing in wit, quick at repartee, and of only too jovial a dis-
> position. My father used to tell of the gay dinners which
> celebrated the not infrequent visits Mr. Dennie made him
> when he was keeping house with his mother. On these
> white days he would summon the flower of the youth of

[26] *Life of Josiah Quincy*, by his son, Edmund Quincy (Boston, 1867), p. 30.

Boston to enjoy the society of their versatile friend, and the festivity which set in at the sober hour of two would reach far into the night before the party were willing to break up.

When *The Portfolio* was established, Dennie summoned all his friends with literary tastes to contribute, and the columns of the journal, if carefully studied, reveal some interesting writers and men of prominence in affairs and science. General Thomas Cadwallader wrote translations from Horace; Joseph Hopkinson contributed both prose and verse; Charles Brockden Brown and his brother-in-law, John Blair Linn, were among the writers whose authorship can be attested. Gouvenor Morris, Samuel Ewing, and Mrs. Sarah E. Hall were other writers of the day who assisted Dennie. Josiah Quincy contributed a series of papers, signed "Climenole," satirical and spicy; their authorship was long a secret.[27] As in previous ventures, Dennie had support from "The Shop of Colon and Spondee;" other writers contributed more serious reviews and accounts of travels. Among the latter sort were "Letters from Silesia," found in earlier issues of *The Portfolio*. These letters were by John Quincy Adams, who was then traveling abroad with his wife, on account of the latter's ill health. The letters came

[27] *Op. cit.,* p. 33.

into Dennie's possession in a peculiar way.[28] They were written to the brother of Mr. Adams in Philadelphia. He was a friend of Dennie, and the latter, when allowed to read the letters, was so delighted that he begged to include them unsigned in his journal. The owner consented, and they appeared in twenty-nine numbers, forming an interesting feature of *The Portfolio*. At first the writer of the letters did not know of their use; later he was powerless or unwilling to interfere. They became so popular that an unknown individual reprinted them in London, for his own profit, in 1804, and three years later they were translated into German and French.

Among the Adams papers, owned by Charles Francis Adams, are two unpublished letters from Dennie to John Quincy Adams, which I have been permitted to use. The first, dated September 17, 1804, refers to the London publication of these *Letters*. It is in Dennie's usual fluent and obsequious style:

I perceive by the Public papers, that "Letters from Silesia," &c., have been published in your name in the city of London. You will add to those numerous acts of kindness, with which you have often obliged and honoured me, if by the return of Post, you will mention whether this book has been thus printed with your consent. Your correspondence with the Port Folio has been for some

[28] See *Memoirs of John Quincy Adams,* edited by Charles Francis Adams (Philadelphia, 1877), Vol. I, p. 240, 241.

time, relinquished. Be assured, Sir, I employ no false, or dissembling compliment, when I express the delight I feel in perusing any of your literary productions, and my sorrow that any cause should for a single week, deprive me of the valued assistance of a classical coadjutor.

Whatever you choose to write for my Journal, I will always promptly impart to the Public. I inhibit no topics, I suggest no style; but I intreat that you will still continue to *benefit* me, by the dictates of your Judgement, and the productions of your Taste.

The second letter was in answer to a word of remonstrance from John Quincy Adams against the publication, in *The Portfolio,* of such unreliable, inferior articles as a series entitled "The British Spy," which had appeared during the autumn of this same year, 1804.[29] The letters had some gossipy passages, designed to ferment political feeling regarding Theophilus Parsons, as tool of a junto and of John Adams. Dennie has made the only defense that I have found in this interesting letter to Mr. Adams:

My dear Friend.

A bundle of lucubrations with the title of the "British Spy," was left at my lodgings, by some person unknown. They were inclosed in a letter, without a signature, and I was requested to give them a place in the Port Folio.

[29] See the *Portfolio,* Letter II, November 10, 1804. The inference was that Parsons refused the appointment offered by John Adams. In a note, after Letter IV, November 24, 1804, Dennie urged the writer to verify his statements, corrected this special one, but praised the letters. There were no more, however.

Occupied with the care of an edition of Shakespeare, and of Sir W. Jones, the only paper I perused was the *first* of the Series. Though I was offended by the tumid and Asiatic stile, which the anonymous author thought proper to employ, I thought it would not be disagreeable to the Public, and possibly might be pleasant to the Bostonians, if I gave a place to what from a very cursory glance, I deemed not dishonourable to my native town.

The *second* letter containing the offensive paragraph, of which you so *justly* complain, was not perused by me, until after publication. The instant that I read it, and some days prior to the receipt of your letter of expostulation, although I did not know with precision, the state of facts, I deemed the paragraph a gossiping anecdote of Jacobinical origin, I estimated it as a *lye,* accordingly, and resolved, at the end of the series, hitherto received, which will be printed, on the Saturday of the current week, to express my frank opinion of the falsity of the article, and to warn the author against hazarding such random calumny. I feel with very acute sensibility wounded, that you should suppose for an instant, that I could willingly lend a *lye* the confidence of Truth. If you knew me more intimately you would very distinctly perceive that I was never found to retail Scandal for any individual, or any *Junto;* and that though I have lived more than Thirty years in a Republic, I have not yet learned to be ungrateful to those who have showed me kindness.

Within the columns of *The Portfolio* were selected passages from contemporary English writers of both prose and verse, with interpretative comments. On December 19, 1801, as an example appeared Wordsworth's "Lucy Gray" and

"Eglantine," with praises for "the genuine poet who has forsaken the necromantic realms of German extravagance, and the torrid zone of Della Cruscan ardour and has recalled erring readers from sounds to things, from fancy to the heart." What a pity that Dennie could not have applied to his own style some of the Wordsworthian simplicity and clearness!

The visit of Thomas Moore to Philadelphia, in the spring of 1812, was an event of great significance in the life of Dennie. Moore's grateful memories of this American writer are almost the only words of recognition given to Dennie by any author outside the narrow circle of his friends. Moore had been disappointed in his reception at New York and Washington, but the cordiality with which he was greeted by Dennie and his coterie did much to soften his bitterness. Not alone was he fêted during the few days of his stay in Philadelphia, but his coming was heralded in *The Portfolio* for some weeks before his arrival. As early as April 21, 1804, Moore's poem "To Julia"—one of many of this title—was printed with the note of praise for "this recent poet who is much admired in England for the singular sweetness of his versification, and for a certain glow in his descriptions, mildly ardent, like the setting suns of Claude," True to his promise, in another issue Dennie selected many examples of Moore's poems, especially from the translations of Anacreon.[80]

Moore appreciated his attentions in Philadelphia, in June, 1804. To Dennie's journal he contributed freely many of the poems, which appeared later in English magazines, but were printed here first, often with the prefatory words, "Printed from the Author's Manuscript." In *The Portfolio* for July 14 is "A Birthday Song" by Moore which refers to these cordial, new-found friends:

> In every eye around I mark,
>   The feelings of the heart o'erflowing;
> From every soul I catch the spark
>   Of sympathy, in friendship flowing.

More familiar, as testimony by Moore, are his "Lines on Leaving Philadelphia," which were sent in a letter to Dennie, July 2, 1804, and first printed in his journal. The poem was dedicated to Mrs. Joseph Hopkinson, whose sympathetic singing of Moore's songs had assured him, though a stranger, that—

> The lays of his boyhood had stol'n to their ear,
>   And they loved what they knew of so humble a name;
> And they told him, with flattery, welcome and dear,
>   That they found in his heart something better than fame.

.   .   .   .   .   .   .   .   .   .   .   .   .   .   .

[30] Copies of *The Portfolio* from April to September, 1804, contain many of Moore's poems, with comment, as "The Wedding Ring," "To the Invisible Girl," "Rondeau," "Written in a Common-Place Book," and many poems "To Julia."

The stranger is gone—but he will not forget,
  When at home he shall talk of the toils he has known,
To tell, with a sigh, what endearments he met.
  As he stray'd by the wave of the Schuylkill alone.[31]

Moore kept his pledge of remembrance. He wrote his mother about his Philadelphia friends and gave them special mention in the metrical "Letter to the Hon. W. R. Spencer," where he extolled

                ye sacred few,
Whom late by Delaware's green banks I knew;
Whom, known and loved through many a social eve,
'Twas bliss to live with and 'twas pain to leave.
Not with more joy the lonely exile scann'd
The writing traced upon the desert's sand,
Where his lone heart but little hop'd to find
One trace of life, one stamp of human kind,
Than did I hail the pure, th' enlightened zeal,
The strength to reason, and the warmth to feel,
The manly polish and th' illumined taste,
Which—mid the melancholy, heartless waste
My foot has travers'd,—oh, ye sacred few!
I found by Delaware's green banks with you.

To his mother, Moore wrote of his reception in Philadelphia: "It is the only place in America which can boast any literary activity." [32] In the

[31] This poem, in Moore's handwriting, and two letters by him to Dennie are owned by Mrs. Oliver Hopkinson. They were printed in the *Critic,* June, 1888.

[32] *Memoirs, Journals and Correspondence of Thomas Moore* (London, 1856), Vol. I, p. 164.

same vein of unjust criticism, but flattering experience, he said in the appendix to his poems:

In the society of Mr. Dennie and his friends at Philadelphia, I passed the few agreeable moments which my tour through the states afforded me. Mr. Dennie has succeeded in diffusing through this cultivated little circle that love for good literature and sound politics which he feels so zealously himself and which is very rarely the characteristic of his countrymen.

Among other allusions in Moore's letters to his mother is one to "two or three little poems of a flattering kind" which were addressed to him in Philadelphia. These may be found in *The Portfolio* for September 8, 22, and 29, 1804. The third was an ambitious ode, sung at a dinner to Moore just as he was leaving the city. In mock-heroic verse, the gods are represented in conclave over the seeming dulness of earth, and the need of some new spirit of poetry to waken man, as did Anacreon of old. To their suggestions Jupiter replies in the concluding stanza:

I love well these mortals, though sometimes they err,
  And blessings abundant upon them will pour;
The promise thus made, not an instant defer,
  You ask for Anacreon, but I will give MOORE.[33]

By inheritance Dennie had slight endurance, and his life of conviviality, while it never became debauchery, tended to reduce his vigor. Without

[33] These poems were signed "Mercutio" and C. H—d.

the restraints or the comforts of a home-life, he was careless and irregular in his hours of meals and sleep, and often seemed desperate to snatch all the zestful pleasures which he could. The inevitable day of reckoning came, and he died in January, 1812, when only forty-three years old. Various eulogistic paragraphs appeared soon after his death in the press of Philadelphia and New York. His own journal devoted much space to a "Mortuary," [34] appended to the February number. A poem, full of absurd over-praise and strained meters, was followed by a prose eulogy somewhat less extravagant, in which his personal traits and his aim throughout life were duly emphasized. Of the former the writer said:

So full of urbanity and gentleness were his manners —so amiable his deportment, that none could approach, without loving a man from whom there never escaped an unkind expression—who, in his graver mood, was an instructive friend, and in his social hours, a most gay and captivating companion.

The chief motive of his life was recalled, in language too ornate to be effective, but with truth in the thought:

The great purpose of all his exertions, the uniform

[34] *The Portfolio*, February, 1812; 12 pages with black border, signed "A." Possibly this was Paul Allen, who was associated with Dennie during the last months of his editorship. Premonitions of Dennie's illness and death were in the last volume of *The Portfolio* which he edited.

pursuit of his life, was to disseminate among his countrymen a taste for elegant literature, to give to education and
to letters their proper elevation in the public esteem, and
reclaiming the youth of America from the low career of
sordid interests to fix steadfastly their ambition on objects
of a more exalted character. In this honourable enterprize,
he stood at first almost alone. But such is the power of a
single mind in awakening the talents of a whole nation, so
easily may the pliant materials of public opinion be
moulded by the plastic hand of genius, that the establishment of his work may be considered as forming an æra
in the literary history of America.[35]

Six years after the death of Dennie an admir-
ing friend tried to publish a series of *New and
Original Lay Sermons*,[36] collected from his writings in *The Portfolio*. The avowed purpose was
to get money for a monument. The price was to
be five cents a copy, or two dollars a year. The
first sermon chosen was one of his boldest in
theme, from the text II Sam. 6:20—the unique
explanation of the treatment of Michal by
David. Whether because of this unfortunate
initial "sermon," or for some other reason, the
scheme did not succeed. The monument was
erected later by friends, but the failure of this
series was symbolized in the bizarre illustration
at the end of this first issue—a monument, a book,

[35] *The Portfolio*, February, 1812, pp. 186–187.
[36] *New and Original Essays by Joseph Dennie* (Philadelphia, 1818). Only one has been found in this series.

and an ink-bottle jumbled together above the phrase, "The Relicks of Dennie."

There are two collective editions of his *Lay Sermons,* which were clearly modeled after those of "Dr. Yorick." They do not include the larger portion of Dennie's essays of this type, but they contain representative examples. The first volume, published at Walpole in 1796, was the expression of the earlier, more spontaneous essays. The second collection, edited by his friend in Philadelphia, John E. Hall, five years after Dennie's death, revealed more care in selection and form. This same friend included others of Dennie's writings, with a sketch of his life, in *The Philadelphia Souvenir* for 1826.[37]

In reading Dennie's *Sermons* the question sometimes arises: Was the author serious or cynical?—for wit and earnestness are mingled throughout. He was sincere in purpose; never cynical with intent to injure. Sometimes he chose an unusual theme, like that used in the first essay of the early collection. Taking for his subject, "Two is Better than One," he makes a plea for second marriages, under fitting conditions, and illustrates his text by examples from history and literature. Another good "Sermon," among the earlier ones, was inspired by political dangers and gave warning, from the text: "In those days

[37] *The Philadelphia Souvenir,* 1826, pp. 70–93, 96–136.

THE

# LAY PREACHER;

OR

*SHORT  SERMONS,*

FOR

IDLE  READERS.

---

" THEREFORE, SEEING WE HAVE THIS MINISTRY—
WE FAINT NOT." ST. *PAUL.*

---

*Published according to* ACT *of* CONGRESS.

*By Joseph Dennie, Esq.*

PRINTED AT *WALPOLE*, NEW-HAMPSHIRE,
BY DAVID CARLISLE, JUN.
And Sold at his BOOKSTORE.

1796.

Title-page of first edition of *The Lay Preacher,* 1796; from
copy in American Antiquarian Society Library.

there was no king in Israel; every man did what
was right in his own eyes." The last essay in this
first collection is worthy of special mention. Here
he chose for a theme the prison experiences of
Joseph. After some passages of exposition, he
applied his text to modern life:

> Yet did not the Chief Butler remember Joseph but
> Forgat him. . . . . Many are the promises of the *chief*
> *butlers*, the CHESTERFIELDS, the smooth-tongued men
> of the world. They *keep* them too, But so close, that when
> the day of performance arrives, not even their owner
> can find them,—mislaid in some obscure corner of mem-
> ory's chest!

There is surely not more ground for the charge
of irreverence against Dennie than there is for
the same accusation regarding the essays by Swift
and Sterne. To some minds there is an objec-
tion to paraphrasing the Bible words in text and
illustration. Beyond this general criticism, there
is no offense against religious sentiment, nor are
the texts treated with levity. Dennie had a true,
lifelong reverence for the Bible; it gave him much
comfort in his last hours, as it had in the earlier
years when, he declared, it brought him "medicine
for the mind." In the later collection of his *Sermons,* the second one, "On the Pleasures of
Study," with text from Rev. 1:1, is a direct plea
for Bible-reading. His exposition of the biblical
stories was reverent and often illumining, as

Paul's voyage to Rome, Samuel and Samson, Ruth and Naomi. Sometimes he used episodes like the sufferings of Job, Jonah's lament for his gourd, or Paul's reproof to Athens, as texts for moralizing upon adversity, fretfulness, and scandal. In reciting the story of Samuel's mother, fashioning yearly the little coat which she carried to the boy, he achieved pictorial effects. Sane precepts on the best ways to keep the sabbath are found in the twentieth "sermon" in the later collection, with text from Amos 8:5. Remonstrating against the formal "yawning" endurance of the sabbath, he urged joyful reverence, whether in service indoors or long walks in the country as a means of healthy worship.

In quantity, the literature of permanent value produced by Dennie is small. As an influence his work was of more importance. His essays were novel and stimulating; uneven in interest, yet seldom wearisome. They lack the epigrammatic value of Franklin's essays and those of the best English writers whom Dennie most admired. They are burdened with verbosity, and sometimes seem affected rather than sincere. On the whole, however, they were written with an earnest desire to elevate the literary tastes of his countrymen, and to stimulate them to read more of the higher literature from which he took his allusions and quotations. His essays give us glimpses of the

intellectual and social tastes of his age. As
journalist and essayist he was animated with a
hope that he might inspire young men to read
more intelligently and write more "elegantly."
As one approaches his monument in St. Peter's
churchyard in Philadelphia, he sees from a distance the wreath which encircles the name, and
testifies to the warm friendship with which Dennie was regarded. The epitaph, a long one, was
written by John Quincy Adams.[38] Many of the
sculptured words seem too effusive for our judgment to accept, but no one can question the truth
of one of the last lines:

He devoted his Life to the Literature of his Country.

[38] *Memoirs of John Quincy Adams,* edited by Charles Francis Adams (Philadelphia, 1877), Vol. IX, p. 239.

# WILLIAM DUNLAP: THE BEGINNINGS
## OF DRAMA

# VII

# WILLIAM DUNLAP: THE BEGINNINGS OF DRAMA

Among the research societies, which seek to find and preserve facts and reminiscences in American history and literature, the Dunlap Society has a specific purpose, as outlined in its first printed report:

> The Dunlap Society has been named in honor of William Dunlap, one of the first of American dramatists, one of the earliest of American managers, and the foremost historian of the American Theatre. It has been founded by a Committee of Students of the American Stage, who are also collectors of American dramatic books and prints.[1]

The engraving from Dunlap's portrait of himself, owned by the National Academy of Design, is a fitting frontispiece to this report. Two of Dunlap's plays, *The Father* and *André*, have been edited and republished by this memorial society.

In order that Dunlap may have his true place among the pioneer dramatists of America, we must review briefly the labored, and almost forgotten, ventures in early drama.[2] Probably the

[1] *Biennial Reports of the Dunlap Society*, 1888, p. 11.

[2] Exhaustive outlines of early American drama have been made by Oscar Wegelin in *Early American Plays* (New York,

first attempt at drama written on American soil was *Cornelia,* by Governor William Berkeley, of Virginia, which was acted in London in 1662, but probably was not printed. Another Colonial governor, Robert Hunter, of New York, wrote a political satire in three acts, in 1714, entitled *Androborus; or, The Man-Hater.* He was assisted by Lewis Morris. This early play was owned for many years by David Garrick, and later was in the library of the Duke of Devonshire. A play, *The Suspected Daughter,* by "T. T.," was printed in Boston in 1751, but it has not been traced. The friend of Franklin, Thomas Godfrey, used the popular myth of buried piratical treasure as theme for a broad farce, *The Prince of Parthia,* in 1759. In London, a few years later, a popular play was *Ponteach,* which related the unique adventures of its author, Major Robert Rogers, an Indian ranger.

The early incidents of the Revolution were recited in bombastic attempts at drama. General John Burgoyne had a little literary talent and more vanity. To please the ladies and British officers, during the military investment of Boston, he wrote a farce, *The Blockheads,* for which Major André composed a comic prologue. When

1905; second edition, with bibliography of Dunlap), and Paul Leicester Ford in *New England Magazine,* February, 1894. ("Beginnings of American Dramatic Literature.")

the fortunes of war were reversed, and the
British were in derision as foolish adventurers,
an answering satire in dialogue form, *The Blockheads,* appeared. Paul Leicester Ford has
assigned this to Mercy Warren. The prologue
suggests her style of invective:

> By Yankees frighted too! Oh, dire to say!
> Why Yankees sure at red coats faint away!
> Oh, yes—they thought so too—for lackaday,
> Their general turn'd the blockade to a play;
> Poor vain poltroons—with justice we'll retort,
> And call them *blockheads* for their idle sport.

Among other plays which recall the earlier
years of the war were *The Battle of Brooklyn,*
an unassigned farce; *The Fall of British Tyranny,*
by John Leacock; *The Battle of Bunker's Hill,*[3]
by Hugh Henry Brackenridge, and *The Motley
Assembly,* a satire on prominent Loyalist families. Possibly this last was by Mrs. Mercy
Warren, who wrote two of the popular dramas
of the same period, *The Adulateur* and *The
Group.*[4] When the stress of feeling had somewhat lessened, there were lighter farces, operas,
and drawing-room dialogues, which portrayed or
satirized national traits. Among such was the

[3] *The Battle of Bunker's Hill: A Dramatic Piece of Five
Acts in Heroic Measure. By a Gentleman of Maryland*
(Philadelphia: Bell, 1776).

[4] *The Adulateur* (Boston, 1773); *The Group* (Boston, 1775;
8vo).

anonymous opera, *The Blockheads; or, the Fortunate Contractor*, acted in 1782–83 in London and
New York.[5]   Some crude plays were written by
the Yale tutor Barnabas Bidwell, which were
acted in the colleges.   One of these, *The Merce-
nary Match*, in 1785, was very popular because
it had a strong American note, in remonstrance
against the marriage of an American girl to a
wealthy foreigner.

With the exception of the patriotic satires, all
plays that were written and acted during the war
were disapproved by the anxious, impoverished
patriots as a waste of money and time.   The
American Company of actors, who had enjoyed
a season of favor in New York and elsewhere
before the war, was forced to the South and to
Jamaica, until 1785, when they reappeared in New
York.   At first, on their return, they gave
"Courses of Lectures," and gradually came into
the field of drama again.   The favorite member
of this company, Hallam, had been joined by his
cousin, Wignell.   The latter made a great success
of the character of Jonathan, a typical Yankee, in
Royall Tyler's *The Contrast,* the first distinctively
American   drama   in   background,   motive,   and

[5] *The Blockheads; or, Fortunate Contractor: An Opera
in Two Acts, as it Was Performed at New York.   Printed at
New York, London.*   (1782).

authorship; this was probably given for the first time in New York, April 16, 1787.[6]

Royall Tyler had written an earlier dramatic sketch, *May Day; or, New York in an Uproar,* which had been acted by Wignell. After the success of *The Contrast,* he tried again to gain applause by a comedy, *The Georgia Spec; or, Land in the Moon;* but this, like his lyric efforts and his *Comic Grammar,* has been forgotten. The student of American literature still finds mild interest in Tyler's fiction, *The Algerine Captive* and *The Yankey in London.* He is, however, generally known as the writer of the first American play that won success and maintained the interest of a later generation.[7] In the reprint by the Dunlap Society, the editor, Thomas J. McKee, said of its general influence:

> The success of "The Contrast" was one of the powerful influences which aided in bringing about in this country a complete revolution of sentiment with respect to the drama and theatrical amusements.[8]

The statement of Tyler in the advertisement of

[6] This date, generally adopted, has been disputed by Rev. Thomas P. Tyler, who says the initial performance was at Park Theater, April 16, 1789. See Gilman, *Bibliography of Vermont* (Montpelier, 1897), pp. 282.

[7] A few of his *Songs* in manuscript are in the Boston Public Library.

[8] *The Contrast,* reprint by the Dunlap Society (New York, 1887), Introduction, p. viii.

his play may be readily believed. He assured the public that he "never critically studied the rules of the drama, and indeed had seen but few exhibitions of the stage." In conclusion, he confessed that the play "was undertaken and finished in the course of three weeks." In spite of the obvious results of such haste and lack of training, there is a tone of vibrant Americanism which won passing favor for the drama, not alone with the public, but also with Washington, whose name appears first upon the list of subscribers to the printed version.[9] The keynote of patriotism is sounded in the first lines of the prologue:

> EXULT, each patriot heart! this night is shewn
> A piece, which we may fairly call our own;
> Where the proud titles of "My Lord!" "Your Grace!"
> To humble Mr. and plain Sir give place.
> Our Author pictures not from foreign climes,
> The fashions or the follies of the times;
> But has confin'd the subject of his work
> To the gay scenes—the circles of New York.

The droll frontispiece was drawn by Dunlap, who recorded his interest in this play and its influence upon him, but who also censured it freely:

It is extremely deficient in plot, dialogue, or incident, but has some marking in the characters, and in that of *Jonathan,* played by Wignell, a degree of humour and a

[9] The title-page of the first edition reads: *The Contrast, A Comedy; in five acts. Written by a citizen of the United States; Performed with applause at the Theatres in New-York, Philadelphia and Maryland* (1790).

knowledge of what is termed Yankee dialect which, in the hands of a favourite performer, was relished by an audience gratified by the appearance of home manufacture—a feeling which was soon exchanged for a most discouraging predilection for foreign articles, and contempt for every home-made literary effort.[10]

The climax of broad humor is in the first scene of the third act of *The Contrast*. Here are allusions to the prejudices, then current, against theaters and actors. Jonathan is describing his experiences in the city. Someone hints that he must have seen "the players," and he exclaims:

Mercy on my soul! Did I see the wicked players? Mayhap that 'ere Darby, that I liked so, was the old serpent himself and had his cloven feet in his pocket. Why, I vow, now I come to think on't, the candles seemed to burn blue, and I'm sure where I sat it smelt tarnally of brimstone.

The three women—Charlotte, Letitia, and Maria —were good types of their own times in manners, but they belong to the universally feminine in sentiments and thoughts. The true motif of the play was summarized in the final speech of Colonel Manly, the priggish hero:

And I have learned that probity, virtue, honour, though they should not have received the polish of Europe, will secure to an honest American the good graces of his countrywomen, and, I hope, the applause of THE PUBLIC.

[10] *History of the American Theatre* (New York, 1832), pp. 71, 72.

This comedy by Tyler has received detailed attention here, both because of its important place in the development of native drama, and also on account of its influence upon William Dunlap. His own assertion was:

> I heard of the success of "The Contrast" and although it was already put on the shelf of the prompter, or buried in his travelling chest, the praises bestowed upon it lit up the inflammable material brought from abroad, and a comedy in five acts was written in a few weeks.[11]

The incidents of Dunlap's youth, as well as his tastes, inclined him toward the two professions with which he was allied—art and the drama. Born at Perth Amboy, February 19, 1776, his earliest memories clustered about scenes of the Revolution. His father, Samuel Dunlap, a native of Ireland, was in Wolfe's army and was seriously wounded on the Plains of Abraham. When he recovered, he left the army, married Margaret Sargent, and became a storekeeper at Perth Amboy, where his only son was born. According to family stories, William Dunlap was an example of an only child of the "spoiled" kind, tyrannizing over family and slaves alike. Beyond the instruction of his "good mother," as he always called her, he had another teacher in

---

[11] *History of the American Theatre* (New York, 1832), p. 77. Dunlap had just returned from four years in England at the time this play was presented.

his birth-town, to whom he owed early fondness for books and pictures. This aged friend and his home were described minutely by Dunlap:

> On the corner of Market and High streets stood the house of Thomas Bartow. He was a small, thin, old man, with straight gray hair hanging in comely guise on each side of his pale face.[12]

In this friend's garden, beside the hickory fire in the library, or speeding over the frozen ground behind the old sorrel horse, Dunlap received many happy and lasting lessons on life and books. In memory he recalled this inspiring guide:

> Patiently he turned over the pages of Homer and Virgil in the translations of Pope and Dryden, and of Milton's poems, and explained the pictures, until I was familiar with the stories of Troy and Latium,—of heaven and hell, as poets tell them. Nor was history strange to me, especially that of Rome. Thus was commenced a love of reading which has been my blessing.[13]

As a boy, Dunlap belonged to a company of "Governor's guards," during the later years of the Revolution. He remembered vividly the arrival of British troops at Perth Amboy, and his desire to follow them far out of town. This

---

[12] William Dunlap, *History of the Rise and Progress of the Arts of Design in the United States* (New York, 1834), Vol. I, p. 245, 246.

[13] Wiiliam A. Whitehead, *Contributions to the Early History of Perth Amboy* (New York, 1856), pp. 139–41, gives further facts about this man, and also "the Dame School" which Dunlap attended, kept by Mrs. Randal.

incident had more than a passing result for
Dunlap, for his family moved to Piscatawa,
that they might be sure of safety in an attack.
Here, on the banks of the Raritan, the boy found
a new teacher in Nature. He made fitful attempts
to study at home, and he browsed much in his
father's library. The lifelong regret of his life
was the lack of any systematic education. But
there were compensations at this time. As he
recalled:

> My time was principally occupied in swimming and
> fishing in the creeks of the Raritan, rambling the fields
> and woods—sailing boats on a mill-pond—visiting the
> miller—and, in short, in the delights of liberty and idle-
> ness,—no, not idleness, for this was as busy a summer
> as I remember.[14]

When his family moved to New York, in
1777, Dunlap's studies were renewed, but only
for a brief time. While playing with some friends
near the home of Andrew Elliot, in 1778, his right
eye was cut by a wood-chip carelessly tossed by
a playmate. At first he was threatened with total
blindness, but gradually he recovered the use of
his left eye. His definite schooling was ended,
and pictures became his only resource during
weeks of recovery. He began to use India ink
in copying prints. His success led to attempts

[14] *History of the Rise and Progress of the Arts of Design
in the United States*, Vol. I, p. 247.

at engravings, and he drew sketches of his relatives "at three guineas a head." In later life he traced his failures in working with color to this early enthusiasm, saying: "My eye became satisfied with light and shadow, and the excitement of color was not necessary to my pleasure." [15]

Dunlap's father thought he could make an artist of his son, if he gave him enough instruction. He sent him as a pupil to William Williams, in New York, who taught him the rudiments of portrait-painting; and the youth experimented upon his family and friends. He was especially anxious to paint the portrait of Washington, and was given the privilege at two different times. The second effort was a crude, full-length portrait, modeled after West's painting of the same subject. The background was the battlefield at Princeton. Beside Washington was the recumbent figure of General Mercer.

To fulfil his ambition for his son, his father sent him to London, in 1784, that he might have the benefit of instruction by Benjamin West. The four years abroad did not much advance Dunlap's progress in his art, for he was idle and conceited, the victim of ill-health and too much

---

[15] *Ibid.*, p. 250. One of the droll efforts in color by Dunlap is at the New York Historical Society: "The Artist Showing a Picture from Hamlet to His Parents."

freedom and dissipation in a large city. Evidently West did not consider him promising as an art-student, although "Rafe" West, the painter's son, was one of Dunlap's intimates during this period. When Dunlap showed one of his portraits to West, the latter's droll comment was: "You have made the two sides of the figure alike—each has the same sweeping swell—he looks like a rolling pin." [16]

On his return to America, Dunlap drifted aimlessly for a time; but, after his marriage to Elizabeth Woolsey he renounced his convivial habits and tried to make his life more noble. In the marriage notice, in *New York Daily Gazette,* February 16, 1789, she is called the amiable and accomplished Miss Nabby Woolsey, of Fairfield, Conn. Dunlap was interested, for a time, in the New York Abolition Society, and freed his father's slaves. Afterward he tried business and visited various cities as a trader in general merchandise. Finally he heard of the success of Tyler's *The Contrast,* and became filled with the idea that he would be a playwright. His boyhood pleasure in witnessing the plays given by the British soldiers, the more recent enjoyment of plays in London, and the promise of American response seemed to assure him that this was his opportunity.

*Op. cit.,* p. 262.

His first attempt, *Modest Soldier; or, Love in New York*, was, he said, "read to critics as young and ignorant as the author, and praised to his heart's content. It has long slept in the tomb of the Capulets, and fortunately no traces remain of its merits or demerits." [17] It is to be regretted that the same fate did not attend many others of his more than sixty plays.

The second effort was more successful in immediate and lasting results. The first performance was at the John Street Theater, September 7, 1789. It was entitled *The Father; or, American Shandyism;* in a later issue the title was *The Father of an Only Child*.[18] The comedy abounds in melodrama, crude and complicated situations, until the reader is prepared to echo the sentiment of the epilogue, which was spoken by Mrs. Henry, of the American Company:

Well, We've got thro' and in good truth I'm glad on't,
A sorry, whining, canting time I've had on't,—
My true love lost and found, and found and lost;
Like shuttlecock my passions pitch'd and toss'd.

There were references to the political situation,

[17] *History of the American Theatre* (New York, 1832), p. 77.

[18] This was reprinted from the original in 1887, by the Dunlap Society, with an introduction by Thomas J. McKee. The original play was first printed in the *Massachusetts Magazine*, October and November, 1789.

especially to the proposed and rejected amendments to the Articles of Confederation, in the speeches by the leading characters, Mr. Racket and his petulant wife.

The response to this first play fired Dunlap with determination to write more. In reminiscence he confessed:

Filled with youthful ardour and pleased with the applause of the public and the encouragement of his associates, he tho't only of future triumphs, and tragedies and comedies, operas and farces, occupied his mind, his time and his pen.[19]

The second play which was acted was a trifle, *Darby's Return*, written as a benefit for the actor Wignell. The character of the poor, genial soldier was long recalled. With a party of guests, Washington attended this play at its first staging in New York, and was embarrassed at first, and then amused, by the references to himself.[20] In homely phrase, Darby told of Washington's service:

A man who fought to free the land from wo,
*Like me*, had left his farm a-soldiering to go,
But having gained his point, he had, *like me*,

[19] *History of the American Theatre* (New York, 1832), p. 114. The long list of his plays as given by Wegelin in *Early American Plays,* including a number of manuscripts, testifies to the truth of this word.

[20] *Ibid.,* p. 85. The same story is in Martha J. Lamb, *History of the City of New York,* Vol. II, p. 352; also in Paul L. Ford, *Washington and the Theatre* (New York, 1899).

Return'd his own potato ground to see.
But there he could not rest. With one accord
He's called to be a kind of,—not a lord,—
I don't know what, he's not a *great man* sure,
For poor men love him just as he were poor.

When Kathleen asked, "How look'd he, Darby? Was he short or tall?" Dunlap said Washington showed embarrassment from the expectation of

one of those eulogies which he had been obliged to hear on many public occasions and which must doubtless have been a severe trial to his feelings; but Darby's answer that he had not seen him, because he had mistaken "a man all lace and glitter, botherum and shine" for him, until the show had passed, relieved the hero from apprehension of further personality, and he indulged in that which was with him extremely rare, a hearty laugh.

Such an anticlimax was often found in Dunlap's plays. He chose this device to bring in humor and, in many cases, to speak a message of democracy.

For the rival of Wignell, the actor Hodgkinson, Dunlap wrote the play that was printed later as *Lord Leicester,* but the title of which, as acted April 24, 1794, was *The Fatal Deception; or, The Progress of Guilt.* This play did not win much applause; so the dramatist created a character akin to that of Darby, in the farce *Shelty's Travels.* This was left among his manuscript plays; but it had temporary fame, and cleared five hundred dollars for the actor's benefit. In the copy of *Lord Leicester* printed in New York, probably in 1807, the author wrote: "To the Reader":

The following poem, my first effort in tragic composition, and the first American tragedy produced upon the stage, was written in the year 1790, and first played at New York, in 1794. Its success confirmed my attachment to the drama.

To most readers, Matilda urging Henry to the murder of Leicester will appear as a copy of lady Macbeth; but she is, in reality, more in situation like the Clytemnestra of the Greek poets; yet essentially different (independent of difference in merit) from both.

May, 1806.      W. Dunlap.

In this play the part of *Leicester* was taken by Hallam, and that of *Cecil* by Hodgkinson.

Soon after Dunlap's plays had begun to attract favorable attention, he was persuaded by Hodgkinson to enter a partnership with him as theatrical manager. This was a fatal error, as regarded the financial future of Dunlap. He hoped, however, to improve the American stage and to educate the public to appreciate native dramas of purity. At sixty-five, with shattered health and fortunes, he still affirmed that he had

the thoughts and wishes of one who, on trial, found circumstances too strong for his desires of reform, and, who, after a struggle (with ruined health and fortunes,) gave up the contest without giving up the wish or hope.[21]

[21] *History of the American Theatre*, p. 143.

Hodgkinson persuaded Dunlap to purchase a share in the John Street Theater, and later to join him in a lease of the Park Theater, with a cost for fittings of one hundred and thirty thousand dollars. He also emphasized to Dunlap the opportunity thus afforded for presenting the latter's plays. The month after Dunlap had assumed management, he brought out his opera *The Archers,* the tale of William Tell. This was an adaptation; Hodgkinson as *William Tell* and his wife as *Cecily* won many plaudits.[22] The "Basket Song" was retained in books of parlor music for many years after the play had been forgotten:

> Come, who'll buy my baskets?
> I've small and I've great,
> They are fit for all uses,
> And suiting each state.
> Chorus: Come, who'll buy my baskets?
>
> Buck-baskets, bread-baskets,
> Of broom and of chip;
> Work baskets for ladies
> Who ne'er have the *hip.*
> Chorus: Come, who'll buy my baskets?
>
> Here's love-letter baskets
> Of willow so trim

[22] This was adapted from "a piece, Helvetic Liberty, left with him." His title reads: *The Archers or Mountaineers of Switzerland. An Opera in 3 acts, as performed by the Old American Company* (New York, 1796).

For the swain who sore sighs
At his mistress's whim.
Chorus: Come, who'll buy my baskets?

Discords soon followed triumphs at the theater. Quarrels arose between Hodgkinson and Hallam, and Dunlap was compelled to borrow and advance money to meet the expenses of his partner while on trips in Boston and Hartford. With quiet sarcasm he wrote of his share in these extravagances of Hodgkinson: "His partner sent on money and advice. The one was taken, the other rejected." [23]

Valuable aid in studying the life of Dunlap during this part of his career, both as manager and as playwright, is found in some volumes of manuscript journals recently acquired by the New York Historical Society. Portions are here printed by permission. The four volumes at this library are numbered 14, 15, 24, and 30, in an evidently broken series. They thus cover not alone the two years of his activity as playwright, 1797–98, but the later volumes reveal his last years of struggle as painter and author. The books are bound in leather, and the handwriting is generally clear and strong.

The first entry, July 27, 1797, is a typical record of a day in Dunlap's life, bringing its own testimony to his energy and varied interests:

[23] *History of the American Theatre,* p. 201.

I arose at half-past 4 O'clock and worked in the garden untill breakfast. Went with the Children to Mr. Parker's where I left Margaret. Read Hume with John Read [24] in the 15th vol. of Enc; which I borrowed on the 25th from Mr. Parker's family; on which evening I read several arts. in it to my Wife; particularly potatoes. Read this morning to my Wife Art. Platonism; finding the opinion of Plato in respect to a first cause of the Universe and co-existing Matter very similar to ideas of my own expressed in *Ufrasia,* I took up ye vol. of my Memoirs & read to my Wife one of the dialogues between Joseph and Abbas. Read Hume with ye boy. Read in Enc. arts. Platonism, Plotinus, Plover, etc. Walk out to my Farm,—the buckwheat is well up.

Following such entries of domestic and personal interest are passages relating to his dramas. He records the opinion of Thomas Holcroft, to whom he had sent some of his plays with a view to publication. The decision was unfavorable; the publisher had read "William Tell first and did not care to read the others." Dunlap accepted the verdict with good grace, saying: "His opinion in respect to the publication is just and the knowledge of that opinion is salutary to me."

Letters from Hodgkinson, dated from Hartford and Boston, brought Dunlap tidings of "expenditures far in excess of receipts." The scattered sentences which follow indicate the stress and anxiety which such mismanagement caused Dunlap: "August 15, Rec'd letters from

[24] This reference is to his son, who died in early manhood.

Hodgkinson filled with ill-fortune—wrote to him —'I can send no more; we may as well stop at once. How I shall pay what I owe here I know not.'" A few days later, after a night of anxiety, he wrote in the journal: "The greater part of this day has been passed in fruitless attempts to borrow money."

Near the close of the first manuscript volume, November 25, 1797, there is a significant entry: "Write on André." The early pages of the second volume of the journal (Volume 15) mention this play in progress of writing; then, later, in presentation. As this was the drama which has given Dunlap his true recognition in later years, it is fitting to speak of it in detail. Reading the story from entries in the journal, we find that in December, 1797, Dunlap returned from Boston, where he had been compelled to give security for Hodgkinson's debts. On his way back to New York he had stopped at New Haven, at his "excellent brother Dwight's," to whom he had read parts of his new play.[25] According to the journal, *André* was finished January 21, 1798, but it was March 27 before final rehearsals began. Cooper, Hallam, and Hodgkinson became involved in a three-cornered quarrel over the parts,

[25] Mrs. Dunlap was the sister of the wife of President Timothy Dwight.

ANDRÉ,

A *TRACEDY*, IN FIVE ACTS

AS PERFORMED BY THE OLD AMERICAN COMPANY,
NEW-YORK, MARCH 30, 1798.

TO WHICH ARE ADDED

AUTHENTIC DOCUMENTS

RESPECTING

*MAJOR ANDRÉ*;

CONSISTING OF

LETTERS TO MISS SEWARD,

THE

COW CHACE,

PROCEEDINGS OF THE COURT MARTIAL, &c.

COPY RIGHT SECURED.

NEW-YORK:
Printed by T. & J. SWORDS, No. 99 Pearl-street.
— 1798.—

Title-page of William Dunlap's play, *Andrè*, 1798.

and the presentation was much delayed. But on March 30 there was this significant diary note:

> Evening, André & poor Soldier in ye house—$817. The play was much applauded, notwithstanding the extreme imperfectness of Cooper & of some others but on Blands throwing down his Cocade there was (*sic*) a few hisses.

This incident of the cockade nearly made the play a fiasco. It was dangerous to choose the character of André and his fate as a subject for drama within eighteen years of the dates of the events, and while partisan spirit was still smoldering. Cooper, in the character of Bland, a young American officer who had been kindly treated by André and became his friend while imprisoned within the British lines, finding that his pleas would not save the life of André, tore the American cockade from his casque and threw it down. This episode in the play was easily misinterpreted at the time it was first given. Afterward Dunlap said:

> This was not, perhaps could not be, understood by a mixed assembly; they thought the country and its defenders insulted, and a hiss ensued—it was soon quieted and the play ended with applause.[20]

The contemporary version of the affair, in his journal, indicates that the feeling was not confined to the first night, but lived for a day or

[20] *History of the American Theatre*, p. 222.

two. April 2, 1798, before the second or third presentation, he wrote: "I am told that the people are so offended at the Cocade business as to threaten to hiss off the play tonight." A severe storm prevented the play from being given that night, and before its next performance Dunlap says that he "made an alteration in the 5th act, by making Bland, on his repentance, receive the cockade again." The play was repeated April 6, "for the Author's benefit and cleared $329."

In spite of many technical defects and "wooden speeches," Dunlap achieved considerable success with the character of André. In the reprint of this play, J. Brander Matthews has said, criticizing its merits: "Of all the plays on the subject of Arnold's treason and André's sad fate, the André of Mr. Dunlap is easily the best, both as literature and as a successful acting drama." [27] The best portion of the play is in Act II, the interview between André and Bland:

> ANDRÉ. Oft in the generous heat of glowing youth,
> Oft have I said how fully I despised
> All bribery base, all treacherous tricks in war:
> Rather my blood should bathe these hostile shores,
> And have it said, "He died a gallant soldier,"

[27] The Original edition was entitled: *André: A Tragedy in 5 acts. By William Dunlap* (New York, 1798; London, 1799); reprint by the Dunlap Society (New York, 1887). Introduction by J. Brander Matthews, p. xxiv.

> Than with my country's gold encourage
>       treason,
> And thereby purchase gratitude and fame.
> BLAND.  Still mays't thou say it, for thy heart's the
>       same. . . . .
> ANDRÉ.  Still is my heart the same.  But there has past
>       A day, an hour, which ne'er can be recall'd,
>       Unhappy man! Tho' all thy life pass pure,
>       Mark'd by benevolence thy every deed;
>       The out-spread map, which shows the way
>             thou'st trod,
>       Without one devious track or doubtful line,
>       It all avails thee naught, if in one hour,
>       One hapless hour, thy feet are led astray;—
>       Thy happy deeds all blotted from remem-
>             brance;
>       Cancell'd the record of thy former good,
>       Is it not hard, my friend? Is't not unjust?
> BLAND.  Not every record cancel'd. O, there are hearts
>       Where Virtue's image, when 'tis once engrav'd,
>       Can never know erasure.

The later lines of this act, in which André
recites the incidents of his treason and capture,
have a sustained interest, although many lines
lack spontaneity and force:

> BLAND.  It was thy duty so to serve thy country.
> ANDRÉ.  Nay, nay; be cautious ever to admit
>       That duty can beget dissimulation.
>       On ground, unoccupied by either part,
>       Neutral esteem'd, I landed, and was met.
>       But ere my conference was with Arnold clos'd,
>       The day began to dawn; I then was told
>       That till the night I must my safety seek

In close concealment. Within your posts con-
vey'd
I found myself involved in unthought dangers,
Night came. I sought the vessel which had
borne
Me to the fatal spot; but she was gone.
Retreat that way cut off, again I sought
Concealment with the traitors of your army.
Arnold now granted passes, and I doff'd
My martial garb, and put on curs'd disguise.
Thus in a peasant's form I pass'd your posts;
And when, as I conceiv'd my danger o'er,
Was stopt and seiz'd by some returning
scouts.
So did ambition lead me, step by step,
To treat with traitors, and encourage treason;
And then, bewilder'd in the guilty scene,
To quit my martial designating badges,
Deny my name and sink into the spy.

The interest awakened by this tragedy induced
Dunlap to introduce some of the same characters
—Washington, Arnold, Paulding, and André—
in a melodrama, *The Glory of Columbia,* which
was first given at the Park Theater, July 4,
1803.[28] Some of the songs, which formed a
prominent feature of this play, were crude, but
spirited, such as the chorus, "Glory of Columbia,"
sung to the tune of "Washington's March":

[28] *The Glory of Columbia; her Yeomanry: A Play in 5
acts. The Songs, Duets and Choruses, intended for the celebration of the Fourth of July at the New-York Theatre* (New
York, 1803).

See, the standards float,
       So proudly gay!
Hark! the trumpet's note,
       With clanging bray.
While every breast with conscious might,
Swells ardent for the coming fight!

·   ·   ·   ·   ·   ·   ·   ·   ·   ·   ·   ·

       The fight is done,
       The battle won!
Our praise is due to him alone,
Who from his bright eternal throne,
The fate of battles and of man decides!
       To him all praise be given!
       And under heaven,
       To great Columbia's son,
       Blest WASHINGTON!
Who o'er the *fight* like fate presides.

As one looks over the list of Dunlap's plays,
with dates of writing, performance, and publication,[29] he will note his years of plenty and of
famine as a playwright. The climax of his popularity was at the close of the eighteenth century.
The year 1800 has a record of eight plays that
were either performed or printed, in addition to
some that failed to win sufficient favor to be produced. Following this period of fecundity there
was an interval of discouragement. A brief
revival of success came in 1803, when he produced *The Voice of Nature*, which was an adapta-

[29] Such lists are to be found in the reprint of *The Father*
by the Dunlap Society, and also in Oscar Wegelin, *Early
American Plays* (2d ed., 1905).

tion from a French play, *Le Jugement de Salomon; Ribbemont; or, The Feudal Baron; The Blind Boy*, later given in London,[30] and *The Glory of Columbia*. Another period of desuetude, as regarded publication, followed for four or five years. Then came an awakening of interest in his plays, as is indicated by the performance and printing, within a few years, of the historical dramas *Rinaldo Rinaldini, The Battle of New Orleans,* and *The Soldier of Seventy-Six,* such translations as *Blue Beard, Lover's Vows,* and *The Africans,* and the opera *Yankee Chronology,* with its "Huzza Song" which long survived its time of composition, in the War of 1812. It had a rollicking refrain:

Then huzza! for the Sons of Columbia so free!
They are lords of the soil—they'll be lords of the sea!

At intervals in his later life Dunlap wrote plays for special occasions, or at the requests of theater managers. One of the last of this type was *A Trip to Niagara*—a farce which was, according to his own explanation in the preface, "intended as a kind of running accompaniment to the more important product of the Scene painter." It illustrated a diorama of New York harbor, the Catskills, and Niagara.[31] It is noteworthy that

[30] For full title and date of these plays, see the Bibliography.

[31] *A Trip to Niagara. Written for the Bowery Theatre, N. Y., by William Dunlap, Historical and Portrait Painter,*

in this mongrel play one of the characters was Leatherstocking. There existed a strong friendship between Cooper and Dunlap, in the latter's last years. To the novelist, Dunlap dedicated his American edition of the *History of the American Theatre*.

After such a general survey of Dunlap's work as playwright, the queries arise: What were his merits as a dramatist, and why does he deserve recognition, in the face of such defects and with such meager literary skill? His defects were obvious; to him they seemed insurmountable. In an address which prefaced *Rinaldo Rinaldini* [32] he thanked the public for past favors, and declared:

I am sensible of disadvantages which I consequently labour under, from a confined education, nor do I expect my style will be thought equal in elegance or energy to the productions of those who, fortunately, from their situation in life, have been instructed in the classics and have reaped both pleasure and improvement, by studying the ancients in their original purity.—I wish to be understood that my pretensions to originality are small.

Dunlap well summarized here his chief faults —lack of a strong style and of much originality. Largely because of his rapid writing, but also

Author of *Memoirs of G. F. Cooke, C. B. Brown, Father of an Only Child*, etc. (New York, 1830).

[32] *Rinaldo Rinaldini or the Great Banditti. By an American and a Citizen of New York* (New York, 1810), p. iii.

from deficient training, his style was often loose
and weak. There are a few passages of dramatic
energy, and occasional characters with marked
portraiture, as we have cited; but the mass of
his plays lapse into mediocrity. His claim to
remembrance cannot rest upon any individual
play, with the possible exception of *André;* but
he deserves some praise for skill in meeting the
demands of his age, and for persistent efforts to
cultivate a taste for pure, American drama.

A critic has used the phrase "well made" to
describe Dunlap's plays.[33] In general construction and adaptation to the fashions of his day, his
plays were cleverly devised. They were always
wholesome morally, whether of his own conception or translated from Kotzebue, Iffland, and
other playwrights. He was sometimes extravagant in sensibility to suit the tastes of the time,
but his tone was not prurient. He exerted a dual
influence as dramatist and theater-manager. He
lost money in the latter experience, and was reduced to penury; but he never lost his patience
nor his confidence in the public. For fifteen years
he struggled, endured bickerings among actors,
debts, sickness; but he still maintained a firm
faith in God and man, and a belief that there was

[33] John Malone in Introduction (p. vi) to Oscar Wegelin,
*Early American Plays* (published by the Dunlap Society, New
York, 1900 and 1905).

a future of appreciation for both playwrights and actors of high ideals.

It may seem almost incredible that sufficient material existed for a bulky *History of the American Theatre* in 1832, when Dunlap published his volume. The style and plan of the history were alike leisurely, with many side-excursions into letters, politics, and society. After two or more pages of rambling reminiscence, the author would halt and admonish his readers: "But let us return to New York and the Drama." In addition to the autobiographical chapters, much valuable information was preserved by Dunlap regarding plays, their writers and actors, without which later studies of the stage would have been inadequate. Comparing himself to Colley Cibber in this work, he quotes from his English model:

> If I have any particular qualification for the task more than another, it is that I am perhaps the only person living (however unworthy) from whom the same materials could be collected.[34]

After we have read, with kindly interest, the portraits of famous actors and authors of that day, and the mingled success and pathos in Dunlap's own life, it is disturbing to meet such a sentence of wholesale disparagement as this by Seilhamer: "Dunlap's statements of facts are

[34] William Dunlap, *History of the American Theatre*. Preface, p. viii (New York, 1832; London, 1833).

almost always misstatements, either in whole or
in part." [35] Nor is this later critic quite justified
in such a sweeping condemnation. Some of Dunlap's dates, and many of his deductions, have
been corrected by later research; but, as a whole,
his *History of the American Theatre* is not alone
entertaining, but reliable, as a portrayal of
characters and a graphic revelation of the dramatic impulse in America which survived the
fierce opposition and many discouragements of
the first half-century of national life.

With greater justice toward Dunlap's under-
lying motives and appreciation of his charm,
Samuel Isham, in his recent *History of American
Painting* has written words which may apply
both to the *History of the American Theatre* and
also to the *History of the Rise and Progress of
the Arts of Design:*

He had a feeling for accuracy rare at the time. Like
Herodotus he relates many fables but relates them as they
were told him and gives his authority. . . . . He had a
good eye for character and he had fixed moral standards.
It is only in his pages that we seem to touch the reality
of West and Stuart and Trumbull, and Allston and Sully.
Men were as sensitive then as today, and the men of
whom he wrote and their friends were displeased at his
frankness; but viewed at the present distance of time, he

[35] George O. Seilhamer, *History of the American Theatre
during the Revolution and after.* (Philadelphia, 1889), Vol.
II, p. 274.

seems rather kindly. He had his dislikes but he was harder on no one than on himself. One of his charms is his old-fashioned style as remote from that of the present day as Bacon's, a little ponderous but clear and animated. Being of his time he had to moralize some, but he does it briefly, and compensates for it by introducing innumerable anecdotes, including some remarkably good ones. All of his successors have poached on his preserves, but none has paraphrased them without loss of point or character.[36]

In Dunlap's *History of the American Theatre* are delightful sidelights upon famous men and women of the past, especially among the actors and playwrights. There is a typical example of his anecdotal quality in this paragraph about the actor Henry:

Henry was the only actor in America who kept a carriage. It was in the form of a coach, but very small, just sufficient to carry himself and wife to the theatre, and it was drawn by one horse and driven by a black boy. Aware of the jealousy towards players, and that it would be said he *kept a coach,* he had caused to be painted on the doors, in the manner of those coats of arms which the aristocracy of Europe display, *two crutches* in heraldic fashion, with the motto, *"This or these."* [37]

The work by Dunlap, as chronicler of both theater and art in America, was done in his last years after he had met virtual defeat in both these

[36] Samuel Isham, *History of American Painting* (New York, 1905), pp. 72, 73.
[37] *History of the American Theatre*, p. 79.

branches of pioneer effort. In his *History of the Rise and Progress of the Arts of Design in the United States,* published two years after his history of the theater, he traced the lives of many early artists, painters, miniaturists, engravers, and teachers of art. He recounted with frankness his own failures. In a tone of sadness he wrote:

> In my history of the American Theatre I believe I proved to my reader's satisfaction that I was not qualified to be a director of a play-house and I now intend to show the causes that, at the age of twenty-three, and after a long residence in London, left me ignorant of anatomy, perspective, drawing and coloring, and returned me home a most incapable painter.

He abandoned painting for many years, while he was writing and presenting plays. After his first severe downfall of favor and loss of income as manager, in 1805, he turned to miniature-painting as a resource. Visiting various cities, he secured orders for miniatures from some people of note, like Josiah Quincy, David Humphreys, Mrs. Darley, James Fennell, and others. Through the assistance of Malbone, the artist, he was instructed in the application of colors and the preparation of ivory. To extend his efforts in art, he went to Philadelphia, Baltimore, and Norfolk, securing commissions for portraits and miniatures, and painting some landscapes. His family was living at this time in his mother's home in Perth Amboy.

For a few years, from about 1807 to 1812, he assumed charge of a theater in New York for his friend the actor T. Apthorp Cooper. As he was engaged on a salary, this experience proved to be more profitable than the earlier management. He moved his family to New York, where they lived on Beekman Street, and he became closely associated with men of affairs and letters in the two clubs of the day, the Drone and the Friendly. During this time he prepared and wrote portions of his memoirs of the actor George Fred Cooke and the novelist Charles Brockden Brown.[38] Another position, with a definite salary affixed, was obtained for him through friends, in 1814, when he was appointed assistant paymaster of the militia of New York. He held this place for three years. Apparently he had difficulty in keeping his accounts accurate, for he was charged with defalcation to the extent of a thousand dollars. A careful examination of his books, etc., revealed the gratifying fact that the mistake was

---

[38] *Memoirs of George Fred Cooke, Esq., Late of the Theatre Royal, Covent Garden; by William Dunlap* (London, 1813; 2 vols.). *The Life of Charles Brockden Brown, together with Selections from the Rarest of his Printed Works, from his Original Letters, and from his Manuscripts Before Unpublished. By William Dunlap* (Philadelphia, 1815; 2 vols.).

accidental and the actual deficit was only one dollar.

The last twenty years of his life were largely given to painting and exhibiting pictures. Thus he gained an income to meet his actual needs. But he was not satisfied with his work, and realized that it would have only temporary appreciation. In the autumn of 1819 he went to Norfolk, where he remained six months. Taking up the story of his life, as found in the last two volumes of manuscript journals in the New York Historical Society, we find many revelations of interest and pathos. He secured commissions for paintings in Norfolk, largely portraits, to the amount of three hundred and fifteen dollars. The first part of his sojourn was alone; but later his wife joined him. The promises of the first weeks failed to be redeemed in some cases. To his journal, March 21, 1820, he confided:

> It is now long since I have begun a picture & I look anxiously to the close of my stay here. I have many visitors, much praise & flattery, and I have been constantly employ'd, but after all shall arrive in N. Y. perhaps as poor as I left it. I have supported myself & my family, & perhaps open'd a source of support (or more) for the future. I ought to be thankful. I am, altho' my spirits sink sometimes.

While in Norfolk he sketched and later painted a picture, "Christ Rejected," which

became very popular as an exhibit. It was sent
on exhibition to Boston, Portland, and elsewhere
in New England, and as far west as Ohio. In
Portland alone the returns financially were three
hundred dollars in two weeks; in New York it
remained fourteen weeks on exhibition and
aggregated six hundred and fifty dollars. Ministers urged their parishioners to see the painting,
and, in spite of marked defects in drawing and
color, it was widely heralded. While in Norfolk, Dunlap wrote, and had printed, a descriptive
pamphlet outlining the characters and motif of
the picture.[39] He acknowledged his indebtedness
to West's painting of the same subject, but said:
"It is scarcely within the limits of possibility, certainly not of probability, that Mr. West's Picture
should ever be seen in the western world." What
seemed to him improbable, however, happened
in a short time; West's painting was sent to
America on exhibition, in charge of his son, and
Dunlap was compelled to make some modifica-
tions in his painting, where the figures resembled
his model too closely.

The success with this religious subject induced
him to paint others—"Christ Bearing the Cross"

[39] *Descriptive Pamphlet of Dunlap's Painting of Christ
Rejected* (Norfolk, no date). See full title in the Bibliography, p. 21.

and "Death on the Pale Horse." [40] According to a descriptive pamphlet printed in Boston after the death of Dunlap, the painting of "Death on the Pale Horse, or Opening of the First Four Seals," reached a high-water mark of popularity and an offer of ten thousand dollars was refused for the painting.[41] Possibly this refers to West's painting of the same subject. "A Child Returning from School" and "The Historic Muse," were painted about the same time, while Dunlap was executing a commission for portraits in Orwell, Vermont.

One who seeks information about Dunlap, the painter, is beset with discouragements. In view of the vast amount of work which he accomplished with his brush and pencil, it is surprising how little can now be traced. On the other hand, his paintings were curios rather than works of art in the true meaning; yet they gained a degree of popularity which would naturally insure them remembrance until the present time. Looking over the catalogues of annual exhibitions of the National Academy of Design, from 1826 to 1836, one finds Dunlap's name attached to scores of

[40] The first was painted in 1824, the latter in 1828. For detailed study, see Isham, *History of American Painting* (New York, 1905), pp. 186-201.

[41] *Descriptive Pamphlet of Painting of Death on the Pale Horse* (Boston, 1840).

paintings of varied kinds; very few of these can now be traced.[42] Among the portraits mentioned on these lists are those of Governor George Clinton, Anthony Bleecker, General P. B. Porter, Bishop Channing Moore, of Virginia, and George P. Morris. Subjects of religious and allegorical paintings by Dunlap, exhibited during these years, include "Cupid Sleeping," "Scene from Cooper's *The Spy*," "Barabbas and the Thieves," "Our Saviour and Mary Magdalene in the Garden," "Richard and Kenneth from Scott's *The Talisman*." In March, 1905, there were sold in Philadelphia a collection of miniatures on ivory and some sketches in oil and water-color by Dunlap. The latter were landscapes in New York, New Jersey, and Philadelphia. There were sixteen miniatures, only four of which could be surely recognized—Mrs. Wignell, Mrs. Darley, James Fennell, and the artist's miniature of himself.[43]

As the years passed, Dunlap was weakened by sickness and more financial reverses. Two benefits were arranged for him—one by his friends among actors and playwrights, the other by his colleagues among artists. The first was in Feb-

[42]Dunlap was the organizer as well as the beneficiary of this academy; see Isham, *op. cit.*, chap. 10.

[43] An attractive catalogue of this sale was compiled by Stan V. Henkels.

ruary, 1833, although Dunlap recorded the month as March; and the sum of twenty-five hundred dollars was netted for his benefit. For this occasion a poem was written by George P. Morris.[44] The second benefit was five years later—a loan exhibition, known as the Dunlap Exhibition, in November, 1838. Paintings were loaned by Trumbull, Cole, Durand, Jarvis, Copley, and the following by Dunlap: "Calvary," "The Historic Muse," "A Child Returning from School," "Scene from *The Spy*," and various portraits. In announcing this exhibition and soliciting the patronage of the public, G. C. Verplanck emphasized its purpose as a benefit to our

estimable fellow-citizen, MR. DUNLAP, who is well known to you, as having rendered great and lasting services to art, history and literature of our state and country. In the decline of an honourable life, devoted mainly to these objects on which he still exerts his remaining strength with unimpaired zeal and patriotism, he finds his old age, which has so many claims to the respect and gratitude of his fellow-citizens, harassed by ill-health and straitened circumstances.[45]

The last volume of Dunlap's manuscript journal, in the New York Historical Society—

[44] This poem is included in *Occasional Addresses*, edited by Laurence Hutton and William Carey (published by the Dunlap Society, 1890), pp. 51–53.

[45] A flattering estimate of Dunlap's ability was in a letter from Verplanck in *The Talisman*, 1829.

evidently the last he ever wrote—is covered with marbled paper and shows, in the feebleness of handwriting, the illness which was upon him. He was ambitious and industrious to the last, however, anxious to finish the histories of New York, and also the history of the progress of art in this country. A few scattered extracts from the journal will be most fitting here:

June 26th, 1833. It will be seen by the last vol. that I was very busy in Phila., that I was not at ease as to health, that I saw many persons to collect materials for my history of the Fine Arts in America, yet I left much undone. This day I sit down again in New York to continue my labours & enjoy the blessings conferred upon me & be thankful.

July 10th, 1833. See Durand & engage him to engrave my portrait for the Hist. of the Arts.

July 20th, 1833. My work appeared to bring on stricture. Is it the effect of natural decay? Must I refrain from this, so delightful to me? Read Gibbon's Rome.

August 26th, 1833. Begun 2 portraits. Met Paulding & Cooper. Bank acc't $123. [Notes on books read for his history and mention of increasing illness.]

Thursday, April 3rd, 1834. [After an operation.] I sincerely believed it to be my duty & the will of God that I should undergo this operation & to his will I hope in all things to resign myself with thanks & gratitude. Read a little & think a little relatively to my Hist. of Art.

In addition to these histories of the theater and of art, Dunlap wrote, during the last years, a school history of New York,[46] in dialogue, and a *History of the New Netherlands,* which appeared almost simultaneously with his death.

Few men were more gracious and generous than Dunlap. It often seems, in reading his life, that he was the victim of the schemes and knavery of others, because of his very kindliness and credulity. An anecdote told by Dr. John Francis illustrates this trait.[47] A French refugee, Dr. Pierre Michaux, had published a tract, with a Latin title, on some surgical subject. In spite of its distorted facts, it attracted much attention. Dr. Wright Post, an eminent but irascible physician, begged Dunlap to write a caricature of the French doctor and his tract. Ready to please his friends and happy to be chosen, Dunlap wrote a satire which was used as an after-piece at the John Street Theater. It was called *Fractura Minimi Digiti.* Michaux, hearing of the caricature, saw it at the theater, and was so exasperated at its mimicry of his features and manners that he attacked Dunlap on the street, beating him so severely that the playwright was ill for several days.

Dunlap's work in both art and drama was

[46] *A History of New York for Schools* (New York, 1837. 2 vols., 16mo). *History of the New Netherlands,* etc. (New York, 1839; 2 vols., 8vo).

[47] John W. Francis, *Old New York,* 1866, pp. 66-8.

ephemeral, judged by modern standards. He
wrote plays rapidly to catch the favor of the hour,
and they were soon forgotten. He lost health
and patrimony in a seemingly futile effort to elevate the theater and cultivate a taste for native
talent. He gave fitful attention to art, in his
youth, gaining only mediocre skill which yielded
him a source of income for his later years. Turn-
ing from an estimate of his personal achievement
to his influence on American drama and art, we
must admit that Dunlap should be honored. His
ideals were rudely treated in the struggle of life,
but he never lost his faith in them nor in his
countrymen. He believed that later workers
would create something worthy, in place of his
own defective products.

CHARLES BROCKDEN BROWN AND
PIONEERS IN FICTION

CHARLES BROCKDEN BROWN.

From a miniature painted by William Dunlap, 1806, engraved
by J. B. Forrest; reproduced from *National Portrait Gallery of
Distinguished Americans*, 1835.

# VIII

## CHARLES BROCKDEN BROWN AND
## PIONEERS IN FICTION

In the history of the world's literature, fiction,
in its modern meaning, has been one of the latest
forms of development. For various reasons, the
novelist came late in America. A realization of
the true relation of man to his neighbors and his
surroundings must precede the creation of the
novel. This grasp of conditions, and the ability
to portray them in vivid narrative, did not exist
in America until the stability of the nation had
been assured. Slowly the colonists had emerged
from repression, and indifference to nature,
beauty, art, until they seemed to have a new
appreciation of such influences. Then this
awakening was retarded by the struggle for freedom. War and its issues were the themes which
commended themselves to the patriot-writers.
When independence had been won, unity was not
yet established, and literature took the forms of
argumentation and satire to secure national harmony and a stable government. Then followed
a period of bombast, an ambition to be original.
Prodigal pens did not wait for training, but wrote
with a braggadocio which took the place of art.

279

Under such conditions, the first products of imaginative type were generally in meter—odes and a few bizarre dramas already mentioned. The beginnings of a national fiction were still delayed. In 1789 Isaiah Thomas printed, at his Boston shop, a novel, *The Power of Sympathy; or, the Triumph of Nature founded in Truth."* This was without name of author, but in the copy at the American Antiquarian Society there is a pencil note, after the title, "by Mrs. Sarah Wentworth (Apthorp) Morton." Like other early tales of this period both in England and in America, this was a story of seduction and deceit, with a pronounced moral. The author dedicated the two tiny volumes—

To the Young Ladies, of United Columbia. These Volumes, Intended to represent the specious Causes and to expose the fatal Consequences of Seduction; To inspire the Female Mind with a Principle of Self Complacency, and to Promote the Economy of Human Life, are Inscribed, with Esteem and Sincerity, By their Friend and Humble Servant.

The Author. Boston. January, 1789.

The tale is in the form of letters from the young women and men introduced—Harrington, Worthy, Harriot, and Myra. A sample of the sentimental style of this pioneer effort at fiction follows:

You may now felicitate me—I have had an interview with the charmer I informed you of. . . . . Her mien is elegant—her disposition inclining to the melancholy, and yet her temper is affable, and her manners easy.  And as I poured my tender vows into the heart of my beloved, a crimson drop stole across her cheek, and thus I construe it in my own favour, as the sweet messenger of hope.[1]

The following year appeared *Charlotte Temple,* published in England in 1790, and four years later in America.  Its author, Mrs. Susanna Rowson, daughter of a British naval officer, had been encouraged to write her impressions of America.  Some of these she had interwoven in her earlier novels, *Victoria* and *The Inquisitor;* but they had meager interest to Americans when compared with the later tear-inciting tale of brass buttons, American war-scenes, and feminine tragedy and sensibility in *Charlotte Temple.*  This maintained a wonderful hold upon the readers of its own and the next generation.[2]

Royall Tyler and Hugh Henry Brackenridge wrote some fiction as well as drama.  Their narratives, *The Algerine Captive* and *Modern Chivalry,*

[1] *The Power of Sympathy; or, the TRIUMPH of NATURE founded in TRUTH.  2 vols.  Printed at Boston, by Isaiah Thomas and Company.  Sold at their Bookstore, No. 45 Newbury Street, and at said Thomas's Bookstore in WORCESTER* (1789), pp. 7–9.

[2] *Charlotte Temple* (London, 1790; New York, 1794).  It has recently been reprinted.  Several editions appeared earlier.  The grave of the heroine is often searched for by tourists in Trinity Churchyard, New York.

seem slow reading to the student today, but they aroused enthusiasm at the time of their appearance, and are still of interest as revelations of the tastes and customs of the period which they portray. Both were of the adventurous type, mingling romance with heavy humor.[3]

During the last years of the eighteenth century several romances were written in England and on the continent, of the sentimental, fantastic kind, like Lewis' *The Monk*, Mrs. Radcliffe's *The Mysteries of Udolpho*, and Godwin's *Caleb Williams*. These novels were published in 1794, and became models for initial efforts in American fiction of the early nineteenth century. While authors advocated originality, and often attempted to achieve it, the earliest Americal novels were really adaptations of English models. The reflex influence of Puritanism was shown in a few stories of this time, fittingly called "melodramatic piety," as Caroline Warren's *The Gamesters; or, The Ruins of Innocence,* and *The Power of Sympathy,* outlined above.

Charles Brockden Brown began his work, as the first American who chose fiction as a special field, at the meeting of the eighteenth and nine-

[3] *The Algerine Captive, or the Adventures of Doctor Updike Underhill, six years a prisoner among the Algerines* (Walpole, 1797) ; *Modern Chivalry, or Adventures of Captain John Farrago and Teague O'Regan, his Servant* (Philadelphia, 1792 ; 1796 ; 2 vols.).

teenth centuries.  His novels show the transitional
influences from romance to realism.  His adher-
ence to English models of his time, and also his
aim to be original in background, are expressed in
a sentence which he wrote after he had finished
his first novel, *Wieland,* in 1798:

> When a mental comparison is made between this
> and the mass of novels, I am inclined to be pleased with
> my own production.  But when the objects of comparison
> are changed, and I revolve the transcendant merits of
> Caleb Williams, my pleasure is diminished, and is pre-
> served from a total extinction only by the reflection that
> this performance is the first.[4]

The life of this first American novelist has
been told discursively, but inadequately as regards
vital information, by his friend, William Dunlap.
Unfortunately, the sources of the biographer's
material—many letters and journals—were not
liberally used by him, and may have perished with
the mass of his own literary remains.  Like the
pioneer painter, Benjamin West, Brown came
from Quaker stock, which seemed to scorn all
aesthetic delights; yet, in the sweet sanity and
peace of temperament which characterize this
sect there existed the best soil for fruitage of
the imagination.  Brown, however, had other
inheritance which gave him strong emotions and

[4] William Dunlap, *Life of Charles Brockden Brown* (1815),
Vol. I, p. 107.

fancies; for in his veins Norman blood mingled with that of England.

His uncle, from whom he derived his middle name, held positions of honor in early Philadelphian history. He was "the skilful conveyancer and great scrivener" who framed the articles of agreement for the Philadelphia Library Company, instituted by Franklin, in 1731. The family story regarding this uncle's youth, and his emigration to America, was a favorite with his nephew, and is of general interest. When he was a lad studying law in England, he was apprenticed to a celebrated barrister who was at odds with the government of Charles II. Accidentally, the apprentice was hidden in the room where his employer and some friends were discussing a plot against the government. When the youth was discovered, various suggestions were made regarding his fate; for he could not be left at liberty with such a weighty secret. To save him from death, his employer testified that he was of "too feeble a mind" to cause any injury to them by his knowledge, but he agreed that the boy, for safety, should be shipped to the American colonies.

Our pioneer novelist was born in Philadelphia, January, 1771, probably at 117 South Second Street; this was his father's home for many years. He was weak physically, but studious at a very early age. According to family tradition, he could be left alone for hours on the floor at home, even as a baby, if he were provided with a book. One of the chief delights of his childhood was to climb upon the chairs and tables and study the few maps upon the walls. At ten years he showed an unusual maturity of mind. An incident is told to illustrate this, which suggests a touch of priggishness in him. A visitor had aroused his resentment by calling him "boy," and questioning his statements of facts. The child replied: "Why does he call me boy? Does he not know that it is neither size nor age, but understanding that makes the man? I could ask him an hundred questions none of which he could answer." [5]

Robert Proud was a famous schoolmaster of Philadelphia, as well as its local historian. To his school young Brown was sent to exert his already strained mind and nerves by close application to classic texts. Fortunately, the schoolmaster had an understanding, rare for that day, of wholesome educational methods. He realized the needs of his pupil, and insisted that he should often leave his books and go into the woods, where nature would be both a doctor and a teacher. Although to the boy the walks often proved a time for lonely, gloomy fancies, yet he

[5] Dunlap's *Life of Brown*, Vol. I, pp. 12, 13. Jared Sparks, *A Library of American Biography*, New York, 1839. Vol. I, pp. 122; article on Brown by William H. Prescott.

gained impressions of fine scenery which were used afterward in his writing.

He was early convinced that he would be an author, and began with imitations of Homer and Virgil, Ossian and Milton. American history next attracted him, and he wrote some epics to celebrate the discovery of America and the deeds of his heroes, Cortez and Pizarro. He did not venture, at first, to break through all custom and distress his family by the choice of literature as a profession; so he followed the example of his father and three brothers, and studied law. Meanwhile he had yearnings for literature, spent much of his time in spinning fancies and literary hopes, and contributed some verses and essays to local journals. He told, with disgust, of the fate of a "Poetical Address to Franklin," which had been sent to an Edentown newspaper:

The blundering printer from his zeal or his ignorance, or perhaps from both, substituted 'he name of Washington for that of Franklin. Washington, therefore, stands arrayed in awkward colours. Philosophy smiles to behold her darling son; she turns with horror and disgust from those who have won the laurel of victory in the field of battle to this her favorite candidate who had never participated in such bloody glory and whose fame was derived from the conquest of philosophy alone.[6]

The most absurd qualities were thus attributed to

[6] William Dunlap, *Life of Charles Brockden Brown* (New York, 1815), Vol. I, p. 17, 18.

Washington, until the poem became an unintelligible farce, and was even regarded by some readers as an intentional insult. More successful was the young author in the series of essays called "The Rhapsodist," which began in the *Columbian Magazine* in April, 1789.

The pleasure which Brown found in writing, and in the companionship of his friends of literary tastes, especially William Wilkinson and Dr. Elihu Smith,[7] induced him to give up law and devote himself exclusively to literature. The effect of this decision upon his family and acquaintances may be realized from a comment of a local historian, after the novelist's death:

Mr. Brown had received an education which qualified him for the profession which secured wealth free from the risks of commerce,—the profession, from which proceeded our statesmen, legislators, and rulers;—yet he preferred the toilsome occupation of book-making, from the pure love of literature and a benevolent desire to benefit his fellow-creatures.[8]

The first year after Brown gave up the law for literature he spent largely in New York,

[7] The death of Wilkinson in early manhood was a great grief to Brown. Dr. Elihu Smith was at this time studying medicine in Philadelphia. With another friend, William Johnson, a lawyer, he made a home in New York, to which Brown came for a part of the year 1797.

[8] See Henry Simpson, *Eminent Philadelphians* (Philadelphia, 1859).

passing some of the time with Dr. Smith, and also becoming an inmate of the home of William Dunlap. Evidence of the latter fact has been found in a manuscript letter from Brown to Dunlap in the possession of the Historical Society of Pennsylvania, which is here given by permission. It was written after Brown's return to Philadelphia. The morose and extravagant tone of self-depreciation was characteristic of the writer:

Philadelphia, Jan'y 1, 1798.
To William Dunlap, Care of Dunlap & Judah, Pearl St., New York.

It is nearly twelve months since I parted from you. I believe I have not written to you nor you written to me since. How shall I account for your silence? The task is an easy one. I was not an object of sufficient importance to justify the trouble. My infirmities & follies were too rooted for you to hope their cure. Admonition & remonstrance under your own hand, would be superfluous to this end. Hence your habitual reserve & silence of the pen suffered no interruption on my account. I lived with you six months. During that time you, no doubt, scrutinized my conduct & character with accuracy. You must have formed some conclusions respecting me, but you thought proper to be silent respecting them. You weighed the opposite advantages of communication & reserve. You decided in favour of the latter. I revere your rectitude, my friend, in as great a degree as I detest my own imbecility: but it is allowable for me to question the propriety of your decision.

Communication, it appears to me, was your duty. Whatever was my depravity, it did not sink me below deserving a mere verbal effort for my restoration. Had I led the way you would have followed. There needed only an introduction of the topic by me. Had I mentioned my opinion of your incommunicative temper & importuned you for a knowledge of your sentiments, the barrier would have been removed. It is true I was criminal in failing to employ this means. Were you exempt from blame in making these means necessary? Think of this, my friend, if I may still call you by that name. Surely, all esteem for me has not perished in your bosom. . . . .

I think upon the life of last winter with self-loathing almost insupportable. Alas! my friend, few consolations of a self-approving mind have fallen to my lot. . . . . I am sometimes apt to think that few human beings have drunk so deeply of the cup of self-abhorrence as I have. . . . . Whether it will end but with my life I know not.

I have written to Elihu and informed him of the transactions of the last few months. You will of course be made acquainted with them. I know not whether your engagements have allowed you to prosecute any similar undertaking. I have longed for a knowledge of your views & situation. I am not entitled to know this but by second hand. I make no demands upon you. As I am, you despise me. I shall die, as I have lived, a victim to perverse and incurable habits. My progress in knowledge has enlightened my judgment, without adding to my power.

I have done nothing to deserve the esteem of your wife. I do not therefore expect it. That is no reason which [sic] I should refuse her my respect. She is in the highest degree entitled to it; present it therefore to her.

C. B. Brown.

In a note, signed "W. Dunlap," below this

letter, is the comment: "So at certain moments could think & write one of the purest & best beloved of men." [9] Such a letter, and others from which we shall quote, are of great assistance in interpreting the strange haunting fancies and moods which assailed Brown as novelist.

Dr. Elihu Smith exerted much influence in giving poise to the emotions of Brown, and in urging him to definite literary work. The two men were contrasts in many ways. The physician was absolutely sane and practical, and his geniality has passed into many literary records. At his apartments in Pine Street the Friendly Club met—a band of young lawyers, physicians, and authors. Literature was becoming fashionable, but the media for its expression were few. Clubs in various centers started magazines, which were generally short-lived, but served their purpose as a means of expression for the members. Such was the aim of the familiar *Medical Repository,* established in 1794 by Dr. Smith and two other physicians. By contact with such patient, wise minds, Brown found an incentive to write both essays and fiction.

Yellow fever was a scourge in America during the last decade of the eighteenth century.

---

[9] A note in Dunlap's manuscript journal, April 12, 1798, says that he was then visiting Brown in Philadelphia at 119 South Second Street.

With other portents of evil, it increased the emotional ferment which was shown in many directions. This disease had raged in Philadelphia in 1793; its scenes of devastation furnished Brown with the germ for his novel *Arthur Mervyn*. His family left the city to escape contagion. When the plague attacked New York in 1798, Brown was there with his friend, Dr. Elihu Smith. His brothers urged him to return to Philadelphia, but he refused to leave his friend. They adopted sanitary safeguards and faced the danger. A strange appeal came to their humanity, and proved a fatal risk. Among the friends who had been in their circle in New York for a year was Dr. Joseph Scandella. Just as he was about to leave for Italy, he learned that two of his compatriots, a young girl and her mother, were ill and in want in Philadelphia. He went to their aid, remained until both had died of yellow fever, and then returned to New York, to find that he could not secure lodging in any inn, as he was already showing signs of the disease. Dr. Smith took this friend to his own home, hoping to cure him and not become infected; but the fever attacked both Dr. Smith and Brown. The latter recovered, but found that both the physicians had died. This loss of friendship was an overwhelming grief to Brown, but he rallied his mental powers and tried to write something worthy of his friend who had been such an inspiration. The home of William Dunlap, at Perth Amboy, again became his residence for a brief time. Afterward he returned to Philadelphia.

Before the death of Dr. Smith, Brown had written a dialogue-essay, "The Rights of Women," which was printed in book-form, under the title *Alcuin*.[10] The "Advertisement" in the front of the book is dated March, 1787, and is signed by "E. H. Smith," who states that the material was "put in his hands for publication by a friend." The argument of *Alcuin* was in behalf of more justice for women, equal suffrage, and better education. The woman maintained that, if the intelligence of men was superior to that of women, it was only a proof "in how mournful a degree that capacity has been neglected or perverted." In the same magazine had appeared, two months earlier and unsigned, "The Man at Home"—a series of rhapsodic musings. In June of the same year the first chapters of *Arthur Mervyn; or, Memoirs of the Year 1793*, were printed in this journal, although the book was not finished and published until the next year.

Such scattering publications in magazines pre-

[10] *Alcuin: A Dialogue* (New York, 1798 ; 77 pages). This was first printed as "The Rights of Women" in the *Weekly Magazine of Original Essays, Fugitive Pieces and Interesting Intelligence*, Vol. I, 1798 (Philadelphia).

faced the printing of his first book in fiction.  On the cover of this *Weekly Magazine* were solicited "Proposals for the publication of a novel, *Sky Walk, or the Man Unknown to Himself*." Brown, who was the author of this story, accepted the most promising of the proposals—namely, that which bore the larger share of the expense—and the publication began.  When the book was nearly completed in press, the printer died.  His executors refused to finish the work, or to sell the sheets at any reasonable price; so the effort was useless for the time.  A reference in the manuscript journal of Dunlap, April 11, 1798, suggests that this first, unfinished novel contained the germ, at least, of Brown's later story *Edgar Huntley,* Dunlap wrote in his journal: "Call on Brown who goes with me to bookseller's & gives me some account of his 'Sky Walk,' he says it is founded on Somnambulism."

More information of a personal nature about Brown, and his romantic interests during this year, is furnished in extracts from Dunlap's manuscript journals.  The first is dated "May 1st; Call with Smith & my wife to see Miss Potts, C. B. B.'s wished-for." Again: "May 3rd; Miss Potts drinks tea with us." For some reason, in spite of the hospitality of his friends and his own ardor of temperament, Brown did not secure his "wished-for" as his wife. Possibly the gloom of spirit which followed during the next few months, and which was indicated in the letter to Dunlap already quoted, was enhanced by this disappointment.

If success be gauged by the praise of a few friends, and by sufficient sale of books to pay the expenses of their publication, then Brown was successful during the next two years; for there issued from the press four volumes of fiction in 1798 and 1799. *Wieland; or, The Transformation,* the first to appear, has remained in memory as Brown's most representative work in fiction. It contained unquestioned evidence of originality and imaginative skill; but his later, rapidly published novels failed to fulfil the promise of this first book. *Wieland* is a pot-pourri of strange sensations, isolated scenes of tragic strength, bits of fine description, and labored, discursive style. It would be hard to find a story with more fantastic, incredible incidents, which the reader is supposed to accept as "supernaturalities," although it is not difficult to find simple explanation for many of the absurd devices of the novelist's imagination. There are serious dissertations upon a theory of self-combustion and the elixir of life; hypnotism and ventriloquism combine to make an interesting villain. The author is not willing, however, to let the reader accept the palpable explanation of the blighting influence, "the diabolical malice," of this character, Carwin. He seeks to wrap about him a veil of mystery and to introduce him in labored narration:

> One afternoon I was standing in the door of my house when I marked a person passing close to the edge of the bank that was in front. His gait was awkward and rustic. His form was ungainly and disproportioned. Shoulders broad and square, breast sunken, his head drooping, his body of uniform breadth, supported by long and lank legs, were the ingredients of his frame. His garb was not ill-adapted to such a figure. A slouched hat, tarnished by the weather, a coat of thick gray cloth, cut and wrought, as it seemed, by a country tailor, blue worsted stockings, and shoes fastened by thongs, and deeply discolored by dust, which brush had never disturbed, constituted his dress.[11]

Following this passage is a minute description of the impression made upon the woman by this passer-by, her surprise at his fascinating face, and especially the tremors which thrilled her at the sound of his voice as he asked for a drink of buttermilk from the dairy-maid: "When he uttered the words 'for sweet charity's sake,' I dropped the cloth which I held in my hand, my heart overflowed with sympathy, and my eyes with unbidden tears." Such florid emotionalism was largely typical of the writing of that period, but it found an extremist in Brown. A recent

[11] *Wieland, or the Transformation* (New York, 1798), chap. 6, pp. 58–60.

historian of American literature has said, with justice: "Brown frequently raised a super-structure of mystery on a basis ludicrously weak." [12]

The real plot of the story was based upon the hallucination of a father that he had received command, from supernatural sources, to murder his family. It is evident that this theme was suggested to him by an occurrence just before the tale was written. This fact is attested in two reviews of Brown's novels, especially of *Wieland*. *The American Review and Literary Journal*, which was edited in part by Brown, said in an extended notice of *Wieland:* "The principal incidents, however incredible and shocking, are founded on well authenticated facts, and sublime and tragical in the highest degree." [13] A tragedy similar in general outlines to that narrated by Brown occurred in New York the year before *Wieland* was published. As late as 1819, in a survey of Brown's work in the *North American Review*,[14] the critic commended the novelist's choice of American scenes and added: "Some-times the author takes advantage of a recent event

[12] Henry A. Beers, *Initial Studies in American Letters*, New York, 1891, p. 65.

[13] *American Review and Literary Journal* (New York, 1801), Vol. I. See also *New York Weekly Magazine*, Vol. II, pp. 20-28, for the actual facts of such tragedy.

[14] *North American Review*, June, 1819, Vol. IX, pp. 58-64.

amongst ourselves, as in Wieland, which is too shocking to receive any aid from exaggeration or to lose any interest from its notoriety."

Within a few months after the first novel was issued the second appeared, *Ormond, or The Secret Witness*. The villain, who gave his name to the title, was clearly modeled after William Godwin's Falkland in *Caleb Williams*. In truth, the two novels are not dissimilar in plan and effect. The theme of seduction was treated awkwardly, amid the peaceful environment of Philadelphia. The character of Constantia Dudley, however, is fairly well drawn; she is superior to his other women. She was too prone to "ardent meditation," but through her words Brown expressed some sensible ideas on women's education.[15] It was this character of Constantia, and the novel in which she was outlined, that especially "delighted and deeply affected" Shelley, when, under the spell of Godwin's influence, he reveled in tales of gruesomeness amid surroundings of real life.[16]

In this second novel there are some sentences descriptive of the yellow fever in Philadelphia, but the third in time, *Arthur Mervyn; or, Memoirs of the Year 1793*, owed its chief interest to a

[15] *Ormond, or The Secret Witness* (New York, 1798), pp. 31, 32.

[16] Edward Dowden, *Life of Shelley* (London, 1886), Vol. I, pp. 472, 473.

dramatic portrayal of this fateful year in Philadelphia.   It was the most ambitious of all his
stories, and at the same time the most involved
and prolix.   In some descriptive passages the
realism is so strong that it stirs the feelings of a
reader today, in spite of his recognition that the
novel is a good example of sensationalism.   In
criticism, discriminating and appreciative, W. P.
Trent has expressd the true attitude of a reader to
this special novel and the general estimate of
Brown in fiction:

It is impossible to surrender one's self to the illusion
that such adventures could have happened in Brown's
prim birthplace; but it is easy under the influence of
his strong imagination to walk the deserted streets of
the plague-stricken city and to enter its forbidding houses
tenanted by the dying and the dead.   If this be true
today, it seems hardly fair to sneer at the men and
women who a century ago regarded Brown as a great
and moving writer.   His models were their standards, and
they were right in perceiving that he measured well up
to the Godwins and the Radcliffes.   They had not progressed
far enough to demand a sense of humor, an artistic order-
ing of material, susceptibility to the charms of nature, and
a subtle psychological analysis.   They knew that their
emotions had been deeply stirred, and that in some particulars at least the life around them had been faithfully
set down.[17]

Doubtless the fearful experiences of the fever,

[17] W. P. Trent, *A History of American Literature* (New
York, 1903), p. 211.

which had come upon Brown in New York, increased his imaginative pictures of the conditions in Philadelphia, although history has verified
many of his statements. His passages of narration have been compared fittingly with Defoe's
picture of the London plague. A selection may be
chosen to illustrate the crude, yet haunting,
portrayal:

. . . . In proportion as I drew near the city, the
tokens of its calamitous condition became more apparent. Every farm-house was filled with supernumerary
tenants; fugitives from home; and haunting the skirts of
the road, eager to detain every passenger with inquiries
after news. . . . . The market-place and each side of this
magnificent avenue were illuminated, as before, by lamps;
but between the verge of the Schuylkill and the heart of
the city, I met not more than a dozen figures; and these
were ghost-like, wrapped in cloaks from behind which they
cast upon me glances of wonder and suspicion; and, as I
approached, changed their course, to avoid touching me.
Their clothes were sprinkled with vinegar; and their nos-
trils defended from contagion by some powerful perfume.[18]

Then follows a description of the entrance of
the dread friend of the infected city—the slow,
stealthily-moving hearse:

The driver was seated on it. I stood still, to mark his
visage, and to observe the course which he proposed to
take. Presently, a coffin, borne by two men, issued from
the house. The driver was a negro but his companions

[18] *Arthur Mervyn; or, Memoirs of the Year 1793* (Philadelphia, 1799), chap. 15, pp. 143-45.

were white. Their features were marked by ferocious indifference to danger or pity.

One of them, as he assisted in thrusting the coffin into the cavity provided for it, said, "I'll be damned if I think the poor dog was quite dead. It wasn't the *fever* that ailed him, but the sight of the girl and her mother on the floor. I wonder how they all got into that room. What carried them there?"

The other surlily muttered, "Their legs to be sure."

"But what should they hug together in one room for?"

"To save us trouble to be sure."

"And I thank them with all my heart; but damn it, it wasn't right to put him in his coffin before the breath was fairly gone. I thought the last look he gave me, told me to stay a few minutes."

"Pshaw! He could not live. The sooner dead the better for him; as well as for us. Did you mark how he eyed us, when we carried away his wife and daughter? I never cried in my life, since I was knee-high, but curse me if I ever felt in better tune for the business than just then. Hey!" continued he, looking up and observing me standing a few paces distant, and listening to their discourse, "What's wanted? Anybody dead?"

Such a narrative of a tragic situation, although overdrawn and melodramatic, has a power which attracts and, also, repels. These low, callous grave-diggers, with their latent humanity, and the villain Welbeck, are depicted with a realism that is painful. During these years, chronicled in Brown's novels, there seemed to be an emotional ferment in many parts of America. Curiosity and semi-fear, not unlike the signs of childhood, assailed

the mind of the country. Contemporaneous with
the new interest in science among the educated
classes were the feverish speculations among the
ignorant about clairvoyance, somnambulism, ventriloquism, and other mysteries on the borderland
between fancy and reality. Quacks of all kinds
were ubiquitous, and credulity reigned. Such
evidences of mental whims and fears were reflected in embryonic drama and fiction. They
characterized many of the newspaper columns
that were satirized by the Hartford Wits in *The
Echo*.

As Brown introduced ventriloquism and speculations on the elixir of life into *Wieland,* so he
chose somnambulism for the germ-idea of his
fourth novel, *Edgar Huntley; or, Memoirs of
a Sleepwalker.*[19] There were also scenes of adventure here, especially of Clithero, sleep-walker
and grave-digger, and culminating in the en-
counter of the hero with a panther. This has
suggested Cooper's famous scene in *The Pioneers.*
In the preface to this fourth novel Brown emphasized his determination to depict American
scenery and foster native fiction:

> One merit the writer may at least claim;—that of
> calling forth the passions and engaging the sympathy of
> the reader by means hitherto unemployed by preceding

[19] *Edgar Huntley; or, Memoirs of a Sleepwalker* (Philadelphia, 1799, 1800).

authors. Puerile superstition and exploded manners, Gothic castles and chimeras, are the materials usually employed for this end. The incidents of Indian hostility, and the perils of the Western wilderness, are far more suitable; and for a native of America to overlook these would admit of no apology.

Brown and Cooper have been compared as painters of Indian character, the claims of Brown being based upon certain scenes in *Edgar Huntley*. Brown overlooked the nobler qualities poetized by Philip Freneau. He portrayed the Indian as cruel and malign, and used him as a means of increasing the elements of horror in his story. Cooper, on the other hand, idealized the Indian type, emphasizing the more romantic traits. These three early authors, Freneau, Brown, and Cooper, portrayed diverse qualities of the Indian and, in their totality, revealed the red man as known to the pioneer settlers, when the Indian still lived on the borders of civilization, and his haunts and habits were familiar.

The wildly incredible adventures of his hero, Edgar Huntley, in the mountain districts of eastern Pennsylvania aroused criticism as well as interest among readers. Brown realized the justice of the former, and wrote to his brother James:

Your remarks upon the gloominess and out-of-nature incidents of "Huntley," if they be not just in their full extent, are doubtless such as some readers will make, which alone is sufficient reason for dropping the doleful tone and assuming a cheerful one, or at least, substituting moral causes and daily incidents in place of the prodigious and the singular. I shall hereafter fall into that strain.

To carry out this intention, he abandoned weird and adventuresome incidents, and adopted a form of tame sentimentality in his last two novels, *Clara Howard* and *Jane Talbot*.[20] The same plot, based upon a lost child and mistaken identity, and some of the same characters were introduced into both *Edgar Huntley* and *Clara Howard*. The heroine, of the latter, Mary Wilmot, supporting herself and her brother by her needle, was a familiar type of womanhood in that day. The letters of Jane Talbot and Henry Colden make a weak love-story.

In *Edgar Huntley* are two sentences worth quoting, for they seem to express the author's own defects in mental poise and emotional restraint:

My judgment was for the time, sunk into imbecility and confusion! . . . . Thus I have told thee a bloody and disastrous tale: when thou reflectest on the mildness of my habits, my antipathy to scenes of violence and bloodshed, my unacquaintance with the use of fire-arms, and the motives of a soldier, thou wilt scarcely allow credit to my story.[21]

[20] *Clara Howard; or, The Enthusiasm of Love* (Philadelphia, 1801); *Jane Talbot* (Philadelphia, New York, London, 1801).

[21] *Edgar Huntley*, Vol. I, p. 210; Vol. II, p. 207.

Upon these six novels rests the reputation of Charles Brockden Brown as a novelist. He failed to meet the requirements of fiction of a high order; he created only a few strong characters; he was discursive and stilted in diction. As an example of the last fault, we recall the sentence on the heroine of *Ormond:* "Constantia enjoyed, in their full extent, the felicities of health and self-approbation." [22] In extenuation, we must remember that these novels were written when Brown was a young man—for he was only thirty when the last appeared; that he wrote with fatal rapidity; and that he lacked the wisdom of rejection and the aid of critical advice. In his mature life he repented, too mournfully, of these early novels, and repressed the fancies with which his imagination was stored. Without question, his mind and imagination could produce effective scenes. The author's temperament, especially shown in his youth and early manhood, and his proneness to attacks of melancholy and gruesome fancies, explain largely the characteristics of his fiction. To these individual traits must be added the fashion of the day in literature, and his at-

[22] *Ormond, or The Secret Witness,* p. 32. Mary Shelley commented on *Jane Talbot* as a "very stupid book," etc; see Edward Dowden's *Life of Shelley* (London, 1886), Vol. I, pp. 472, 473.

tempts to follow the English imaginative writers who were favorites of the hour.

Brown entered the field of fiction with diffidence and fear of censure from Americans whom he esteemed; for this form of literature was then often condemned as immoral, or too frivolous to be read. In the *Jefferson Papers,* at the Library of Congress, there is an interesting letter from Brown to Thomas Jefferson, asking his acceptance of *Wieland,* and explaining, with tiresome verbosity, the reasons why he ventured to write a novel, and to present it to the statesman, whom he much admired. By permission, I quote extracts here from the letter:

After some hesitation, a stranger to the person, though not to the character of Thomas Jefferson, ventures to intreat his acceptance of the volume by which this is accompanied. . . . . I am conscious, however, that this form of composition may be regarded by you with indifference and contempt, that social & intellectual theories, that the history of facts in the processes of nature & the operations of government may appear to you the only laudable pursuits: that fictitious narratives, in their own nature, or in the manner in which they have been hitherto conducted, may be thought not to deserve notice, & that, consequently, whatever may be the merit of my book as a fiction yet it is to be condemn'd because it is a fiction.

I need not say that my own opinions are different. I am therefore obliged to hope that an artful display of incidents, the powerful delineation of characters & the train of eloquent & judicious reasoning which may be

combined in a fictitious work will be regarded by Thomas
Jefferson with as much respect as they are regarded by
me. . . . .

No man holds a performance which he has deliberately
offered to the world in contempt: but, if he be a man of
candour & discernment, his favourable judgment of his
own work will always be diffidence and fluctuation. I
confess I foster the hope that Mr. Jefferson will be induced to open the book that is here offered him: that
when he has begun it, he will find himself prompted to
continue & that he will not think the time employ'd upon it
tediously or uselessly consumed.

With *more* than this I dare not flatter myself. That he
will be pleased in any uncommon degree & that, by his
recommendation, he will contribute to diffuse the knowledge of its author, & faciliate a favorable reception to
future performances, is a benefit far beyond the expectations, though certainly, the object of the fondest wishes of
Charles B. Brown.[23]

One who reads this letter by Brown is naturally curious to know what reception the letter and
book won from Jefferson. His answer was brief,
noncommittal in a way, yet promising some
degree of appreciation. The answer, however,
was delayed until Jefferson's return to Philadelphia, and was dated January 15, 1800—more than
a year after Brown's letter.

I receiv'd on my arrival here some days ago the copy
of the book you were so kind as to send me together with
your letter, for which be pleased to accept my thanks.

<hr>

[23] *Jefferson Papers*, Series II, Vol. V, No. 46. The letter is
dated December 25, 1798 (45 Pine Street, New York).

As soon as I am in a situation to admit it (which is hardly the case here) I shall read it, & I doubt not with great pleasure, some of the most agreeable moments of my life have been spent in reading works of imagination, which have this advantage over history that the incidents of the former may be dressed in the most interesting form, while those of the latter must be confined to fact: they cannot therefore present virtue in the best & vice in the worst forms possible, as the former may.

I have the honor to be with great consideration, Sir,

Your most obed' serv't,

Th. Jefferson.[24]

Although classified as America's first novelist, Brown by his personality exerted as great influence upon early literature as by this concrete form of writing. For the youth of his own day and the next generation he left a potent example by renouncing opportunities in law and business, and devoting himself to letters as a profession, in spite of censure and sacrifices. Prescott lays special stress upon Brown's influence in this way upon the young men of the next generation, who were inspired to test their gifts.[25] After he had finished his brief career as novelist, he devoted the rest of his life to editing journals, designed especially to create a taste for good reading among the common people.

[24] *Jefferson Papers,* Series I, Vol. VII, No. 305 (Library of Congress).

[25] *A Library of American Biography,* Vol. I, p. 180: Prescott on Brown.

Beginning in the year of his greatest success as novelist, 1799, he ventured as editor of *The Monthly Magazine and American Review,* published in New York. This survived only a year. The previous year he had contributed papers to *The Weekly Magazine of Original Essays, Fugitive Pieces and Interesting Intelligence* of Philadelphia.[26] He may have assisted in editing this journal. The most fruitful years of his work as editor were from 1803 to 1808, when he edited *The Literary Magazine and American Register.*[27] In his opening "Address to the Public," dated September 1, 1803, he made a persuasive plea for support, urging that

there is not, at present, any other monthly publication in America, and that a plan of this kind, if well conducted, cannot fail of being highly conducive to amusement and instruction. There are many, therefore, it is hoped, who, when such a herald as this knocks at their door, will open it without reluctance, and admit a visitant who calls only once a month; who talks upon every topic; whose company may be dismissed or resumed, and who may be made to prate or to hold his tongue at pleasure; a companion he will be, possessing one companionable property, in the highest degree, that is to say, a desire to please.

True to his promise, the editor seemed to "talk upon every topic," but, amid much that was

[26] See earlier pages of this chapter for his contributions.

[27] This journal was issued from the press of Conrad, of Philadelphia. The publishing house had branches for distribution in Norfolk and Baltimore.

trivial, there were some scholarly papers on affairs and letters, showing the editor's information along both lines. Brown was deeply interested in American politics, and wrote clearly and forcefully upon such themes, in a manner quite unlike his florid style in fiction and letters. Throughout his life he was a firm Federalist, yet a great admirer of Jefferson and Hamilton. In later years he criticized the former for his Democratic policies. An excellent linguist, he was able to speak and read French and Spanish with ease. Two of his essays, with translated passages, attracted attention and have been preserved. The first was *An Address to the Government of the United States on the Cession of Louisiana to the French and on the Late Breach of Treaty by the Spaniards, including the Translation of a Memorial on the War of St. Domingo, and Cession of Mississippi to France.* This passed into a second and revised edition. The next year (1804) he published a translation of *A View of the Soil and Climate of the United States of America, with Supplementary Remarks upon Florida, maps etc., by C. F. Volney.*[28]

As such studies in broader fields increased his culture, they caused him to regret his earlier, more puerile attempts at fiction. In the prospec-

[28] Both these pamphlets were published in Philadelphia, 1803, and 1804.

tus of his *Literary Magazine* he expressed the true humilty of a man who was acquiring scholarship and looked back upon his work with keen disapproval:

> I am far from wishing that my readers should judge of my exertions by my former ones. I have written much, but take much blame to myself for something which I have written and take no praise for anything. I should enjoy a larger share of my own respect, at the present moment, if nothing had ever flowed from my pen, the production of which could be traced to me. A variety of causes induce me to form such a wish, but I am particularly influenced by the consideration that time can scarcely fail of enlarging and refining the powers of a man; while the world is sure to judge of his capabilities and principles at fifty by what he has written at fifteen.

Brown's magazine acquired a fair circulation in New York, as well as in Philadelphia. Joseph Dennie welcomed Brown into the ranks of journalists by a kind reference, in *The Portfolio*, February 11, 1804, to the editor as "a gentleman whose talents are acknowledged to be of a superior order. As author of the novel, 'Wieland,' he acquired considerable celebrity." Brown had not signed his name either to his "Address to the Public" or to his articles, but his work was quickly recognized. Of this reticence he said in the "Address":

> I shall take no pains to conceal my name. Any body may know it who chooses to ask my publisher. I shall not,

however, put it at the bottom of this address. My diffidence, as my friends would call it, and my discretion, as
my enemies (if I have any) would term it, hinder me
from calling out my name in a crowd.

He wrote some historical and literary essays, and
secured contributions on natural history, travels,
etc. A department of "Remarkable Occurrences"
was one feature of the journal, and a column of
"Anecdotes" sought to lighten the mass of serious
writing. Unfortunately, Brown lacked the sense
of humor. Such a faculty would have aided him
in giving a more entertaining touch to his journal.
In earlier years it might have saved him from
some of his more extravagant passages of melodrama. This lack of buoyancy was due, in a
measure, to his physical nature. He confessed
that he had never known "that lightness and
vivacity of mind which the divine flow of health,
even in calamity, produces in some men." [29]

Outwardly his life brightened as the years
passed. In 1804 he married Elizabeth Linn, of
New York, daughter of a well-known clergyman
and sister of another, Rev. John Blair Linn, of
Philadelphia. The latter was a man of literary
tastes, who had written two books of passing
fame.[30]    The year after his marriage, Brown

[29] W. H. Prescott's *Sketch of Brown*, Jared Sparks, *A
Library of American Biography*, Vol. I, p. 169.

[30] *The Powers of Genius:    A Poem by John Blair Linn,
A.M., Co-Pastor of First Presbyterian Church in the City of*

wrote to Dunlap of his home happiness, but also of his haunting fear that it might not last.[31] The birth of twin sons seemed to rouse him, for a time, from his morbid fancies. He found a new incentive in living, and edited and wrote with zeal and encouragement. Proof of this more normal state of mind is given in a manuscript letter, in the possession of the Historical Society of Pennsylvania, which is printed by permission. The letter was written to his wife from Albany, June 17, 1806, where he had gone to visit his sisters. He begins the letter with an account of the journey by boat:

I left New York last Thursday morning & on Monday about twelve got within twelve miles of this place. There being no expectation of reaching town before night, I gladly got on shore & walked the rest of the way. I had scarcely begun my walk when the eclipse began. I sat down on the side of a hill from whence there was a wide prospect of this great river and its lofty shores & enjoyed the grandest and most awful spectacle which I ever witnessed. . . . . I have had a great deal of conversation with our sisters, in which, however, as yet all the talk was on my side. They seem'd to partake of all your pride and fondness for our little ones. . . . .

*Philadelphia* (Philadelphia, 1801; *Bourville Castle*, Philadelphia, 1802 (?)).

[31] "My companion is all that an husband can wish for, and, in short, as to my own personal situation, I have nothing to wish for but that it may last (*Life of Brown*, Vol. II, p. 113).

My fond anticipations of a letter from you were not
disappointed. I found one here on my arrival, which as-
sures me of your welfare. You confirm my prognostics
that the lovely babes will scamper about house, by the
time of my return. I am grieved that you still enjoy so
little assistance & I am very glad you have Susan D. I
have no doubt we shall soon have Massy back again &
her excellence will only show the brighter by comparison
with the defects of others. I will write every day. Love
to thy dear self.

In a postscript his wife is told to "send the
Reflector to the printer," with specific directions
as to his office. Like all of Brown's handwriting,
this letter shows wonderful delicacy and evenness
both in the formation of the letters and also in
the spacing.

The evidence of fatal disease of the lungs, in
1808, brought on a return of brooding. After a
journey through New York and western New
England he seemed to have temporary relief, and
undertook more writing with a zeal which was
almost desperate. Two years before, he had
arranged with his publisher, Conrad, to bring out
a semiannual compendium of reprinted articles
on politics, science, art, and literature. This was
known as *The American Register or General Repository of History, Politics, and Science.* It
lived through seven volumes, from 1806 to 1810.
It may be found at many libraries, and evidently
had a wide circulation for that period, and an

influence in promoting intelligence on world-affairs in an age that was provincial.

The increase of his family by two more children gave Brown added joy, but also anxiety, for he realized that his own years of life were few, and that he could leave no adequate income for his family. He disliked the phrases allied with death, and always spoke of the future for his wife in euphemisms, such as: "You must do this when I am asleep," or, "Remember this when I am absent." [32] As his physical power grew less, his mind seemed more alert and productive. He wrote until the last day of life.

Among the many literary remains were French classics in translation, maps and data for a work on geography, architectural drawings, and the romantic *History of Carsol, Sketches of a History of the Carrils and Ormes* included with *Jessica* and *Memoirs of Stephen Calvert,* in the memoir by Dunlap.[33] A manuscript poem, "L'Amoroso," which was given by his son, William Linn Brown, to Frank M. Etting, Esq., is in the Chamberlain collection at the Boston Public Library. It illustrates the prevailing sentimentality of his writing. A portion is here quoted:

[32] Dunlap, *Life of Brown*, Vol. II, p. 188.
[33] *Ibid.*, Vol. I, pp. 170-262.

From  pleasure's  walks  and  market-places;
  Stilly Groves and lonely Hills;
From gay carousals, thronging faces,
  Moonlight Glades and warbling rills;
From fighting fields and stormy Seas;
  From courtly pomp and war's array;
From State turmoils and letter'd Ease;
  Come, my enamoured Soul! away!
From haunts that moonstruck Fancy wooes·
  Where Nymphs resort, and Muses roam,
From all that vulgar dreams abuse,
  Come home, Exstatic Thought, come home!

The death of Brown, in February, 1810,
attracted very little attention in the newspapers of
Philadelphia and New York. Brief notices
only may be found in the journals of the day.
Even his burial-place was not located with abso-
lute certainty until a short time ago, when a question elicited the following statement from Mr.
George Vaux:

The interment was in Friends' Burial Ground, Arch &
Fourth Streets, Philadelphia, 2nd mo. 22, 1810; age thirty-
nine years; disease, decay; Locality, row 18, Grave 16;
District, Southern. The locality has no significance—all
the early grave mounds in this ground were levelled about
seventy years ago and no interments earlier than 1848 can
be identified.[34]

Two attempts to revive an interest in Brown's

[34] See *Pennsylvania Magazine of History and Biography*,
Vol. XXX, No. 118 (1906), p. 242. This fact was found in an
original record in *Friends' Library*.

personality and novels met with only limited success. A complete edition of his fiction was issued in Boston in 1827, and an edition, edited by Mr. David McKay, was published in Philadelphia in 1887. During the last five years more research has been made for facts about his life and influence, in accord with the general awakening to the historical value of such literary data.[35] There can be no doubt that English readers and reviewers showed more interest in Brown, for a century and a half after his death, than Americans have ever proclaimed. Three volumes of his fiction, including some tales already printed and other posthumous writing, were published in London in 1822, under the title *Carwin, the Biloquist and Other American Tales and Pieces By Charles Brockden Brown, Author of Wieland, Ormond, Arthur Mervyn, &c.*[36]

Because of this dearth of interest among Americans in the past, there is a special significance in a highly-colored article in Blackwood's *Edinburgh Review* for October, 1824, signed "X. Y. Z.," treating the life and writings of Brown. The tone is one of reproach to America for her indifference, until England had brought

[35] A monograph with detailed study of Brown's novels has been written by Martin S. Vilas (1904) ; see the Bibliography.

[36] These volumes may be found in the Library of Congress.

Brown to public notice. Of the personality of the novelist the reviewer wrote:

He lived in Eleventh street (we mention this for the information of his townsmen—not one in a thousand of whom knew it; of his countrymen not one in a million of whom, out of *ATHENS,* ever would know it, but for us) between Walnut and Chestnut—on the eastern side—in a low, dirty, two-story brick house; standing a little *in* from the street, with never a tree nor a shrub near it—lately in the occupation of—or as a Yankee would say *improved by* an actor-man, whose name was Darling.[37]

He was a tall man—with a powerful frame—and little or no flesh. It was impossible to pass him in the street, without stopping to look at him. His pale, sallow, strange complexion, straight black hair—"black as death,"—the melancholy, broken-hearted look of his eyes, his altogether extraordinary face,—if seen once, has never been forgotten. He would be met, week after week,—month after month,—walking to and fro in his native town, for hours and hours together on some unfrequented street—generally at a very early hour in the morning, lost in thought and looking like a shipwrecked man. Nobody knew him, nobody cared for him (till we took up his cause) he was only an author—yet, when we have described him, everybody in Philadelphia will recollect him.

Much of this description sounds like the figment of a modern journalist's imagination; yet many of the facts, are correct, and some of the surmises cannot easily be disproved.

---

[37] This account tallies with the description of Brown by Sully, the artist; see Scharf and Westcott, *History of Philadelphia,* Vol. III, p. 1981.

The novels of Brown are of historical interest in tracing the development of American fiction which followed within a few years—the work of Irving, Cooper, Poe, and Hawthorne. Before the death of Brown, the *Salmagundi Papers* and *Knickerbocker History of New York* had been published. Minor ventures in fiction had been made by Irving, Paulding, and their comrades. Irving met Brown, and was impressed by his patience and aspiration. He acknowledged his indebtedness to this early fictionist for an example of courage and literary purpose. The masters of fiction who followed Brown were able to use material similar to his, in fancy and character-delineation; but they gave to their fiction both reality and effectiveness. It was the lack of such artistic execution that reduced Brown's romances to extravaganzas. He had a fertile fancy but lacked constructive faculty. His power of imagination was often virile, but it was never fully developed and trained. He produced only the germs of national fiction, from which there evolved, within a few years, such effective tales as *Rip Van Winkle, The Gold Bug,* and *The Hall of Fantasy.* In both fiction and essays on political and literary themes, Brown evidenced some originality of thought and an impulse of patriotism which helped to promulgate a love of literature among his countrymen.

BIBLIOGRAPHY

# BIBLIOGRAPHY

## I. GENERAL BOOKS OF REFERENCE AND INTRODUCTORY CHAPTER

The author, in preparing this Bibliography, has included only the books, periodicals, letters, manuscripts, etc., which she has consulted by personal research or by correspondence; the list is far from exhaustive, but may prove helpful for further studies upon these subjects.

American Poems, Selected and Original. Anon. Litchfield (Connecticut). Preface is dated 1793. This was edited by Dr. Elihu Smith. 8vo.

American Museum, The; or Repository of Ancient and Modern Fugitive Pieces. Philadelphia: Carey, 1787–92.

Columbian Muse, The: A Selection of American Poetry from Various Authors of Established Reputation. Philadelphia, 1794. 12mo.

Columbian Songster, The, and Jovial Companion. New York, 1797. 8vo.

Cyclopaedia of American Literature. By Evert A. Duyckinck, New York, 1866.

The National Portrait Gallery of Distinguished Americans. Compiled by James B. Longacre (Philadelphia), and James Herring (New York), 1835.

Specimens of American Poetry. By Samuel Kettell. Boston, 1829. 12mo. 3 vols.

A Library of American Literature. By E. C. Stedman and E. M. Hutchinson. New York, 1900. 8vo. (Vol. I.)

Illustrated Ballad History of the American Revolution. By Frank Moore. New York, 1870. 4to.

Songs and Ballads of the Revolution. By Frank Moore. New York, 1856. 12mo.

American Lands and Letters. By Donald G. Mitchell. New York, 1890. (Vol. I, chaps. 3 and 4.)

A History of American Literature. By W. P. Trent. New York, 1903. 8vo. (Pp. 22–66.)

The Literary History of the American Revolution, 1763–1783. By Moses Coit Tyler. 2 vols. New York, 1897. 8vo.

American Literature (1607–1885). By Charles F. Richardson. New York, 1898. 2 vols. in 1. (Vol. I, chaps. 1–7.)

Proposals Relating to the Education of Youth in Pensilvania. By Benjamin Franklin. Philadelphia, 1749. 32 pp. (In library of the Historical Society of Pennsylvania and Boston Public Library.)

A List of Books Written by, or Relating to Benjamin Franklin. Edited by Paul Leicester Ford. Brooklyn, 1889. 8vo.

The Complete Works of Benjamin Franklin. Edited and compiled by John Bigelow. 10 vols. New York, 1888. Federal Edition, 1906–7.

The Writings of Benjamin Franklin. Edited by Albert Henry Smyth. 9 vols. New York, 1905–6.

Benjamin Franklin. By John Bach MacMaster. Boston, 1887. (Chaps. 8, 9.)

Letters from a Farmer in Pennsylvania to the Inhabitants of the British Colonies. Philadelphia, 1768; printed same year in Boston and London. 8vo.

The Boston Gazette and The Country Journal, July 18, 1768: "A Song Now Much in Vogue in North America." (By John Dickinson.)

Essays on the Constitution of the United States, 1787–1788. Edited by Paul Leicester Ford. Brooklyn, 1892.

Pamphlets on the Constitution of the United States. Published during Its Discussion by the People, 1787–1788. Edited, with Notes and a Bibliography, by Paul Leicester Ford. Brooklyn, 1888.

The American Nation: A History. Edited by Albert Bushnell Hart. New York, 1906–7. (Vols. IX, X.)

A History of the American People. By Woodrow Wilson. New York, 1902. (Vol. III.)

A History of the People of the United States, from the Revolution to the Civil War. By John Bach MacMaster. New York, 1883. (Vol. I, chaps. 1–4.)

History of the Republic, as Traced in the Writings of Alexander Hamilton and His Contemporaries. Edited by John C. Hamilton. New York, 1859.

Writings of George Washington. Edited by Worthington C. Ford. New York, 1899. 14 vols.

## II. FRANCIS HOPKINSON
### WRITINGS BY HOPKINSON

An Exercise containing a Dialogue and Ode Sacred to the Memory of his Late Majesty Geo. II. Performed at the College of Philadelphia, May 23, 1761. The Ode written and set to Music by Francis Hopkinson, Esq. M.A. of said College. Philadelphia, 1761. 8 pp., sq. 8vo.

Science. A Poem by Francis Hopkinson. Dedicated to the Trustees and Profs. of College & Academy. Philadelphia, 1762. 4to.

Two early poems in manuscript: L'Allegro, dedicated to Benjamin Chew, and Il Penseroso, dedicated to Rev. Dr. Smith. Also: An Elegy sacred to the Memory of Mrs. Ann Graeme, July, 1765. (These manuscripts are in the library of the Historical Society of Pennsylvania.)

Four Dissertations, on the Reciprocal Advantages of a Perpetual Union between Great Britain and her American Colonies. Written for Mr. Sargent's Prize-Medal. To Which (by Desire) is prefixed an Eulogium, spoken on Delivery of the Medal. Philadelphia, 1766; London, 1766. (Hopkinson wrote one of these dissertations.)

A Pretty Story Written in the Year of Our Lord 1774 by Peter Grievous, Esq. A.B.C.D.E. Veluti in Speculo. Philadelphia, 1774.

Reprint as The Old Farm and the New Farm: A Political Allegory, with Introduction and Historic Notes by Benson J. Lossing. New York, 1857; 2d ed., 1864.

A Prophecy. Philadelphia, 1776.

The Pennsylvania Magazine or American Monthly Museum. (R. Aitkin.) Philadelphia, 1775. (This contains many of Hopkinson's early writings.)

Prose Account of the Battle of the Kegs (unsigned). In New Jersey Gazette, January 21, 1778.

The Pennsylvania Packet, March 4, 1778 ("The Battle of the Kegs"). December 29, 1787, ("The New Roof").

Battle of the Kegs. A ballad broadside. (No date or place.) In American Antiquarian Society Library.

Battle of the Kegs. Philadelphia: Oakwood Press, 1866. 8vo.

Seven Songs for the Harpsichord or Forte Piano. The Words and Music Composed by Francis Hopkinson. Philadelphia, 1788. 8vo.

An Oration which Might have been Delivered to the Students in Anatomy on the Late Rupture between the Two Schools in this City. Philadelphia, 1789. 19 pp., 4to.

The Miscellaneous Essays and Occasional Writings of Francis Hopkinson. 3 vols. Philadelphia, 1792. 8vo.

Two manuscript volumes of "Miscellanies," owned by
Mrs. Florence Scovel Shinn, a descendant of Hopkinson.

Five manuscript volumes of prose writings (many printed
in "The Miscellaneous Essays," etc.), owned by the
American Philosophical Society.

One volume of collected writings (some in manuscript,
some in print), made by Hopkinson, owned by the
Historical Society of Pennsylvania.

Manuscript letters by Hopkinson to Jefferson in Library
of Congress, Jefferson Papers, Series II; also letters
to Hopkinson, Series I.

Manuscript letters by Francis Hopkinson to Franklin,
owned by the American Philosophical Society; also
letters to Hopkinson.

Manuscript letters by Hopkinson to several men of his
day, and to his family, owned by Mrs. Oliver Hopkinson; also letters to Hopkinson by Washington, Jefferson, Robert Morris, and others.

The American Museum; or Repository of Ancient &
Modern Fugitive Pieces, Prose & Poetical. Philadelphia: Carey. January, 1787: "On Annual Whitewashings." February, 1787: "Modern Learning
exemplified by a Specimen of Collegiate Examination.
By the Hon. Francis Hopkinson, esq."

The Columbian Magazine, May, 1787 (Philadelphia).
Design for a candle-case, etc., by Hopkinson.

Account of the Grand Federal Procession, Philadelphia,
July 4, 1788; to which is added a Letter on the same
Subject. Philadelphia, 1788.

The Pennsylvania Packet or The General Advertiser.
Philadelphia, 1782–88. Many articles by Hopkinson,
signed "Calamus," "Cautious," "One of the People,"
"A Lover of Candour," "F. H.," etc.

BIOGRAPHICAL AND CRITICAL ON HOPKINSON

The American Museum, etc. Vol. IX, Appendix, p. 38, 39. (Elegy by John Swanwick.)

The Columbian Magazine, May, 1791. Philadelphia. (Obituary and elegies.)

The Complete Works of Benjamin Franklin. Edited by John Bigelow. New York, 1888. (Vol. VII, p. 294.)

Delaplaine's Repository of the Lives and Portraits of Distinguished American Characters. Philadelphia, 1815. (Vol. III, pp. 125–39.)

The National Portrait Gallery of Distinguished Americans, conducted by John B. Longacre (Philadelphia) and James Herring (New York), 1835. (Vol. III.)

Biography of the Signers of the Declaration of Independence. By John Sanderson. Philadelphia, 1823. (Vol. II, pp. 187–201.)

Historic Houses of New Jersey. By W. Jay Mills. Philadelphia, 1902. (Pp. 285–89.)

The Journals of Hugh Gaine, Printer. Edited by Paul Leicester Ford. New York, 1902. (Vol. I, p. 108.)

The New York Mercury, Printed by Hugh Gaine, Bookseller, Printer and Stationer at the Bible & Crown, in Hanover Square. April 19, 1762. (Advertisement of new edition of "Science: A Poem.")

The Literary History of Philadelphia. By Ellis Paxson Oberholtzer. Philadelphia, 1906. (Pp. 44, 56, 61, 67, 106, 113, 114.)

The Pennsylvania Magazine of History and Biography. 1878. (Vol. II, pp. 314–24; Sketch of Hopkinson by Charles R. Hildeburne.)

Pennsylvania State Trials. Philadelphia, 1794. (Vol. I, edited by Edmund Hogan. The impeachment and trial of Francis Hopkinson, judge of the Admiralty.)

Francis Hopkinson and James Lyon. By O. G. Sonneck. Washington, 1905. Large 8vo.

Military Journal during the American Revolutionary War. By James Thacher. Boston, 1823. (Pp. 146–150; notes about Battle of the Kegs.)

The Washington-Duché Letters. Edited by Worthington C. Ford. Brooklyn, 1890.

The Writings of Thomas Jefferson. Edited by Paul L. Ford, New York, 1892–9. Vol. III, p. 495, Vol. V, pp. 75–8.

Letters of John Adams Addressed to his Wife. Edited by Charles Francis Adams. Boston, 1841. (Vol. I, pp. 156, 157.)

The Literary History of the American Revolution. By Moses Coit Tyler. New York, 1897. (Vol. I, pp. 164–71, 225, 226, 279–92; Vol. II, pp. 134–57, etc.)

## III. PHILIP FRENEAU

### WRITINGS BY PHILIP FRENEAU

(A full bibliography of Freneau has been compiled by Victor Hugo Paltsits. New York, 1903.)

Father Bumbo's Pilgrimage to Mecca in Arabia. Vol. II. Written by H. B. and P. F. 1770. (This is a manuscript quarto of 55 leaves, in the history of the Historical Society of Pennsylvania.)

The American Village, a Poem. To which are added, Several other Original Pieces in Verse. By Philip Freneau, A.B. New York, 1772. 12mo.

The first printed poem by Freneau, after his commencement poem, is in an original copy in the Library of Congress; also in John Carter Brown Library, Brown University. From the latter copy a reprint was made, facsimile, Providence, 1906. (Club for Colonial Reprints), with an introduction by Harry Lyman Koopman, and bibliographical data by Victor Hugo Paltsits.

A Poem on the Rising Glory of America: Being an Exercise Delivered at the Public Commencement at Nassau-Hall, September 25, 1771. Philadelphia: Aitkin, 1772. 12mo. (Copies of this poem are in the Library of Congress, the Historical Society of Pennsylvania, Lenox Library, New York Historical Society, and Massachusetts Historical Society. The manuscript is in Princeton University Library.)

American Liberty. A Poem. New York, 1775. 12mo.

The Last Words, Dying Speech and Confession of J—s R—g—n, P—t—r. (Broadside in Lenox Library. Mr. Paltsits says "in the style of Freneau's earlier verse, and perhaps by him" [Bibliography of Freneau].)

General Gage's Soliloquy. New York: Hugh Gaine, 1775. (Manuscript copy in the Library Company of Philadelphia. For further notes see Bibliography of Freneau by Paltsits, p. 28.)

A Voyage to Boston. A Poem. By the Author of American Liberty, a Poem. New York: Anderson. 12mo.

A Voyage to Boston. A Poem. By the Author of American Liberty, a Poem, Gen. Gage's Soliloquy, &c. Philadelphia: Woodhouse, 1775. 12mo. (At American Antiquarian Society, Historical Society of Pennsylvania.)

General Gage's Confession: Being the Substance of His Excellency's last Conference, With his Ghostly Father, Friar Francis. By the Author of the Voyage to Boston. Printed in the Year, 1775 (Gaine). Small 8vo.

American Independence, an everlasting Deliverance from British Tyranny: a Poem. Philadelphia, 1778. 12mo. (This poem "By Philip F———, Author of the

American Village, Voyage to Boston, &c," is found in
the library of the Historical Society of Pennsylvania,
in The Travels of the Imagination, pp. 113–26.)

The British Prison-Ship: A Poem, in four Cantos. Philadelphia: Bailey, 1791. 12mo. (Found at Brown
University, Library Company of Philadelphia.)

A Journey from Philadelphia to New York, by Way of
Burlington and South-Amboy. By Robert Slender,
Stocking Weaver. Philadelphia: Bailey, 1787. 12mo.
(This edition is in the library of Brown University,
Library of Congress, and New York Historical So-
ciety. Another edition, entitled, A Laughable Poem;
or Robert Slender's Journey, etc. By Philip Freneau,
[Philadelphia: Neversink, 1809. 12mo], is in the
Historical Society of Pennsylvania, Library Company
of Philadelphia, and Brown University.)

The Village Merchant: A Poem. To which is added The
Country Printer. Philadelphia, 1794. Small 8vo.
(Copies in the Historical Society of Pennsylvania and
Brown University.)

The Poems of Philip Freneau. Written chiefly during the
late War. Philadelphia, 1786. Small 8vo.

The Miscellaneous Works of Mr. Philip Freneau containing his Essays, and additional Poems. Philadelphia,
1788. Small 12mo.

Poems written between the years 1768 & 1794. By Philip
Freneau of New Jersey. A New Edition. Revised
and Corrected by the Author. Monmouth (N. J.).
Printed at the Press of the Author, at Mount-Pleasant, near Middetown-Point, MDCC,XCV; and, of
American Independence, XIX. (Fifteen stars in
pyramid.) 8vo.

Letters on Various interesting and important Subjects,
many of which have appeared in the AURORA. By

Robert Slender, O.S.M. Philadelphia: Hogan. December 30, 1799. 12mo.

Poems written and published during the American Revolutionary War, and now republished from the original Manuscripts; interspersed with Translations from the Ancients, and other Pieces not heretofore in Print. By Philip Freneau. Philadelphia: Lydia Bailey, 1809. 2 vols. 12mo.

A Collection of Poems, on American Affairs, and a variety of other Subjects, chiefly moral and political; written between the Year 1797 and the present Time. By Philip Freneau. New York, 1815. Longworth. 2 vols. Small 12mo.

Poems on various Subjects, but chiefly illustrative of the Events and Actors in the American War of Independence. By Philip Freneau. London: Smith, 1861. Small 8vo. Reprint of 1786 edition.

Poems relating to the American Revolution. By Philip Freneau. New York, 1865. 12mo and royal 8vo. (Memoir and notes by Duyckinck.)

Some Account of the Capture of the Ship Aurora. New York, 1899. 8vo. (Reprinted from manuscript.)

The Poems of Philip Freneau. Edited by Fred L. Pattee. Princeton, N. J., 1902-7. 3 vols.

NEWSPAPERS AND JOURNALS WHICH FRENEAU EDITED OR TO WHICH HE CONTRIBUTED

The Freeman's Journal; or, The North-American Intelligencer. Published by Francis Bailey. Philadelphia. Weekly newspaper. (Freneau's verse and occasional essays from 1781 to 1789. Files in Philadelphia Library Company, Historical Society of Pennsylvania, Lenox Library, Library of Congress, American Antiquarian Society.)

National Gazette. Edited by Freneau. Philadelphia, October 3, 1791, to October 26, 1793. Semi-weekly.

Jersey Chronicle. Edited by Freneau. Mount-Pleasant (Monmouth), May 2, 1795, to April 30, 1796. (File at New York Historical Society; scattered numbers at American Antiquarian Society and elsewhere.)

The Time-Piece; and Literary Companion. Edited by Freneau. New York, March 1797, to March, 1798. Tri-weekly.

The Pennsylvania Packet and Daily Advertiser. Philadelphia. (Many poems by Freneau from 1782 to 1788.)

The United States Magazine: A Repository of History, Politics and Literature. Vol. I, for the year 1779. Edited by H. H. Brackenridge. Philadelphia. (Many contributions by Freneau.)

The American Museum, Vol. I, p. 77 (January, 1787. Under "Original Poetry," attributed to Freneau, is "The Death-Song of the Cherokee Indian.")

BIOGRAPHICAL AND CRITICAL ON FRENEAU

A Bibliography of the Separate and Collected Works of Philip Freneau, Together with an Account of His Newspapers. By Victor Hugo Paltsits. New York, 1903.

Philip Freneau: The Poet of the Revolution. A History of His Life and Times. By Mary S. Austin. Edited by Helen Kearny Vreeland. New York, 1901.

The Political Activities of Philip Freneau. By Samuel E. Forman, Ph.D. The Johns Hopkins University Studies, in Historical and Political Science. Series XX, Nos. 9, 10. Baltimore, 1902.

Obituary Notices of Freneau in:

The Monmouth Inquirer, December 19, 1832.

The New York Evening Post, December 27, 1832.

The New York Spectator, December 31, 1832.

The New York Mirror, January 12, 1833.

Philip Freneau: The Huguenot Patriot-Poet of the Revolution. By Edward F. DeLancey. New York, 1898. Also in Proceedings of the Huguenot Society, Vol. II, No. 2.

The Memorial History of the City of New York. By James Grant Wilson. New York, 1893. 4 vols. (Several references in Vols. II, III, and IV.)

Writings of Thomas Jefferson. Edited by Paul Leicester Ford. (Vol. I, p. 231; Vol. V, pp. 330, 336; Vol. VI, pp. 101-9, 134, 328, 438, 443.)

Jefferson Papers, Series I and II. Manuscript in Library of Congress.

Madison Papers. Library of Congress.

The Character of Thomas Jefferson as Exhibited in His Own Writings. By Theodore Dwight. New York, 1839. (Pp. 129-49.)

The Literary History of Philadelphia. By Ellis Paxson Oberholtzer. Philadelphia, 1906, pp. 115-29.

The Journals of Hugh Gaine, Printer. Edited by Paul Leicester Ford. New York, 1902. (Vol. I, pp. 9, 34, 55, 63, 73, 138.)

Manuscript Letters by and about Philip Freneau. In Pickering Papers, in Massachusetts Historical Society. (Vols. XXIX and LV.)

The Issues of the Press of Pennsylvania, 1685-1785. By Charles R. Hildeburne. Philadelphia, 1885. (Vol. II, p. 148.)

Historic Houses of New Jersey. By W. Jay Mills. Philadelphia, 1902. (Pp. 75, 145, 180, 195.)

History of the College of New Jersey, from Its Origin in 1746 to the Commencement of 1854. By John Mac-

Lean. Philadelphia, 1877. (Vol. I, chap. 15, pp. 309–22.)

A History of Journalism in the United States from 1690 to 1872. By Frederic Hudson. New York, 1873. (Pp. 103, 111, 134–36, 175, 185–87.)

Narrative of a Journey down the Ohio and Mississippi in 1789–1790, by Major Samuel S. Forman. (With a Memoir and Illustrative Notes.) By Lyman C. Draper. Cincinnati, 1888. (Pp. 9–11.)

The Southern Literary Messenger. (Vol. VIII, No. 1, pp. 2, 3. Note about commencement poem written with Brackenridge.)

Personal Memoirs and Recollections of Editorial Life. By Joseph T. Buckingham. Boston, 1852. (Vol. II, pp. 137–46.)

American Poems. Litchfield, 1793. (Scattered poems.)

The Literary History of the American Revolution. By Moses Coit Tyler. New York, 1897. (Vol. I, pp. 171–83; 413–25; Vol. II, pp. 249–76.)

Magazine of American History. Vol. XVII, 1887, pp. 120–7.

---

## IV. JOHN TRUMBULL

### WRITINGS BY JOHN TRUMBULL

An Essay on the Use and Advantages of the Fine Arts; Delivered at the Public Commencement in New Haven, Sept. 12, 1770. New Haven, 1770. Pp. 16. 8vo. (Copies of this essay are in the libraries of Yale University, Massachusetts Historical Society, Library of Congress, and Watkinson Library, Hartford.)

The Progress of Dulness, Part First: or the Rare Adventures of Tom Brainless; Printed in the Year 1772. New Haven. Pp. 19. 8vo. (Second edition, New Haven, 1773. Pp. 20. 8vo.)

The Progress of Dulness, Part Second: or An Essay on the Life and Character of Dick Hairbrain. New Haven, 1773. Pp. 27. 8vo.

The Progress of Dulness, Part Third; or the The Adventures of Miss Harriet Simple. New Haven, 1773. Pp. 28. 8vo.

The Progress of Dulness: or the Rare Adventures of Tom Brainless. By the celebrated author of McFINGAL. Exeter, 1794. Pp. 72. 16mo. (3 parts.)

M'Fingal: A Modern Epic Poem. Canto First, or The Town-Meeting. Philadelphia. Printed and Sold by William and Thomas Bradford, at the London Coffee-House, 1775. 16mo.

M'Fingal: A Modern Epic Poem. Cantos First and Second. The Town-Meeting. Hartford, Philadelphia, and Boston, 1776; London, 1776. 16mo.

M'Fingal: A Modern Epic Poem, in Four Cantos. Hartford, 1782. Pp. 100. 8vo. (This first edition was printed by Hudson & Goodwin. Two other editions appeared in Hartford the same year; one printed by Nathaniel Patten; the other, by Bavil Webster.)

Later editions of M'Fingal, to be found in the Watkinson Library of Hartford, the Boston Public Library, the Lenox Library, Brown University, Massachusetts Historical Society, and the Library of Congress, are:

M'Fingal: A Modern Epic Poem, in Four Cantos. Philadelphia, 1791. Pp. 95. 12mo.

M'Fingal: A Modern Epic Poem. London: (Jordan), 1792. Pp. 142. 8vo.

M'Fingal: A Modern Epic Poem; Embellished with Nine Copper plates; designed and engraved by E. Tisdale. The first edition with plates and explanatory notes. New York, 1795. Pp. 136. 8vo.

M'Fingal: With explanatory notes. Boston, 1799. 16mo.

M'Fingal: A Modern Epic Poem. Baltimore, 1812. Pp. 146. 24mo.

M'Fingal, etc., Albany, 1813. Hallowell, 1813; Boston, 1826. Philadelphia, 1839.

M'Fingal: A Modern Poem. With Notes by Benson J. Lossing. New York, 1864. 16mo.

M'Fingal, etc. New York, 1857, 1860, 1881.

An Elegy on the Times: First Printed at Boston, Sept. 20th, A.D. 1774. Reprinted New Haven, 1775. Pp. 15. 8vo.

The Poetical Works of John Trumbull, LL.D., containing M'Fingal, a Modern Epic Poem, revised and corrected, with copious explanatory notes: The Progress of Dulness; and a Collection of Poems on Various Subjects written before and during the Revolutionary War. Hartford, 1820. Printed for Samuel G. Goodrich, by Lincoln & Stone. 2 vols. 8vo.

Selected poems by Trumbull may be found in:

American Poems; Selected and Original (1793). Litchfield. (Edited by Dr. Elihu Smith.)

The Poets of Connecticut. By Rev. Charles W. Everest. Hartford, 1843.

Specimens of American Poetry. By Samuel Kettell. Boston, 1829. Vols I, II.

Early essays by Trumbull may be found in:

Boston Chronicle, September, 1769, to January, 1770. ("The Meddler" and "The Schemer." A large number of these essays were by him.)

Connecticut Journal, February to July, 1770. ("The Correspondent.")

Connecticut Courant and Weekly Intelligencer, August 7 and 14, 1775. (Parodies in verse on General Gage's proclamations.)

BIOGRAPHICAL AND CRITICAL ON TRUMBULL

Federalism Triumphant in the Steady Habits of Connecticut Alone, or, the Turnpike Road to a Fortune. A Comic Opera, or Political Farce in Six Acts, as performed at the Theatres Royal and Aristocratic at Hartford and New Haven, October, 1801. Printed in the Year, 1802. (no place.) Trumbull is one of the characters.

Connecticut Journal, September 30, 1770. (Reference to his Essay on the Fine Arts.)

The Origin of M'Fingal. By J. Hammond Trumbull. Historical Magazine, January, 1868.

Memorial History of Hartford County, 1633–1884. By J. Hammond Trumbull, LL.D. Boston, 1886. 2 vols. (Several references.)

The Town and City of Waterbury, Connecticut, from the Aboriginal Period to the Year Eighteen Hundred and Ninety-Five. Edited by Joseph Anderson, D.D. New Haven, 1896. (Vol. I, pp. 326–29; Vol. II, pp. 9, 546; Vol. III, pp. 923–26.)

Brinton Eliot; From Yale to Yorktown. By James Eugene Farmer. New York, 1902. (Chap. 7.)

The Literary History of the American Revolution. By Tyler. New York, 1897. (Vol. I, pp. 188–221, 427–50.)

List of Books Printed in Connecticut from 1709 to 1800. By James Hammond Trumbull, LL.D., L.H.D. 1904. (Acorn Club.)

Letters among Oliver Wolcott, Jr., Papers, at Connecticut Historical Society.

Biographical Sketches of the Graduates of Yale College, with Annals of the College History. By Franklin B. Dexter. New York. Third Series, 1903, pp. 251–7, etc.

## V. THE "HARTFORD WITS"

WRITINGS BY AND ABOUT THE "HARTFORD WITS"

The New Haven Gazette and the Connecticut Magazine, October 19, 1786, to February 5, 1787. ("The American Antiquities," later collected as "The Anarchiad.")

The Anarchiad. A New England Poem. Written in concert by David Humphreys, Joel Barlow, John Trumbull, and Dr. Lemuel Hopkins. Now first published in book form. Edited, with notes and appendices, by Luther G. Riggs, New Haven, 1861. Pp. 120. 24mo.

The American Mercury, Printed by Elisha Babcock. Hartford. August 8, 1791, to March 12, 1792. (Numbers of "The Echo.")

The Echo with Other Poems. Printed at the Porcupine Press by Pasquin Petronius. New York, 1807. 8vo. (The printer was Isaac Riley.)

The Political Green-House for the Year 1798. Addressed to the Readers of the Connecticut Courant, January 1st, 1799. Hartford, no date. (Written by Theodore Dwight, Richard Alsop, and Lemuel Hopkins. Small 8vo. Included in "Echo," pp. 233–59.)

Guillotina for 1797. Addressed to the Readers of the Connecticut Courant. Hartford, January 1, 1797. (A broadside, unidentified, in Connecticut Historica Society.)

The Democratiad. A Poem in Retaliation, for the Philadelphia Jockey Club. By a Gentleman of Connecticut. Philadelphia, 1795. Pp. 22. 8vo. (In "The Echo," pp. 127–40; supposed to be by Dr. Hopkins.)

The Guillotina, or a Democratic Dirge: A Poem. By the Author of Democratiad. Philadelphia. Pp. 14. 8vo. (Probably by Hopkins.)

The last two pamphlets may be found at the Connecticut
Historical Society, Lenox Library, and Library of
Congress.

Aristocracy; an Epic Poem by De Bellare Superbos. Bk.
I. Philadelphia, 1795. (At Library of Congress cata-
logued as Richard Alsop's [?].)

The Poets of Connecticut. By Rev. Charles W. Everest.
Hartford, 1843. 8vo.

A Sketch of the History of Yale College. By William
L. Kingsley. Boston, 1835. (Vol. I.)

List of Books Printed in Connecticut from 1709 to 1800.
By James Hammond Trumbull, LL.D., L.H.D., 1904.
(Acorn Club.)

American Poems; Selected and Original. Litchfield,
1793.

Atlantic Monthly, Vol. XX, 1865, pp. 187–201. The New
Englander, January, 1882.

### WRITINGS BY AND ABOUT JOEL BARLOW

The Prospect of Peace, a Poetical Composition delivered
in Yale College, at the Public Examination, July 23,
1778. New Haven, 1788. Pp. 12. 8vo.

The Vision of Columbus; a Poem in Nine Books. Hartford, 1787. Pp. 258. 8vo. (2d ed. Hartford, 1787;
12mo.)

Conspiracy of Kings. London, 1792; Paris, 1793. Pp. 32.
4to.

Advice to the Privileged Orders in Several States of
Europe. Part I. Pp. 156. 8vo. London (2d ed.),
1792–93.

Hasty Pudding; a Poem. In three cantos. Written at
Chambery, in Savoy, January 1, 1793. New Haven,
1796; Salem, 1799; Albany, 1807; Boston, 1810. Pp.
16. 8vo.

Joel Barlow to his Fellow Citizens of the United States of America. Paris, 1799. Pp. 27. 8vo.

The Political Writings of Joel Barlow: A new edition. New York, 1796. Pp. 258. 16mo.

The Columbiad. A Poem by Joel Barlow. Philadelphia, 1807; Philadelphia, 1809; London, 1809; Paris, 1813; Washington, 1825. Pp. 454. 8vo.

Critical Observations on the Poem of Joel Barlow, The Columbiad. By M. Gregoire. Reply by Joel Barlow. Washington City, 1809. (This last, as well as other writings mentioned, is in the Library of Congress.)

Life and Letters of Joel Barlow; Poet, Statesman, Philosopher. By Charles B. Todd. New York, 1886.

Three Men of Letters. By Moses Coit Tyler. New York, 1895.

Manuscript letters to Oliver Wolcott, Jr., in folio at Connecticut Historical Society.

Manuscript letters to wife and friends; also an unfinished poem, "The Canal;" at Pequot Library, Southport, Conn.

Memorial History of Hartford County. By J. Hammond Trumbull. New Haven, 1886. (Several references to Barlow and the other "wits.")

### WRITINGS OF DAVID HUMPHREYS

The Miscellaneous Works of David Humphreys, Late Minister Plenipotentiary from the United States of America to the Court of Madrid. New York, 1804. 8vo.

Miscellaneous Works, etc., (containing Poems and Life of Israel Putnam). New York, 1790. (In this volume is the play, "The Widow of Malabar," which was not included in the Miscellaneous Works, 1804.)

A Poem addressed to the Armies of the United States of America. By a Gentleman of the Army. New Haven, 1780. Pp. 16. 8vo. Reprinted, New Haven, 1785; Paris, 1786 as—Discours en vers, addressé aux officiers et aux soldats des différentes armées américaines. Paris, 1786.

A Poem on the Happiness of America; addressed to the Citizens of the United States by David Humphreys, LL.D. London, 1786; Hartford, 1786. Pp. 51. 4to.

An Essay on the Life of the Honourable Major-General Israel Putnam; addressed to the State Society of the Cincinnati in Connecticut. Hartford, 1788; Middletown, 1794; Philadelphia, 1798; Boston, 1818. 12mo.

Life and Exploits of Israel Putnam. New York, 1834. 24mo.

Memoirs of the life, adventures & military exploits of Israel Putnam, Senior Major-general in the Revolutionary army of the United States, and next in rank to Gen. Washington (by David Humphreys). New York: Duyckinck, 1815. Pp. 108. 24mo.

A Poem on Industry; addressed to the Citizens of the United States of America. By Col. David Humphreys, Minister Resident at the Court of Lisbon. Philadelphia, 1794. 8vo.

Valedictory Discourse delivered before the Cincinnati of Connecticut, in Hartford, July 4, 1804, at the Dissolution of the Society. By Col. David Humphreys.

Letters from the Hon. David Humphreys, F.R.S. to the Rt. Hon. Sir Joseph Banks, President of the Royal Society, London, containing some ACCOUNT of the SERPENT of the OCEAN, frequently seen in Gloucester Bay. New York, 1817.

The Yankey in England, a Drama, in Five Acts. By
General Humphreys. (No date, nor place, but the
preface signed D. Humphreys, Humphreysville, Sept.
1, 1815.) A copy is in Boston Athenaeum.

BIOGRAPHICAL AND CRITICAL ON DAVID HUMPHREYS

Yale and Her Honor-Roll in the American Revolution,
1775-1783. By Henry P. Johnston. New York, 1888.
Seymour; Past and Present. By Rev. Hollis A. Campbell,
William C. Sharpe, and Frank G. Basset, Seymour,
1902.
Chapter Sketches, Connecticut D. A. R. Edited by Mary
Philotheta Root. New Haven. (1900.)
The Writings of Thomas Jefferson. Edited by Paul L.
Ford. (Vol. I, pp. 216, 233; Vol. IX, p. 225, 226.)
The Writings of Washington. Collected and edited by
Worthington C. Ford, New York, 1891. (Vol. X, pp.
473, 474.)
The Veil Removed; or, Reflections on Humphrey's Essay
on the Life of Putnam. By John Fellows. New
York, 1843.
Manuscript letters in Pickering Papers. Vol. XXI.
(Massachusetts Historical Society.)

WRITINGS BY AND ABOUT THEODORE DWIGHT

An Oration before the Connecticut Society for the Promotion of Freedom convened at Hartford, May 8,
1794. Hartford, 1794. Pp. 24. 8vo.
An Oration spoken at Hartford, July 4th, 1798. Hartford,
1798. Pp. 31. 8vo.
The Triumph of Democracy, a Poem. January 1, 1801.
(No name nor place; in "The Echo," pp. 267-82.)
History of the Hartford Convention with a Review of
the Policy of the United States Government which led
to the War of 1812. New York, 1833. 8vo.

The Character of Thomas Jefferson as Exhibited in his
Own Writings. Boston, 1839. 12mo.

Memorial History of Hartford County. By J. Hammond
Trumbull, LL.D. Boston, 1886. (Vol. I, pp. 124, 157,
160, 385, 516, 612.)

### WRITINGS BY AND ABOUT RICHARD ALSOP

To the Freemen of the State of Connecticut. (Anon.,
no place; 1803. In copy at Massachusetts Historical
Society, a note is written in ink, "By Richard Alsop;
Middletown, Sept. 12, 1803.")

The Charms of Fancy. A Poem in Four Cantos.
Edited from the original manuscript by Theodore
Dwight. New York, 1856. Pp. 214. 8vo.

A Poem Sacred to the Memory of George Washington,
Late President of the United States and Commander-
in-Chief of the Armies of the United States, by
Richard Alsop. Hartford, 1800. Pp. 23. 8vo.

Verses to a Shearwater, in Specimens of American Poetry.
By Samuel Kettell. (Vol. II, p. 60.)

Runic translation; Twilight of the Gods, in American
Poems; Selected and Original (1793). Pp. 265-272.

Translations:

The Enchanted Lake of the Fairy Morgana. From the
Orlando Inamorata of Francisco Berni. New
York, 1806. 8vo.

An Appendix to the Civil and Political History of Chili;
translated from Juan Ignacio Molina. New York,
1808. 8vo.

Selections in The Poets of Connecticut. By Rev. Charles
W. Everest. 1843. (Pp. 73-91.)

Manuscript letter to Dr. Mason Cogswell about The Echo,
at Connecticut Historical Society, in John Trumbull's copy of The Echo.

Possibly the author of Aristocracy, an Epic Poem by De Bellare Superbos. Philadelphia, 1795.

### WRITINGS BY AND ABOUT LEMUEL HOPKINS

The Democratiad. A Poem in Retaliation, for the Philadelphia Jockey Club. By a Gentleman of Connecticut. Philadelphia, 1795. Pp. 22. 8vo. (Reprinted in The Echo.)

The Guillotina, or a Democratic Dirge. A Poem. By the Author of Democratiad. Philadelphia. Pp. 14. (Reprinted in The Echo.)

New Year's Verses, For the Connecticut Courant, January 1, 1795. Hartford, 1795. (Reprinted in The Echo.)

Specimens of American Poetry. By Samuel Kettell. (Vol. I, pp. 272–83.)

The Poets of Connecticut. By Charles W. Everest. 1843. (Pp. 51–58.)

American Medical Biography; or, Memoirs of Eminent Physicians. By James Thacher, M.D. Boston, 1828. (Vol. I, pp. 298–306.)

Manuscript letters to Oliver Wolcott, Jr., at Connecticut Historical Society.

The Town and City of Waterbury, Connecticut, from the Aboriginal Period to the Year Eighteen Hundred and Ninety-Five. Edited by Joseph Anderson, D.D. New Haven, 1896. 3 vols. (Many references to Hopkins.)

Memorial History of Hartford County. By J. Hammond Trumbull, LL.D. Boston, 1886. Vol. I, pp. 139–58.

------

## VI.  JOSEPH DENNIE

### WRITINGS BY DENNIE

The Lay Preacher; or Short Sermons for Idle Readers. Walpole (N. H.), 1796. Pp. 132. 16mo.

The Spirit of the Farmer's Museum and Lay Preacher's Gazette. Walpole. Carlyle, printer for Thomas & Thomas. 1801. Pp. 318. 12mo.

The Lay Preacher, collected and arranged by John E. Hall, Esq. Counsellor at Law. Published at Philadelphia by Harrison Hall, at the Portfolio Office, 1817. Pp. 168. 16mo.

New and Original Essays by Joseph Dennie. Philadelphia, 1818. (Only one in the series appeared, so far as known.)

The New Hampshire Journal; or The Farmer's Weekly Museum. Walpole, 1793–97. (Contributions by Dennie during these years. Some later issues were entitled The Farmer's Museum: New Hampshire & Vermont Journal, 1797–1810.)

The Tablet: A Miscellaneous Paper devoted to the Belles-Lettres. (Edited by Dennie.) Boston. 4to. May 19, 1795, to August 11, 1795. (No more issued.)

The Port Folio by Oliver Oldschool. Philadelphia. 1801–12. (Started and edited by Dennie.) Weekly, 1801–8; monthly 1809–12. (The journal continued in various forms until 1827; published by Maxwell; 4to of 8 pages as weekly.)

Two letters from Dennie to Hon. Jeremiah Mason. Massachusetts Historical Society Proceedings, March, 1880, Vol. XVII, pp. 362–65.)

Letters by Dennie to Timothy Pickering, in Pickering Papers (Massachusetts Historical Society, Vol. X, XIII, XXIV.)

Letters and manuscript, in Adams Papers, from Dennie to John Quincy Adams. (In the possession of Charles Francis Adams.)

### CRITICAL AND BIOGRAPHICAL ON DENNIE

Sketch of Dennie. [By Colonel W. W. Clapp.] Cambridge, 1880. 8vo.

The Philadelphia Souvenir: A Collection of Fugitive Pieces from The Philadelphia Press, with Biographical and Explanatory Notes by J. E. Hall. Philadelphia, 1826. (Pp. 70–136.)

Walpole as It Was and as It Is, containing the Complete Civil History of the Town from 1749 to 1879. By George Aldrich. Claremont, N. H., 1880. (Pp. 74–82.)

History of Philadelphia. By Scharf and Westcott. Philadelphia, 1884. (Vol. I, pp. 508, 509; Vol. III, p. 1979.)

The Literary History of Philadelphia. By Ellis Paxson Oberholtzer. Philadelphia, 1906. (Pp. 168–83, 189, 264.)

Memoirs, Journal and Correspondence of Thomas Moore. Edited by Lord John Russell. London, 1856. (Various passing references in Vols. I, II, III, IV, V, VI, VII, VIII.)

Poetical Works of Thomas Moore. Leipzig, 1842. (Collected and annotated by himself. Vol. I, references in Preface and notes.)

Life of Josiah Quincy by His Son, Edmund Quincy. Boston, 1867. (Pp. 30–33.)

Memoirs of John Quincy Adams. Edited by Charles Francis Adams. Philadelphia, 1877. (Vol. I, p. 240; Vol. IX, p. 239.)

Personal Memoirs, Anecdotes and Reminiscences. By J. T. Buckingham. Boston, 1850, 1852. Vol. II, pp. 175–90, 195–202, 226.) Some editions have title, Specimens of Newspaper Literature, with Memoirs, etc.

A History of Journalism in the United States from 1690 to 1872. By Frederic Hudson. New York, 1873. (Vol. II, pp. 51–64, 708–18.)

The New Englander Galaxy, July 24, 1818. (Anecdote of
Dennie's law-experience as given by Royall Tyler.)

Benjamin's Collector, February, 1896; article by Charles
Henry Hart. (Two letters from Moore to J. E. Hall,
with many references to Dennie.)

The Critic, June, 1888. (Two Letters from Moore to
Dennie.)

New England Magazine, August, 1896. ("Damon and
Pythias among our Early Journalists.")

Curiosities of Literature. By D'Israeli and Griswold. New
York, 1848. (Pp. 51, 52.)

Magazine of American History, Vol. XVII, 1887. Pp. 117,
118.

The Historical Magazine, December, 1857, p. 379. Rufus
Griswold's reference to Dennie's portrait.

American Historical and Literary Curiosities. Collected
and edited by J. Jay Smith and John F. Watson. New
York, 1850. Plate XLI. (Letter and song sent by
Moore to Dennie.)

---

## VII.  WILLIAM DUNLAP

### WRITINGS BY DUNLAP

Complete lists of Dunlap's plays may be found in:

Second edition of Early American Plays by Oscar
Wegelin, with Introduction by John Malone. New
York, 1905. The first edition, 1900, has only a
partial list.

Introduction to The Father, or American Shandyism,
reprinted by the Dunlap Society. New York, 1887.
(Pp. x, xi.)

The following are some of Dunlap's most representative plays, to be found generally at libraries with a collection of Americana:

The Father, or American Shandyism. A Comedy in five acts. Written by a Citizen of New York. New York, 1789. 8vo. Reprint of the above by the Dunlap Society, New York, 1887. Introduction by Thomas J. McKee. The same play was printed later as The Father of an Only Child, by William Dunlap. New York, 1807. 12mo.

Darby's Return: a Comic Sketch. New York, 1789.

Darby's Return, an Interlude. New York, 1806. 8vo.

The Archers, or Mountaineers of Switzerland, an Opera, in Three Acts, by an American. New York, 1796. 8vo.

Tell Truth and Shame the Devil; a comedy in 2 acts, as performed by the old American Company, New York, 1797.

André: A Tragedy in Five Acts. New York, 1798. Reprint of this edition by the Dunlap Society, New York, 1887; Introduction by J. Brander Matthews.)

André: A Tragedy in Five Acts; To which are added Authentic Documents respecting Major André, Consisting of letters to Miss Seward, The Cow Chase; a Satirical poem by Major John André; with the proceedings of court martial. New York: Swords, 1798. London, 1799.

False Shame, or The American Orphan in Germany. A Comedy in Four acts, translated from the German of Kotzebue. New York, 1800; Charleston, 1800. 12mo.

Abaellino; the Great Bandit. Translated from the German of Tschokke and adapted to the New York Theatre. New York, 1802; Boston and New York, 1803. 12mo.

Ribbemont, or the Feudal Baron. A Tragedy in Five Acts. New York, 1803. 18mo.

The Glory of Columbia; her Yoemanry. A Play in Five
Acts. The Songs, Duets, and Choruses, intended for
the celebration of the Fourth of July at the New
York Theatre. New York, 1803, 1817. 12mo.

The Voice of Nature; A Drama in 3 Acts from French
Melodrama, Le Jugement de Salomon. New York,
1803. 18mo.

Blue Beard; or Female Curiosity; a dramatic romance in
three acts, as altered for the New York Theatre, with
additional songs, by William Dunlap. New York,
1803, 1806. 18mo.

Lord Leicester; a Tragedy. New York, 1807. 16mo.

Fontaineville Abbey. A Tragedy. New York, 1807. 18mo.

The Blind Boy; a Melodrama as performed at the
Theatre Royal, Covent Garden. London, 1808; New
York, 1808. 12mo. (Altered from Kotzebue's Epi-
gram.)

Rinaldo Rinaldini, or the Great Banditti, New York, 1810.

The Africans or War, Love and Duty. Philadelphia, 1811;
Hartford, 1814.

Yankee Chronology: a musical interlude in one Act to
which is added Patriotic Songs of the Freedom of
the Seas & Yankee Tars. New York, 1812. 16mo.

Yankee Chronology or Huzza for the American Navy.
(Broadside, 1813–14.) In American Antiquarian
Society.

The Italian Father; a comedy in Five Acts. New York,
1810.

Lover's Vows, a play in five acts. New York, 1814. 12mo.
(From the German of Kotzebue.)

A Trip to Niagara, or Travellers in America. A Farce in
Three Acts written for the Bowery Theatre, N. Y.
By William Dunlap, Historical and Portrait Painter;

author of Memoirs of G. F. Cooke, C. B. Brown,
Father of an Only Child, etc. New York, 1830. 18mo.

Ella: a Norwegian Tale, in American Poems, Litchfield,
(1793), pp. 226–31.

Memoirs of George Fred Cooke, Esq., Late of the
Theatre Royal, Covent Garden, by William Dunlap,
Esq. London, 1813. 2 vols.

The Life of Charles Brockden Brown, together with Selections from the Rarest of his Printed Works, from
His Original Letters, and from his Manuscripts Before Unpublished. By William Dunlap. In two volumes. Philadelphia, 1815.

Thirty Years Ago; or, Memoirs of a Water Drinker.
New York, 1836. 2 vols.

A History of the American Theatre by William Dunlap,
Vice-President of the National Academy of Design,
Author of Memoirs of George Fred Cooke, C. B.
Brown, etc. New York, 1832.

History of the Rise and Progress of the Arts of Design
in the United States; by William Dunlap. New York,
1834. 2 vols.

A History of New York for Schools, by William Dunlap. In two volumes. New York, 1837. 16mo.

History of the New Netherlands, Province of New
York and State of New York, to Adoption of the
Federal Constitution; by William Dunlap. In two
volumes. New York, 1839.

Four volumes of manuscript journals, in New York Historical Society: 15, 16, 24, 30.

### BIOGRAPHICAL AND CRITICAL ON DUNLAP

The best biographical material is found in many references to himself in his History of the American
Theatre, and also in History of the Rise and Progress

of the Arts of Design in the United States; also in the manuscript journals at the New York Historical Society.

Early American Plays (1714–1830). By Oscar Wegelin. Introduction by John Malone. Dunlap Society Publication. New York, 1900; 2d ed., 1905.

New England Magazine, February, 1894: Beginnings of American Dramatic Literature. By Paul Leicester Ford.

Occasional Addresses. Edited by Laurence Hutton and William Carey. Published by the Dunlap Society. New York, 1890. (Pp. 51–53.)

Washington and the Theatre. By Paul Leicester Ford. Published by the Dunlap Society. New York, 1899.

History of New York City. By Martha J. Lamb. New York, 1850. (Vol. II, pp. 352, 353.)

Old New York. By John W. Francis. New York, 1866. Pp. 66–68, and scattered notes.)

References in The Memorial History of the City of New York. By James Grant Wilson. New York, 1893. (Vols. II, III, IV.)

Contributions to the Early History of Perth Amboy. By W. A. Whitehead. New York, 1856. (Pp. 97, 126–28, 139–43, 243, 292–94, 328, 329, 343.)

Descriptive Pamphlet of Christ Rejected by the High Priests, Elders and People. Shields, Ashburn & Co., Norfolk. (No date.)

History of New York City. By William L. Stone. New York, 1872. (Pp. 134, 151, 241–48.)

History of the American Theatre during the Revolution and After. By George O. Seilhamer. Philadelphia, 1889. (Vol. I, pp. 3, 19, 72, 73, 81, 141–43; Vol. II, 274–80.)

## VIII. CHARLES BROCKDEN BROWN

### WRITINGS BY BROWN

History of American Painting. By Samuel Isham. New York, 1905. Pp. 11, 17–24, 43–49, 72–79, 186–89.

The Columbian Magazine. Philadelphia, April, 1789. (Contains Brown's "The Rhapsodist.")

The Weekly Magazine of Original Essays, Fugitive Pieces and Interesting Intelligence. Philadelphia. Vol. I, 1798–99. (Contains Brown's "The Man at Home" and "The Rights of Women.") The latter was printed as Alcuin: a Dialogue. New York: Swords, 1798. 16mo.

Wieland or the Transformation: An American Tale. New York, 1798. 12mo.

Ormond, or the Secret Witness. New York, 1798.

Arthur Mervyn or the Memoirs of the Year 1793. Philadelphia, 1799. 12mo.

Edgar Huntley or the Memoirs of a Sleepwalker. Philadelphia, 1799–1800. 2 vols. 12mo.

Clara Howard or the Enthusiasm of Love. Philadelphia, 1801.

Jane Talbot. London, New York, and Philadelphia, 1801.

The Novels of Brown were reprinted by Goodrich, Boston, 1827, in uniform edition, 7 vols. in 6. 12mo.

Complete edition of the Novels of Charles Brockden Brown. Edited and published by David McKay. Philadelphia, 1887.

Carwin, the Biloquist, and other American Tales & Pieces by Charles Brockden Brown, Author of Wieland, Ormond, Arthur Mervyn, &c. In Three Volumes. London, 1822. 12mo.

An Address to the Government on the Utility and Justice
of Restrictions upon foreign Commerce. (Anon.)
Philadelphia, 1809. 8vo.

An Address to the Government of the United States on
the Cession of Louisiana to the French and on the
Late Breach of Treaty by the Spaniards, including the
Translation of a Memorial, on the War of St. Do-
mingo, and Cession of the Mississippi to France.
Drawn up by a French Counsellor of State. A new
edition, revised, corrected, and improved. (Anon.)
Philadelphia, 1803.

A View of the Soil and Climate of the United States of
America with supplementary Remarks upon Florida,
etc., by C. F. Volney. Translated, with occasional remarks, by C. B. Brown. Philadelphia, 1804.

Editor of and Contributor to:

The Monthly Magazine and American Review, Vols.
I-III, April, 1799, to December, 1800. New York:
Swords.

The American Review and Literary Journal for the
Year, 1801. New York: Swords.

The Literary Magazine and American Register, Vols.
I-VIII. Philadelphia: Conrad, 1803-7.

The American Register or General Repository of History, Politics, and Science. Philadelphia, 1806-10.

Manuscript letters in Historical Society of Pennsylvania.

Manuscript letter to Jefferson, and reply, in Jefferson
papers (Library of Congress).

### BIOGRAPHICAL AND CRITICAL ON BROWN

Life of Charles Brockden Brown. By William Dunlap.
2 vols. New York, 1815. (Together with Selections

from the Rarest of his Printed Works, from his Original Letters, and from his Manuscripts Before Unpublished.)

A Library of American Biography. Edited by Jared Sparks. New York, 1834. (Vol. I, sketch of Brown by W. H. Prescott.)

Charles Brockden Brown: A Study of Early American Fiction. By Martin S. Vilas. Burlington, Vt., 1904.

The National Portrait Gallery of Distinguished Americans. Conducted by James B. Longacre and James Herring. New York, 1835. (Vol. III, from miniature by Dunlap, engraved by Forrest.)

The Memorial History of the City of New York. By James Grant Wilson. New York, 1893. (Many references in Vols. III and IV.)

A History of Philadelphia. By Scharf & Westcott, Philadelphia, 1884. (Vol. III, p. 1981.)

The Literary History of Philadelphia. By Ellis Paxson Oberholtzer. Philadelphia, 1906. (Many references.)

The Pennsylvania Magazine of History and Biography. Philadelphia, 1906. Vol. 30, p. 242.

North American Review, June, 1819. (Vol. IX, p. 58–64.)

Blackwood's Magazine, February, 1820. (Vol. VII, p. 554.)

Blackwood's Edinburgh Review, October, 1824. Vol. XVI, p. 421–26. (Signed "X. Y. Z.")

Fortnightly Review, September, 1878, Vol. 30, pp. 399, 400.

INDEX

# INDEX

## A

"A. B.," 38
"A Bone to Gnaw for the Democrats," 173
"A Child Returning from School," painting, 270, 272
A Group of Hartford Wits, 149–89
*A History of American Literature,* 298, 322
*A History of New York, for Schools,* 274, 349
"A Laughable Poem," 91, 92, 329
*A Library of American Literature,* 62, 321
"A Lover of Candour," 38
"A Poem Addressed to the Armies," 177, 340
"A Poem on Industry," 178, 340
"A Poem on the Happiness of America," 181, 340
"A Poem on the Restoration of Chaos and Night," 152, 154
"A Poem on the Rising Glory," 66, 67, 328
"A Poem Sacred to the Memory of George Washington," 185, 342
"A Political Catechism," 41
"A Pretty Story," 28, 129, 324
"A Prophecy," 28, 30, 31, 129, 324
"A Speech of a Standing Member," 53
"A Sketch of the History of Yale College," 112, 338
"A Trip to Niagara," 260, 348
"A View of the Soil," etc., 309, 352
"A Voyage to Boston," 69, 70, 328
*Abaellino,* 347
Adams, Charles Francis, 219, 231, 344, 345
Adams, John, references to, 51, 83, 125, 127, 130, 138, 139, 163, 203, 208, 220; *Letters to His Wife,* 21, 51, 327
Adams, John Quincy, references to, 218, 220, 231, 344, 345; *Memoirs* of, 219, 231, 345
Adams, Samuel, 9
Addison, Joseph, 19, 111, 114
"Advertisement of a Coquette," 117, 119

357

Anderson, Rev. Joseph, 108, 336, 343
André, Major John, 236, 258
*André*, play, 235, 254–58, 262, 347
*Androborus*, 236
Anti-Federalists, 45, 46, 78, 81
"Aquiline Nimblechops," 167
*Appeal to the World*, 9
"Apostrophe to Fancy," 99
Arbuthnot's *History of John Bull*, 30
"Aristocracy," an epic poem, 338, 343
*Arthur Mervyn*, 291, 292, 297–300, 351
*Atlantic Monthly, The*, 338
*Aurora, The*, 98, 164
Austin, Mary S., 73, 87, 331

B

Babcock, Elisha, 337
Bache, Benjamin Franklin, 98, 164, 165
Bailey, Francis, 76, 89
"Ballads of Taxes and Tea," 11
Banks, Sir Joseph, 340
"Barabbas and the Thieves," painting, 271
Barlow, Joel, 143, 150, 152, 157, 161, 162, 169, 170–73, 181, 203, 338, 339
Barrell, Joseph, 207
Bartow, Thomas, 242, 243
"Basket Song," 251, 252
Basset, Frank G., 341
"Battle of the Kegs," 39, 40, 41, 95, 324
"Beauties of Santa Cruz," 72
Beers, Henry A., 296
Berkeley, Governor William, 236
Berni, Francisco, 342
Bibliography of the Works of Philip Freneau, 129, 327
*Bibliography of Vermont*, 239
Bidwell, Barnabas, 238
*Biennial Reports of the Dunlap Society*, 235
*Biglow Papers, The*, 136

## C

T